Mister Rogers Talks With Parents

Mister Rogers Talks With Parents

By Fred Rogers
and Barry Head

With Drawings by Jim Prokell

Berkley Books, New York

The authors gratefully acknowledge permission to quote from the following:
"The Working Mother and Her Children," by Eda LeShan, whose article appeared in the booklet *Childhood*, copyright © 1976 by the Blue Cross Association.

Your Child's Self-Esteem by Dorothy Corkille Briggs. Copyright © 1970 by Dorothy Corkille Briggs. Reprinted by permission of Doubleday & Company, Inc.

The Magic Years by Selma H. Fraiberg. Copyright © 1959 Selma H. Fraiberg. Reprinted with the permission of Charles Scribner's Sons.

"Come Back, Mister Rogers, Come Back," by Jerome L. Singer and Dorothy G. Singer. Reprinted from *Psychology Today*, copyright © 1979 Ziff-Davis Publishing Co. Reprinted with their permission and permission of the authors.

"Is Human Imagination Going Down the Tube?" by Dorothy G. Singer and Jerome L. Singer. Reprinted from *The Chronicle of Higher Education*, April 23, 1979, with their permission and permission of the authors.

Article on the South Bronx by William Gale, 1982, from *The New York Times*. Copyright © 1982 by The New York Times Company. Reprinted by permission.

The Widening World of Childhood: Paths Toward Mastery, by Lois Murphy, Copyright © 1962. Reprinted with permission of the publishers, Basic Books, Inc.

"Be the Best of Whatever You Are," by Douglas Malloch, copyright © 1925 McClure Newspaper Syndicate. Reprinted by permission of United Features Syndicate.

MISTER ROGERS TALKS WITH PARENTS

A Berkley Book/published by arrangement with Family Communications, Inc.

PRINTING HISTORY
Berkley trade paperback edition/June 1983
Fourth printing / April 1985

ISBN 0-425-08220-2

A BERKLEY BOOK® TM 757,375
The name "Berkley" and the stylized "B" with design are trademarks belonging to Berkley Publishing Corporation.
PRINTED IN THE UNITED STATES OF AMERICA

To our teacher and friend,
Margaret B. McFarland, Ph.D.,
whose wisdom and encouragement
made this book possible.

Acknowledgments

So much patient, hard work by so many people goes into the making of a book! At Family Communications, Sally Decker kept us organized and on track as the manuscript grew through several stages of revision. Margaret Fuller typed and re-typed unflaggingly and with good humor. Barbara Davis, a long-time associate, has provided the book with a helpful index. William P. Barker, D.D., provided italics. Musical arrangements for the songs are the work of John Costa—our brilliant Musical Director who has added to our Neighborhood with his music for almost twenty years. To these co-workers we are deeply grateful.

It has been our good fortune at Family Communications to have worked for several years with Jim Prokell. His illustrations enhance our work, and we give him our thanks for the artistry he brings to these pages.

Then there is the Berkley team—Beverly Lewis, Linda Healey, Elisabeth Jakab, Suzanne Corber, Donald Richardson, and Molly Katz—to whom we'd like to express our gratitude for their constructive suggestions, expertise, and sensitivity to what we were trying to say in this book. Its shortcomings are ours alone, but fewer because of the thoughtful editorial support Barry Head and I received.

Finally, I'd like to express my personal thanks to my family and to Dr. Albert Corrado, who have been such a help to me in so many ways. And my great thanks to Barry Head, whose writing skills and personal dedication to every phase of this work allowed this book to come to life.

FRED ROGERS

CONTENTS

CHAPTER 1:

PARENTS ARE SPECIAL, TOO

When I was starting out in television, that grand old character actor, Gabby Hayes, was hosting an afternoon film program at NBC in New York, where I had my first job. One day I asked him how he felt when he sat there talking to a huge audience of children. "Freddy," he told me, "I just think of one little buckaroo."

That's what I've been doing ever since on *Mister Rogers' Neighborhood*—imagining that I'm talking with one "television friend." And that's how I want to write this book—imagining that I'm writing it for one fellow parent.

By "parent" I don't mean just a biological parent, but rather anyone who has primary responsibility for the care of a young child or young children. One definition of parent is "a source from which other things are derived," and that's how I'd like to think of you—as a source from which a young child is deriving nourishment, shelter, character, and love. To provide all that is an enormous job. "You are special" is something I often say to my young television friend on *Mister Rogers' Neighborhood*, but parents are special, too.

Looking back over the twenty and more years of parenting that my wife and I have done with our two boys, I feel good about who we are and what we've done. I don't mean we were perfect parents. Not at all. Our years with our children were marked by plenty of inappropriate responses. Both Joanne and I can recall many times when we wish now we'd said or done something different. But we didn't, and we've learned not to feel too guilty about that. What gives me my good feelings is that we always cared and always tried to do our best. Our two sons are in their twenties now. They are very different one from the other; yet, at the core of each of them there seems to be a basic kindness, a caring, and a willingness to try, which already gives me a good feeling about who they will be if and when they become parents.

For many parents, the arrival of a baby comes as the fulfillment of a dream. But it often comes at the expense of other dreams, as it did for my wife. In our family, our first son's birth meant the interruption of her career as a concert pianist, an interruption that lasted twenty years. I wonder how things would have turned out if she had not made that decision. I wonder how our sons would have turned out. And I wonder how my own life would have been different. She made a very special choice. I know that she, too, has wondered what would have happened had she chosen otherwise, even though now she is active in concert work again. We are all bound to wonder, along with Robert Frost, about "the road not taken" and where it might have led.

Not everyone who has children has chosen to have them; but once we have accepted the role of parent, we have made a choice that will change our lives as few other choices can. Inevitably there follows the daily round of practical necessities associated with child rearing, the constant demands on our time, and new financial considerations. There's something much more than that, though. It's hard to put into words, but it lies at the root of my wanting to offer this book to you after so many years of talking with children. It has to do with a word that will turn up often in this book, and that word is *growth*. When we choose to be parents, we accept another human being as part of ourselves, and a large part of our emotional selves will stay with that person as long as we live. From that time on, there will be another person on this earth whose orbit around us will affect us as surely as the moon affects the tides, and affect us in some ways more deeply than anyone else can. Our children are extensions of ourselves in ways our parents are not, nor our brothers and sisters, nor our spouses. That doesn't mean that we love our children more or less than these other people who are so dear to us, but I do believe our feelings about our children are different from those we have about anybody else in this life, and those feelings touch the very core of who we are. When good things happen to our children, we do more than rejoice on their behalf. Because of the unique emotional bond between ourselves and our children, their joys are inseparable from our joys. And of course the same is true of their sorrows.

When we parents were ourselves very little children, we, like all children, went through a busy and often turbulent first few years of life. From having no sense of what we were, let alone who we were or where we were, we gradually forged an understanding of our bodies and our feelings, our place in space and time, and our relationships with people around us (see Chapter 2). That journey laid the foundations of our personalities. Along the way, it introduced us to pleasure, joy, and laughter; and it also introduced us to anger, fear, and guilt.

Many of the steps we took during the first years are the same steps our children will take, because *all* children have to take them. In that sense all human beings are related. Learning to deal with both emotional and physical separations from the ones we love, for instance, is a big step. The way our parents helped us with tasks like that will affect how we help our children. Old feelings may resurface as we do so. When we leave our child in nursery school for the first time, it won't be just our child's feelings about separation that we will have to cope with, but our own feelings as well—from our present *and* from our past. Parents are extra-vulnerable to new tremors from old earthquakes.

When young people tell me that they're going to "settle down and raise a family," as though it were the most natural thing in the world, I always feel some anxiety. Of course, in some ways it *is* the most natural thing in the world, but I long to be able to give them at least an inkling of what lies ahead—not so much to warn them of difficulties, but to prepare them a little for the new growth tasks they are undertaking for themselves. I'd like them to be able, at least, to sense the depth and

MISTER ROGERS TALKS WITH PARENTS

intensity of parenting. But even that doesn't seem possible to get across, any more than conveying our complex feelings when we catch our aging reflections in a store window. It's only if you've "been there" that you'll know what I mean. *Essentially parenthood is not learned: Parenthood is an inner change.*

Often we may be tempted to say to our children, "You're just too young to understand!" as though there were something deficient about being young. We might do better to say, "You just see it differently at your age than I do at mine." We have all been children and have had children's feelings...but many of us have forgotten. It's not our fault, but we *have* forgotten. We've forgotten what it's like not to be able to reach the light switch. We've forgotten a lot of the monsters that seemed to live in our room at night. Nevertheless, those memories are still there, somewhere inside us, and can sometimes be brought to the surface by events, sights, sounds, or smells. Children, though, can never have grown-up feelings until they've been allowed to do the growing.

Feelings *are* closely tied to age, and that's one reason for the so-called generation gap. The best and surest bridge across the gap is trust. In fact, sometimes trust may be the only possible bridge. We need to trust that our children's feelings are honest and true for their particular age, and we need to help them learn that ours are honest and true, too.

One reason I want to offer you this book is to help with the remembering—and with the trust as well. I believe that rediscovering yourself as the trustworthy person you are is one of the greatest gifts you can give yourself *and* your child.

Family Shapes

From what I've seen and heard and read, I have come to believe that a child is most likely to thrive emotionally when he or she, for the first three years of life, has the full-time care of a consistent motherperson and the close participation in that care of a consistent fatherperson.

I also know from experience that emotionally healthy, compassionate, and fulfilled adults can grow from childhoods in families of almost any conceivable shape and circumstance. That includes children whose childhoods were, by any standards, traumatic.

I'd like to be able to tell you for sure why this is so, but I can't. For every dollar that's been spent on research about why children fail, about the causes of mental illness and the origins of delinquency, I doubt that a nickel has been spent on finding out why some children in high-risk situations thrive. Until we know more, we have to guess and speculate.

Here's what I think: The roots of a child's ability to cope and thrive, regardless of circumstance, lie in that child's having had at least a small, safe place (an apartment? a room? a *lap*?) in which, in the companionship of a loving person, that child could discover that he or she was lovable and capable of loving in return. If a child finds this during the first years of life, he or she *can* grow up to be a competent, healthy person.

That's why a child's closest caregivers—the people I think of as parents—are very, very special. They are the people who are best able to provide that security, sense of worth, and belief that life is worth the effort to live.

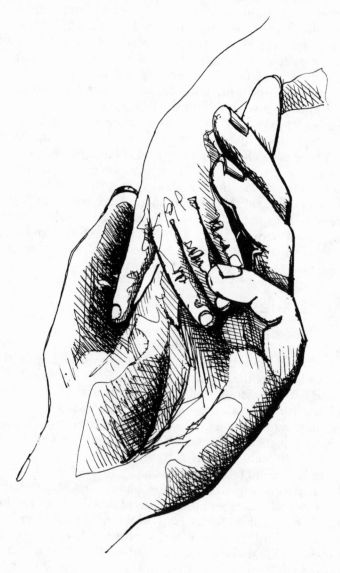

MISTER ROGERS TALKS WITH PARENTS

It is parents who are special and who help children to grow, not family shapes. The nuclear family, with mother, father, and 2.2 children, is perfectly capable of harboring misery, mental illness, and violence, and is not necessarily blessed with love, pleasure, and resilience, even if it is part of an ideal extended family of aunts, uncles, and grandparents all living nearby. Extended family, intact nuclear family, adoptive family, foster family, single-parent family...none of these shapes can tell us how the children within them will grow—whether they will thrive or fail. What can tell us a great deal, on the other hand, is the quality of the relationships between the children and the adults within these shapes, particularly those relationships during the first and most formative years of the children's lives.

A psychologist friend of mine told me of a two-and-a-half-year-old boy he worked with who had been in a car accident that killed his mother and grandmother. My friend was particularly struck by the way Matthew at only two and a half could already use play to cope with his grief, creating dramatic situations with his puppets and miniature life figures that let him work through his feelings of anger and sadness, separation and loss. "I can only assume," my friend told me, "that Matthew had some really superb mothering in those two and a half years." (After the accident, Matthew's grandfather moved in, so that the household consisted of Matthew, his older brother, their father, and their grandfather—an unusual family shape, but one that supplied them all, in their grief, with the kind of loving support they needed right then.)

One of the most unusual families I have come across is the family of Our Little Brothers and Sisters—an orphanage in Cuernavaca, Mexico. The orphanage was started more than twenty years ago by an American priest, Father William Wasson. Over the years, Father Wasson has legally adopted more than four thousand orphans of all ages from infancy up. The children receive care, food and shelter, schooling and job training. In return, each is expected to give a year of service to the orphanage after his or her high school graduation. They help look after the younger children and maintain the orphanage grounds and farm. While there is a small professional staff, it is the "brothers" and "sisters" who do most of the parenting for one another. From childhoods of tragedy and deprivation, many of Father Wasson's children grow into adulthoods of courage, compassion, and fulfillment. Why? Why some and not others?

If we could answer those "whys," we'd know a lot more than we know now about the way human beings develop, and consequently we'd know a lot more about parenting. Some people may say, "It's just the way a person's born," but I'm not comfortable with that. Yes, our biological makeup at birth has much to do with who we become, but so do our environment and our psychological development from one stage to another. And how we grow with all our unique endowments will influence how other people will respond to us. It's all this and more, I feel sure.

Last summer I attended a neighborhood child's birthday party. The children at this party were very much at ease talking to me about what was important in their lives right then. Most of them were five years old. One little girl wanted me to see her baby brother who was asleep next door. "But if we go, Mister Rogers, we'll have to be very quiet so we won't wake him up," she told me. We went, and we were quiet, and she showed me her sleeping brother, as well as her own room next door. "But we have to be quiet here, too," she cautioned me, "because these are paper walls."

Obviously this little girl's parents talk with her, and she feels comfortably included in the comings and goings of her family. What's more, she seems to have acquired, through her parents, a sense of partnership in her family's well-being and the early foundations of responsibility.

Working Mothers

Some mothers want to work and many others have to work. I hope that from what I've already said you will know that I don't think it's "wrong" for mothers to work or that children are bound to suffer emotional damage if they don't have full-time mothers. I do think, though, that if a mother has a choice about working during her baby's first years, she does well to think long and carefully about what that choice will mean. There are reasons why close and consistent mothering are very beneficial to a baby's earliest growth, but it's the *mother's* growth I want us to think about here.

Eda LeShan is a well-known educator and family counselor, a mother, and a friend of mine. I'd like you to know how she feels about it:

> From my own experience, I would like to suggest that sometimes the decision to work during the first year or two of a child's life is made in too much haste. I had already worked for a number of years; I had an advanced degree. How could I possibly stop, midstream, and take a few years off? My brain would atrophy! I would lose my momentum; I was meant for better things. There are few decisions that I now regret more. Not for my child's sake, but for mine. She had much to teach me about wonder and curiosity, about joy and loving—and most of all about the refreshment of play. I wasn't mature enough to see that. What I could not comprehend was that when she left home at eighteen, I would be as vigorous as ever and have at least another twenty-five years of creative work ahead of me. I might have waited

until she was three, or even two, and lost nothing and gained something I can't have now.

The child-raising years are relatively short in our increased lifespan. It is hard for young women caught between diapers and formulas to believe, but there are years and years of freedom ahead. I regret my impatience to get on with my career. I wish I'd relaxed, allowed myself the luxury of watching the world through my little girl's eyes.

Choice, I realize, is a real luxury these days, and millions of mothers are faced with the need to leave their very young children in someone else's care for long periods of the working day. If you're one of them, you'll know how hard that kind of separation can be.

If I were looking for day care for my child, there are several things I'd want to be sure of—as sure as I possibly could be.

First of all, I'd want to know if the people offering day care had experience with both the emotional and physical needs of very young children. Where else have they worked? What makes them qualified to look after infants and toddlers?

I'd want to be assured that one specific person in that day-care center was going to be responsible for my particular baby every day. It would be important to me to know that my baby would be adjusting to only one main caretaker besides myself.

If I were dropping off a toddler, I'd look around to make sure there were plenty of toddler-type spaces, toys, and activities as well as the things that infants need. I'd want someone to be in charge of my toddler who didn't have to be in charge of infants as well.

I'd want to feel that the person taking care of my child really cared about *my* relationship with my child, was a kind of parenting partner with me, and understood that these times of separation were difficult for both my child *and* me. If I couldn't feel these things, I'd look for somewhere and someone else.

If you've already been out looking for day care for your child, you'll probably have learned that my few "wants" are really hard to find in one place. If you can find them, it may be an expensive day-care service. It is not only sad but *serious* that there are so few healthy alternatives for working mothers. Not many couples can arrange their schedules so as to share work and day-care responsibilities. Not many couples live close to other family members who can take over during the day. Sometimes it's possible to find a motherly person in the neighborhood who likes children and will take three or four into her house and give them truly loving and individual care. But whatever the options, there are two choices I would find very difficult to accept: One would be a setting where my baby was looked after by a lot of different people; and the other would be a setting where a single person looked after many different babies.

I believe that fragmented care in the early years *can* lead to a fragmented personality later on. It is through a strong relationship with one main caregiver in infancy and toddlerhood that a child can best develop a strong sense of self and later become capable of forming healthy relationships with others.

Parents' Special Role

No one tells us when we're ready to be parents. Often the role comes as a surprise, with only a little lead time for us to prepare. Then suddenly we have a child in our care, and what we've got to work with is who we are. That's all our children have to work with, too. Becoming a first-time parent can bring us new uncertainties about who we are, but of one thing we can be quite certain: There is nothing as important for a newborn's growth as the close loving care of another human being.

Parents must confront their feelings continuously and intensely, and that confrontation goes on as long as we are parents. Parenting forces us to get to know ourselves better than we ever might have imagined we could—and in many new ways. We're bound to discover some surprising thoughts and feelings inside ourselves—some that will give us pleasure and others that will worry and maybe even frighten us. We'll discover talents we never dreamed we had and fervently wish for others at moments we feel we desperately need them. As time goes on, we'll probably discover that we have more to give and can give more than we ever imagined. But we'll also find that there are limits to our giving, and that may be hard for us to accept. So...

Being a parent is a complex thing. It involves not only trying to feel what our children are feeling, trying to know just how much to do to help them with what they cannot yet do for themselves, but also how much *not* to do. We must also learn to recognize our children's real capacities and respect their need to do things for themselves.

As we discover more and more of the truth about ourselves and our children, what our needs and capacities are and what theirs are, we become more effective caregivers. There is one universal need that we all share, though: We all long to be cared for, and that longing lies at the root of our ability to care for our children. If the day ever came when we were able to accept ourselves and our children exactly as we and they are, then I believe we would have come very close to an ultimate understanding of what "good" parenting means.

It's part of being human to fall short of that total acceptance and that ultimate understanding—and often far short. But one of the most important gifts a parent can give a child is the gift of that child's uniqueness. That may sound strange to you, because, of course, each child is born unique. But it is natural for young children to want to be like other people, particularly the people they love. Being different may seem to them to be wrong and even scary. Children's parents are the very best people to let them know that they are different, that there are no others in the whole world who are exactly like them, and that their differences are part of what makes them special and lovable. When parents put value on their child's uniqueness, that child can learn self-worth and the worth of others as well.

I don't believe that children can develop in a healthy way unless they feel that they have value apart from anything that they own or any skill that they learn. They need to feel they enhance the life of someone else, that they are needed. Who, better than parents, can let them know that?

Giving a child his or her uniqueness is a basic step in encouraging a child to deal with the issue of identity. It is one of the paradoxes of parenting, and often a painful paradox, that even as our children need us for love and trust, they also need us for honest differing. It's not only differing over limits and rules. It may be differing about what we represent in the way of culture, traditions, and values. We owe it to our children to let them know what we believe, and if they differ with us, we owe it to them to be honest adversaries, for it is through this honest confrontation that children can grow into adults who have a firm sense of their place in the sequence of the generations.

Each generation, in its turn, is a link between all that has gone before and all that comes after. That is so genetically, and it is equally true in the transmission of identity. Our parents gave us what they were able to give, and we took what we could of it and made it part of ourselves. If we knew our grandparents and even great-grandparents, we will have taken from what they could offer us, too. All that helped to make us who we are. We, in our turn, will offer what we can of ourselves to our children and their offspring.

Our own differences over identity are likely to have been greatest with our immediate parents. Often grandparents are calm and wise mediators in that conflict, and so the generations interweave. Already I find myself looking forward to the time when I can be a grandparent. I know how important my own grandparents were in my becoming who I am. I already feel like a grandfather to some of my television friends — those people who once watched *Mister Rogers' Neighborhood* as children and now have their own children who are watching. Can you imagine how special that is to me?

MISTER ROGERS TALKS WITH PARENTS

Parents are like shuttles on a loom. They join the threads of the past with the threads of the future and leave their own bright patterns as they go. Providing continuity to succeeding ages—that's a special role indeed!

About This Book

Over the more than twenty years of *Mister Rogers' Neighborhood* we have heard from thousands of parents who have made the effort to write us or call us about special feelings and events in their families. Many of them have shared with us very personal moments, although we have never met except through television. I feel truly privileged to have been able to be a daily part of so many children's early growth and development.

After all these years I continue to try to talk honestly with children about the concerns of early childhood, and in the last two or three years I've been trying to talk directly to parents also about contemporary concerns such as divorce and superheroes and day care, as well as timeless issues such as friendship, competition, and discipline. In all that I do today, just as when I began more than twenty years ago, my goal is to facilitate communication *within* families. I've never tried to compete with parents for their children's attention, but rather to strengthen, to the extent I could, the bond between them. It is my belief that parents (with few exceptions) are the very best people to raise their children, and that their parenting styles should be determined by the traditions from which they have come and the people they have grown to be.

So this book will not try to tell anyone how to raise a child. It is, instead, a response to all those parents who have shared part of their lives and their children's lives with me, who have trusted me with their feelings—and the feelings of their children. I like to think it's my turn now to share some of my experiences, thoughts, and feelings with you. I hope that just as I have come to feel that I know many of you, you will feel, when we have traveled these pages together, that you know me better, too.

Of course, it is also my hope that some of what I have seen and heard and learned over the years may be useful to you. I have had some superb teachers in my life—in grade school, in high school, in college, seminary, graduate school, and in the television industry. One outstanding one is Margaret McFarland, who has been our program's chief consultant for two decades and to whom this book is dedicated. Margaret's ability to understand complex dynamics in the development of human personality and make her understanding comprehensible to her students is a rare and precious gift—which she shares unselfishly with those who want to learn. Another of our teachers is Helen Ross, whom I knew in the later years of her life. Helen taught and consulted with professionals working with children and families all over the world. She was a great help to me and other participants in preparing our testimony for the 1970 White House Conference on Children. Her credits and honors are so many that I won't begin to list them. She was simply one of the great people of our age in the understanding of human beings.

After one operation for cancer and some subsequent therapy, Helen chose to refuse treatment when the cancer reappeared. I visited her in the spring of 1978, just before she died, and during that visit she left me with a memorable summation of her life's work. I happened to be in Washington, D.C., where Helen lived, and I telephoned to see how she was doing. Her sister answered. "Helen's having a pretty good day," she told me, and then she asked if I would like to come for a short visit.

I found Helen very frail yet very interested in all that I had to tell her about our work and her friends in Pittsburgh. Some of the time I just held her hand and we said nothing. We didn't have to. After one of those silences, Helen said to me, "Do you ever pray for people, Fred?" I told her that I did, and I simply said, "Dear God, encircle us with thy love wherever we may be."

Helen was eighty-eight. She had spent most of her adult life working with, and caring for, people of all ages in all walks of life. She turned to me and said: "That's what it is, isn't it? It's love. *That's what it's all about.*"

Love is a word to use with care. It means many different things and can be expressed in many different ways. But I think I know what Helen meant when she said that. She meant that a person can grow to his or her fullest capacity only in mutually caring relationships with other human beings.

Mutually caring relationships require kindness and patience, tolerance, optimism, joy in the other's achievements, confidence in oneself, and the ability to give without undue thought of gain. We need to accept the fact that it is not in the power of any human being to provide all these things all the time. For any of us, mutually caring relationships will also always include some measure of unkindness and impatience, intolerance, pessimism, envy, self-doubt, and disappointment.

I don't believe that to Helen love meant a state of perfect caring. I think it was to her, as it is to me, an active noun like *struggle*. To love someone is to strive to accept that person exactly the way he or she is, right here and now—and to go on caring even through times that may bring us pain.

No one is more involved in the struggles and strivings of love than a parent. That's why we're special, and that's why I wanted to invest a part of my life in order to be able to offer you this book.

It's incomplete, as any book about human development is bound to be. There are certainly subjects on my mind that I would like to have talked with you about—adoption, gifted children, relationships with stepparents—and I'm sure there are many on your mind as well, but they're for another time. Please go on letting me know what they are. My address is Family Communications, Inc., 4802 Fifth Avenue, Pittsburgh, Pennsylvania 15213. We'll go on trying to be responsive to your concerns, not just because it's our work, but because our continuing dialogue may really be a way in which, together, we can help other parents and their children grow.

CHAPTER 2:

IN THE BEGINNING

The Early Months

Many parents, especially first-time parents, worry that their every move has to be just right. During the sixties and seventies there were many books on the market offering how-to advice and recipes for parenting. It was a time when there was a sudden interest in early-childhood research, and out of that, to be sure, came some new, useful information; nevertheless, I wonder how really useful that information was in the way it was presented to parents. So much of it suggested there was a right way and a wrong way to raise children. With the exception of parents who are cruel, abusive, or neglectful, there are about as many acceptable ways to raise children as there are families.

Most childhood problems don't result from "bad" parenting, but are the inevitable result of the growing that parents and children do together. The point isn't to head off these problems or find ways around them, but rather to work through them together and in doing so to develop a relationship of mutual trust to rely on when the next problem comes along.

Each of our life journeys is unique. No child will take the same journey as the parent and no parent can determine what a child's journey will be. Although that's a truism, we all know parents who desperately want one or more of their children to "follow in their footsteps" or "continue the family tradition." We all know parents, too, who push their children into careers that they themselves didn't choose but wish they had, and who now try to find that lost fulfillment through the lives of the next generation. We can have hopes for our children, and we all do. But I think the very best hope of all is that they will find fulfillment in their lives in their own ways, in accord with their distinct individualities, learning to feel good about who they are so that they're able to feel good about people they meet. Finding that kind of fulfillment requires a child to have the courage to be who he or she is, and requires a parent to have the courage to help the child do so.

The issue is really one of healthy separation—our children from us and we from them.

Separation is something we work on all our lives. That work begins in the very first weeks of our lives and is, perhaps, *the* major task of the first two years of our growing.

When we are conceived, the combination of genes from our father's millions of forebears and from our mother's millions of forebears already defines a very broad range of possibilities for us. There are possibilities for how we can look, how tall we can be, how fast we can run, what we can understand, how we can express ourselves, what we can invent, and what we can create.

From the moment of our conception, what we *could* be starts getting changed into what we *will* be by circumstances, and no two sets of circumstances are the same, even for any two as yet unborn children. To begin with, the body of each mother is different in its chemistry and rhythms. In addition, each mother eats differently, drinks different things, takes different medications or none at all, engages in different physical activities. There is much concern over the effects of smoking on an unborn child and real alarm over the effects of mind- and body-altering drugs. It may be a long time before we know exactly how the things that happen to an unborn child affect the child-to-be, but we can be certain that life in the womb is full of its own kinds of experiences that somehow influence the kind of person we will become.

And so, already at birth, there's no way we can be just like anybody else who has ever lived before. Right at the beginning we may be very, very different even from those people who are about to become our first caregivers. I sometimes wonder whether those caregivers are ready to accept such difference. How natural it is for a parent to want "my baby to be just like me" and to expect from that baby similar behaviors and reactions, similar likes and dislikes!

The cutting of the umbilical cord is life's first big separation for the new individual. It's a tremendously important separation for the mother, too. The ending of the *physical* attachment between the mother and the baby is the beginning of an increased *emotional* closeness as care and feeding begin. It's an attachment that, though invisible, is as strong and real as the umbilical cord itself. Even for mothers who cannot keep their babies or who never even see their babies, the emotional tie is there. If you have ever been close to a mother who has made the decision to give up her child for adoption, you have probably seen how deeply painful the severing of that emotional tie can be. The loss of any part of ourselves—an actual physical part of our bodies, or the loss of the people and places and things that give meaning to who we are—is always the most difficult kind of loss for people to cope with.

For most mothers, the emotional tie that begins before birth grows more and more intense from birth on. We take that for granted on the mother's side, but how does it look from the baby's point of view? We can't really know, of course, but many researchers think that the relationship between child and mother progresses something like this:

For nine months the newborn has been a physical part of the mother, just as the mother's eye or hand is a part of her. They have shared the same oxygen, the same nutrients. They have been one organism. Once the umbilical has been cut, *we* know that they are now two separate people because our eyes and minds tell us so, but that separateness has no meaning to the newborn. The baby probably feels *something* has happened, but has no way of making sense of the sudden sensation of breathing, the sudden bombardment of lights and sounds and smells and tastes, the bumps and jars, the discomfort of itching and wetness,

sensations of hot and cold, the hurt of hunger pangs, the comfort of feeding. The newborn probably can't even tell that some of these things are going on outside the body and some inside. Everything just *is*.

It's the mother who begins to sort out the general confusion for her baby. She regulates what's going on, and with the help of her baby's crying cues, she tries to keep her baby comfortable. When I see a newborn close against a mother's breast, I wonder if that baby is hearing long-familiar sounds—the heartbeat, the rumblings of the mother's body—and if, in this strange new world, those echoes of the old one are comforting. Certainly, in the earliest days and weeks, the new smells and sounds and touches of "mother" must become comforting because they are so closely associated with feeling warm and dry and full and content.

(Of course, it isn't always the biological mother who "mothers" the child, and when we talk of mother here I mean it in the widest sense—the person who does the mothering.)

Watching mothers and babies together, you can see how each mother responds to the needs of her particular infant in her own unique ways. Each mother's style of mothering reflects how she herself was mothered. It's not something that's taught. It's just inside waiting to be expressed. Like language, mothering styles do tend to get passed down from generation to generation. And if you watch long enough, you can see how the infant adapts to the mothering style of his or her particular mother and how the mother adapts to her unique infant. Little by little each brings about changes in the other's behavior. Some babies seem more comfortable being held one way than another or more at ease on their tummies or on their backs. Some mothers nurse or feed their babies on regular schedules, while others do so whenever their babies cry or when they themselves feel like it. Together, the baby and the mother work things out between them. That time lays the foundation for all of that baby's future relationships.

Even as a baby appears to recognize the mother's face and to smile, there is probably still little sense (on the baby's part) of "you" and "me." That comes later and slowly. There is certainly pleasure for the baby in the mother's smile, her laughing eyes, or affectionate talk. Often babies kick and coo, as well as smile, in response. When they do, their mothers are likely to step up their own responses because they in turn feel pleased. It's like enjoying a ride on a seesaw. Mother and baby each seem to be trying to increase the other's joy because the joy of the other brings joy to the self. This striving for mutual pleasure is a very basic part of the mother-child relationship, basic to both the mother and the baby. The fact that it is such a strong and fundamental urge may in part explain why, all through life, when children and parents bring *dis*pleasure to one another, it is so fundamentally painful.

Many professionals think that the baby's sense of *self* begins with the awareness of inside sensations such as the hurts of hunger and bowel distress, and the good feelings that come with relief from these hurts. Researchers even speculate that when babies find that these hurts are regularly relieved, they come to *expect* relief and so experience the very earliest beginnings of hope and optimism.

Babies take a giant step when they watch their own hands moving and then actually stop their motion. In that control of eye and mind and hand there must be a new sense of "me" beginning, an awareness that those things that have been waving around out there all this time are "things that I can start and stop and even bring to my mouth when I want to." Whatever "me" is, those hands have to be part of it. And when I bring "my" hand to my mouth and chomp on it, or when "my" hands find each other and squeeze...why, that's a new sensation. It feels different from when I squeeze a rattle or chomp on it. I have the feeling of touching something, but at the very same time I have the feeling of being touched, too. *I'm* touching *me!*

(For the baby, of course, these discoveries come slowly and quietly, as a natural part of everyday growing during the first three months or so. It is only when we are much more grown up that we begin to get a feeling of *eureka!* when we discover new parts of ourselves, and there are new aspects of ourselves to discover as long as we live. Often, people surprise themselves with what they can do with their creativity—did *I* really make that cabinet? Was that idea really *mine*? Did *I* actually paint that painting or write that song? It's true of physical discoveries about ourselves, too. Some years ago I was introduced to biofeedback at the Menninger Foundation in Topeka, Kansas. With coaching, I found that I could change the temperature in my fingertips, and that seemed like magic. I'd never really considered my body temperature part of the *me* who had thoughts and feelings, who made choices and who did things.)

In the early months comes the awareness that "I" can have an effect on the things that are outside of me. Babies in high chairs love to throw things onto the floor, and as soon as the something is picked up and given back, the baby throws it down again...and again. It can be an irritating game for a mother, particularly when, if she doesn't give the object back, her baby sets up a howl. For the mother it looks like willfulness, but for her baby it's a way to come to understand something new about what's me and what's not-me. This kind of understanding takes much practice.

In this game of throw and retrieve, there may also be an awareness that "I" can separate myself from things that are not-me. Certainly, when babies start to crawl and then toddle, they learn that they can separate themselves from their mothers, fathers, and other caretakers. They learn that they can go back to them, too. They practice going away and coming back over and over. They learn that something can still exist even when they can't see it (see page 96) and this, in turn, helps them cope with those times when their closest caretakers go away from them. Of course, it helps that their caretakers do come back, so that babies learn that separation can be followed by return rather than abandonment. In fact, they come to *trust* that this is so.

It's only toward the end of the first year that a child may really see "mother" as a separate person who is different from "me." A striking demonstration of this evolving awareness was caught on videotape by two of our colleagues at Family Communications—Dr. Margaret McFarland and Dr. Naomi Ragins—in the course of a year-long observational study they were conducting with a child they called "T."

When T was five months old, her mother held her up to a mirror in the studio where the taping was taking place. T, in her mother's arms, gazed primarily at her mother's familiar face. The baby in the mirror didn't seem to have either interest or meaning for her.

By the time T was six and a half months old, she was showing clear pleasure at the sight of her mother *and* herself in the mirror. In fact, it seemed to be precisely the sight of *both at once* that produced the pleasure, because when she was held at the mirror by someone else, T grew very solemn.

At seven and a half months, T crawled over to the mirror, pulling

herself upright beneath it. When her mother held her up, she looked at her mother and herself one at a time and seemed delighted at her own image. When, for instance, her mother lifted her up to the mirror and then lowered her out of sight, up and down, up and down, in a game of peekaboo, T laughed and squealed with joy.

At eight and a half months, T clearly seemed to recognize herself in the mirror, and that recognition brought her delight no matter who was holding her. Excitedly, she would look at herself and reach out to the mirror to pat herself.

The significance of the separated umbilical cord is clearer at this age. Although mother and child, even from the child's point of view, are physically separate, the emotional bond is likely to have become even stronger after all those months of care and nurturing and mutual adaptation. Yet this is just the time for the child to start "hatching" from complete dependence on the mother and the mother's way of organizing the world. Even as a child comes to organize and understand the world in his or her own way, the structure the mother first provided remains the foundation on which the child will build. That foundation won't determine completely the growing child's view of the world, but it will influence it profoundly all life long.

For the child it will be a lifelong source of tension as well.

That first year is a big journey, and it's one we've all taken and most likely forgotten: from literal oneness with our mothers to a physical twoness; to the gradual awareness of our insides and our outsides; to the sense of where our bodies begin and end and the sense of what is me and not-me; to the feeling that we are physically separate from our mothers (though we are still emotionally bound together); to the knowledge that we can make choices and have effects on the people and things around us; to the beginnings of emotional as well as physical separateness.

The awareness of our separate selves brings a lot of excitement and the need to try it out and play with it many times and in many different ways. How else can we find out what it means? Sometimes it can be scary for a child, who may wonder: Am I so separate I can lose my mother? Lose her smiles, her laughing eyes, lose her loving voice? All those things that showed her joy in me and brought me joy in myself? I know that I need to be *me*, but I also need to be *us*!

And the mother? She may take real pleasure in watching her child grow and learn new things. She may be delighted to see her child roll over, crawl, and then walk, excited to hear her baby start to babble and then talk, proud to see her child start to manage small tasks.... But she is also likely to feel: Where has my baby gone? The one who was helpless and cuddly, who lay in my arms and nursed, who smiled when I cooed, who brought me such joy and made me feel so needed? Mother as well as child is feeling: I know we're separate people but I also need to be *us*!

So far I haven't mentioned fathers, and that's because during the first year of life it's the mothering person who is likely to be a baby's primary caretaker, even though a male can be a mothering person, too. One thing is sure: A baby needs *one primary caretaker* with whom to take those first early steps toward selfhood—one person to feel part of and then grow separate from. Some experts even believe that how children take those first steps has much to do with whether they will be able to form strong, healthy relationships as they grow. That's one reason many people, myself included, are concerned about the effects of group infant day care—settings where this one-to-one developmental journey may be difficult if not impossible (see page 16).

A mother and child, as they work through their earliest relationships with each other, are both vastly enriched if there is a loving, supportive, and participating husband and father in the home. From the mother's viewpoint, one obvious reason is that child care is hard work and it helps to have an extra pair of hands to spell you when you need it. And of course a mother can feel more secure in her mothering when she has a partner to provide food and shelter during the time of her healthy preoccupation with her baby.

But as important as these practical considerations may be, there are equally compelling emotional reasons mothers need helping fathers for their children. Having a child forces change and growth whether we want it or not. Few things remain the same after a birth in the family. Any major change like that brings uncertainty and anxiety, doubts about who we are, what we are doing, and what we are becoming. At such times, we all need, most of all, a trusted partner who can help us keep our sense of self together, who can support us at times of discouragement or depression, and share our joys, discoveries, and successes. Needing that kind of reinforcement is a very real part of being human. It's emotionally as well as physically draining to be a single parent.

There is also the problem all single parents have of trying to be both mother and father to the child. Just what "being mother" and "being father" means is not clear at all. It seems to depend on what the societies we live in expect it to mean; and on how we experienced the difference when we were growing up; and on what each of us decides we want it to mean. Whether male or female, we all have our own unique ways of expressing ourselves as parents.

We all worry about how much firmness and how much permissiveness we should provide, or whether we are showing more anger than love. We may feel less guilty about scolding, for instance, when we know there is another loving parent at hand who can provide comfort. So much that we do as parents is like seesawing, and it's hard to seesaw

MISTER ROGERS TALKS WITH PARENTS

alone. In short, a mother is likely to feel more confident about providing her mothering (whatever form it takes) when she knows there is a father there to provide his fathering (whatever form *it* takes).

For an infant, having a father as well as a mother caretaker means an early exposure to differences—differences in smells and voices, different ways of being held or hugged, different ways of being diapered and fed, different ways of being comforted—in other words, different ways of experiencing love. A baby may not be able to *make* comparisons, but a baby can certainly *feel* comparisons, and comparing things that are similar and things that are different is a large part of the way we learn about our world and about ourselves. I've come to believe that it is the children who are most secure in the primary mother-child bond who can best use the relationship with the father—and who then are best able to extend that relationship to older and younger brothers and sisters, to grandparents, aunts, uncles, and people beyond the family. And when children get to be two, three, four, and are working on what it means to be a boy or a girl, having a male parent as well as a female one of course takes on new and important meanings.

The Two-Year-Old

I know that many parents look to their child's second birthday with very mixed feelings. They've been warned that along about that time begin the "terrible two's," and they're expecting the worst. It's true that there's likely to be a change even in children who have seemed easy and docile until then, but how could there not be? Each child needs to practice the new feelings of being a separate self, and so often that's all that a child's "stubbornness" means. Children have to practice their newly acquired language abilities, too, and the two kinds of practicing may come together again and again in the use of the word *no*. Perhaps you've noticed that children frequently are quite willing to do the things they say no to. Even your suggestion to do something you know your child likes to do may be greeted with a firm "no," and that's part of what makes these refusals perplexing and irritating. Some parents read into them a real challenge and clash of wills and decide they'd better show their child who is boss, right then and there, so they counter with punishment or physical force. But, more often than not, the "no" isn't a "no" of defiance and the issue isn't one of "who's boss?" The issue, once again, is separateness. The child is trying to find out whether his or her new feelings of separateness are all right. I think most parents would agree that such feelings are not only all right but are necessary for healthy growth. If that's the case, these feelings need to be acknowledged and supported—even as family life has to go on, too.

Here's a description of the problem—one that may sound familiar if you've had a two-year-old in the house. It's from a book called *Your Child's Self-Esteem: The Key to Life* by Dorothy Corkille Briggs. Mrs. Briggs is a teacher, psychologist, family counselor...and mother.

The child's cooperation up into the second year results from his not knowing any other way to behave. Awareness of autonomy, however, opens whole new vistas. He has a brand-new perception of his little universe.

Down go the heels, out goes the chin, and the "No's!" flow fast and furiously. No matter that it gets him into hot water, the flag of independence is raised and family peace goes by the boards. The revolutionary discovery that he has a mind of his own must be tested and experimented with in all its dimensions, particularly with mother. Even if she doesn't give the "two" opportunities to resist, he's undaunted—he manufactures them tirelessly.

Only by *practicing* separateness can the child capture the feeling of autonomy. It is as if the two says, "To find me, I must defy you. I have to prove my realness."

"But," asks Mrs. T., "if I accept defiance, don't I teach my child to be disrespectful?"

A child's capacity to respect others later on is measured by his capacity to respect himself now. During the second year of life the child's primary psychological assignment is to forge a sense of self. To do so,

he needs recognition that this self exists.

Awkward and bombastic as his efforts may be, autonomy must be respected. Life with a two is life with a tiny despot. But it is life with a little human being taking his first step toward selfhood.

It is no accident that this is called "The Age of Negativism," or "The Terrible Two's." Actually, these negative labels becloud the fact that an extremely important task in the child's life is under way. It would be more helpful to parents if this period were labeled, "The Age of Separateness."

Just because two's need practice in autonomy doesn't mean throwing out all rules and cowering in the corner. The goal is to avoid head-on collisions when certain behavior is necessary, to accept defiant *feelings* without making the child feel guilty...and to channel defiant acts into acceptable outlets.

Whenever a child feels guilty because of his emerging selfhood, he concludes, "I'm separate, and this gets me into trouble. Safety lies in being a 'yes-man.'" And he may fail to develop a sense of separateness altogether.

How vigorously any one child goes through this state depends on inherited characteristics and temperament, the number of frustrations he has faced in his early months, and how cooperative he's found the world around him. If as an infant, Bobby learned that he had to scream bloody murder before anyone came, he's more likely to use dynamite to declare separateness at two.

The degree to which the environment meets his needs, the intensity of competition, how parental power is used, the extent of defiance he sees around him and how it is handled, physical health, and the intensity of home tensions all play a part in the child's handling of this stage.

Unless you know the priority that independence has for the two, his behavior can be confusing. Mrs. G. was puzzled when Walter announced firmly, "Don't wanna ice cream!" But he screamed like a stuck pig when she removed the dish he'd just refused. Bewildered, his mother was downright determined not to give the dessert back.

"I've read about this conditioning stuff and I certainly don't want a spoiled brat. Giving the ice cream back would only reward his being contrary," she said.

From Walter's point of view, his actions were entirely rational; he was not being a brat. One part of him was busy on the task of selfhood; another part wanted the ice cream, but only *after* his separateness was recognized.

Developmental "homework" comes first, but you can imagine Walter's frustration when doing his job caused him to lose out. His "no" to the ice cream was his naive way of saying, "Mommy, I must defy even when you offer me a goody because my 'person homework' comes first." His "no" was a code for "I'm separate."

Awareness of the job they're doing doesn't make two's any easier to live with; but knowing the purpose of their defiance makes it easier to avoid getting in the way of growth. Their rebellion is *not* disrespect.

Parents find many different ways to work their way through the assertiveness of their two-year-olds, but seeing that assertiveness as positive energy being directed toward growth as a competent individual may open up some new possibilities. It seems to me that the times in life that are the hardest on our own sense of separateness and individuality are those times when we feel we have no choices about what happens to us: times at work or at home when we feel schedules and regulations and circumstances are deciding our lives for us and leaving no room for us to be ourselves. If you think about a time like that, you're likely to remember feelings of frustration and itchiness at best, and, at worst, a good deal of anger and rebelliousness or despair and depression. We all need to feel that we are, to some degree, in charge of our lives. We need structure and limits and purposes, too; but, like everything, we need a healthy balance. It's that balance that we need to try to provide for our two-year-olds.

There *are* choices that two-year-olds can make, and giving them that opportunity whenever we can seems to be one way to handle their need to assert themselves. There are choices of things to eat and drink, choices of clothes to wear, and choices of things to do. There can even be choices about chores that *have* to be done—for instance, "Do you want to pick up your toys now or after lunch?" The best choices are those that are limited, specific, and real, ones that you can settle for, too. "Bedtime, okay?" isn't a real choice for most children. On the other hand, "Do you want to wear your blue or your yellow jammies to bed?" is. There are many times, too, when a firm "no" may be perfectly acceptable to everyone, and it's worth making the most of those times— even creating them. "How about putting on your sneakers to go out- doors?" could be a useful question when wearing something else is just as good an alternative.

I'm often impressed by the reports of large companies that have found ways to give their employees some decision-making power over their work lives—flexibility, for instance, over when to arrive at work and when to leave. There always seems to be a noticeable rise in morale and in output, even though the choice *doesn't* include whether or not to come to work. I think that's because it always feels good when some- one recognizes our individual needs and preferences and in doing so confirms that we are different and unique human beings. I know it feels good at fifty... and I'm sure it felt good at two as well.

The Continuing Journey

Two-year-old behavior can be such a clear expression of the struggle between the urge to be different and separate and the continuing need to be a loved part of someone else. Here's what Selma Fraiberg says of the two-year-old in her classic book on early childhood, *The Magic Years*:

> He loves, deeply, tenderly, extravagantly, and he holds the love of his parents more dearly than anything in the world. To be fair about it, he also loves himself very, very much and the conflict between self-love and love of others is the source of

much of his difficulty at this age. But when put to the test, it is his love for his parents which wins out. When he has displeased them he is disconsolate and even his self-love is diminished when he feels the displeasure of his parents. He wants to be good in order to earn their love and approval; he wants to be good so that he can love himself. (This is what we mean, later, by self-esteem.)

As children grow, much of the time they want to be like their parents, probably even wishing they could marry one of them at some point (see page 69). Then they want to be like their friends—to have the same clothes and toys their friends have, and to do the same things their friends do. In early childhood, they may not even see how different their friends are from one another—that one may have a different color skin or speak a different language or have a physical disability. Learning to accept differences in ourselves and others, and coming to value each person's uniqueness, are not attitudes that suddenly spring full-blown into being. In fact, one of the most deeply rooted tensions in anyone's life is wanting to be the same as other people and knowing that we can't be. The origins of this tension may very well go way, way back to that time before memory when, as infants, we felt we were actually a physical part of the person who first held us, fed us, and cared for us. As we grew, we learned that our bodies had boundaries that separated us from everyone else, that we had our own thoughts and feelings, that we could move away, get left behind, or even get lost from the people we loved. We learned we were physically separate and could be physically independent. The trouble is, physical separateness does not always bring equivalent emotional separation and independence. Emotionally, we have ties with the people we love all life long. That's part of what loving them means.

By adolescence, children are usually trying on a lot of different identities and often seem to reject being like their families in favor of being like certain of their friends. So much of the so-called adolescent rebellion is really trying to be the same and trying to be different and the search for a comfortable compromise. And so it goes as we choose professions and spouses and life-styles. It's a lifelong challenge.

I went through grade school and high school with a girl who lived two blocks away. We took the same course of studies with the very same teachers. Not surprisingly, we went in different directions as we followed our different interests. For both of us there were to be surprises ahead. My friend became a medical doctor in Maine, but after fifteen years of practice, she found a totally unexpected and unique way to combine her interests in science and the humanities. Throughout the state of Maine she set up closed-circuit television systems on which visiting

nurses could telecast routine checkups to doctors in Portland. X rays could be shown on the television screen, as well as actual patient examinations. Through this system, leading doctors in large medical centers have been able to make diagnoses from afar, thus helping many patients they would not have been able to help otherwise. And all because of the pioneering work of Dr. Doris Stewart Pennoyer.

I think, too, of another friend of mine, Hoagy Carmichael, who is the son of the famous songwriter. Young Hoagy probably could have been a fine professional jazz drummer, but he wanted to go into television production, and he did, working with us at Family Communications for several years. His work in television led him to want to become a filmmaker, and he went to New York to start his own film production company. Hoagy loves fly-fishing, too, and in the course of his film career he made a documentary about one of the grand masters of fly rod making—Mr. William Garrison. Mr. Garrison was in his eighties at the time Hoagy produced the film, and the two became such close friends that when Mr. Garrison died, he willed Hoagy his special equipment and priceless know-how. Now Hoagy doesn't do much filmmaking. He makes fly rods, and a Carmichael rod is one of the finest

IN THE BEGINNING

you can buy. His creative energy, like his father's before him, is invested in his own special field.

For me, the focus for my life came ever so slowly, but I think I always trusted that it would emerge. I was interested in songwriting, languages, telecommunications, and in human psychological and spiritual development. I'll never forget the sense of wholeness I felt when I finally realized that all these things and more could be used to enhance the healthy growth and development of children. And the more I think about it now, the more convinced I am that my choice to work with children reflects the attitudes of the adults around me as I was growing up. I must have sensed that children were valuable—otherwise I don't think I would have chosen to spend a great part of my professional life working with and for children. Pediatricians, teachers, child-care specialists of all kinds, must have come to the conclusion that childhood is a time worth adults' long-term investment. I'm grateful to those who somehow "communicated" that so strongly to me.

Maybe you've found a way to combine what you've learned with who you are. Perhaps, out of all your explorations and experiences, you've chosen what it is you want to call *yourself*. For most of us it's a process that will go on as long as we live, and often it won't be easy. But something I hope my wife and I have given our children is this: the conviction that they are unique and valuable individuals and that finding meaning in their lives *is* worth the while.

I hope for my sons, too, that they will find as much pleasure as I have in the exhilarating diversity of people in different countries, in different parts of the United States, in different members of my own family. The tapestry of human possibilities is so rich and varied. It is a continuing source of wonder. And the weaving of it goes on with the birth of each new child.

One of the mysteries is that as unalike as we are, one human being from another, we also share much in common. Our lives begin the same way, by birth. The love and interdependence of parents and children is universal, and so are the many difficulties parents and children have in becoming separate from one another. As we grow we laugh and cry at many of the same things, fear many of the same things. At the end we all leave the same way—by death. Yet no two threads—no two lives—in that vast tapestry of existence have ever been, or will ever be, the same.

*   *   *

Several years ago we introduced a story into the Neighborhood of Make-Believe parts of our television programs about a place where each person was *not* unique. In fact, everyone was the same. It was a planet called Planet Purple, and Lady Elaine Fairchilde, one of our puppet characters, discovered it quite by accident while she was on her way to explore another planet. What follows is a version of that story, which, along with the other stories in this book, I'd like to offer as a gift to your children. "The Story of Planet Purple" could be a way for you to talk with them about the delights to be found in human differences.

The Story of Planet Purple

If you lie on your back and look way up in the sky, you won't see it. If you stand on tiptoes and listen very carefully, you won't hear it. But, if you close your eyes and close your ears and think of everything you can think of *purple*, you can imagine a place so far away that only make-believe can get you there. A place called Planet Purple.

Planet Purple was called Planet Purple because the sky was purple, the streets were purple, the houses were purple, the people were purple, everything was purple. And what's more, everything was the same. The cars were the same, the chairs were the same, the food was the same. Everybody ate purple pumpernickel pudding. Even the people were the same. They looked the same, they talked the same, they walked the same, they played the same games, they had the same friends.

Planet Purple people even had the same names. Every boy's name was Paul and every man's name was Paul. Every girl's name was Pauline and every woman's name was Pauline.

And every single panda on the whole planet was called Purple Panda. That's all that lived on Planet Purple: Pauls, Paulines, and Purple Pandas.

Well, for years and years and years, everybody on Planet Purple dreamed the same dreams. But never once did they dream that a strange-looking make-believe pink woman astronaut would discover their planet and surprise their lives.

It was neither morning nor afternoon nor evening nor night, because the times on Planet Purple were all the same. All the Pauls and Paulines and all the Purple Pandas were sitting around in a circle singing: "Planet Purple, Planet Purple, we all live on Planet Purple."

And right in the middle of their song, and right in the middle of their circle, landed this strange-looking make-believe pink woman astronaut by the name of Lady Elaine Fairchilde.

Her spaceship was made of green leaves and her astronaut suit was all white. The Planet Purple people had never seen the color green or white, much less a pink woman whose name was Lady Elaine Fairchilde, so they all ran and hid behind their purple houses. All of them except one Paul and one Pauline and one Purple Panda.

When Lady Elaine stepped off her spaceship, the first words she said were: "Where am I?"

Paul and Pauline and Purple Panda said all together: "Planet Purple."

"You mean I've discovered a new planet?" asked Lady Elaine.

Paul, Pauline, and Purple Panda said: "You've discovered a new planet."

"Whoopee, whoopee!" shouted Lady Elaine.

Lady Elaine hopped back on her spaceship and flew to her own home, the Neighborhood of Make-Believe, where she told all her friends about her great discovery. What she didn't know was that Paul and Pauline and Purple Panda watched where she was going. They had a new idea that no other Paul or Pauline or Purple Panda had ever had. It was the first new idea on Planet Purple.

Now, the Purple way to travel is the thinking way. If you are a Planet Purple person or panda, all you have to do is to think that you're someplace and you will be there. So Paul and Pauline and Purple Panda all thought about the pink woman and where she was, and immediately they arrived in the Neighborhood of Make-Believe.

They could hardly make themselves believe what they saw and what they heard. Things were *different*! Streets and houses and cars and chairs and even people were different. Some could fly, some could crawl, some could speak two languages, some could wear crowns, some could wind clocks, some could even make rocking chairs. Nobody was exactly the same, everyone was *different*!

Purple Panda was so excited with all the new colors and all the new faces and voices and feelings that he just sat down on a rocking chair and rocked and rocked and rocked. But all of a sudden, he remembered one of the Planet Purple laws: Anyone who rocks on a rocking chair may not live on Planet Purple. It was too late, he had already rocked. Now he couldn't go back. He wasn't sad, though. He liked the new neighborhood much better than Planet Purple. Then he thought, "Maybe that's why I sat down and rocked in the first place—so I really would have to stay."

Purple Panda's new neighbors loved him. They had not known anybody like him. He soon found a good job with the nearby circus. It was a good job because the circus people really needed him. Paul and Pauline liked the Neighborhood of Make-Believe, too, but they wanted to help make things different in their old land. They decided to go back, but

MISTER ROGERS TALKS WITH PARENTS

to do some exploring first.

They went as far and as near as they could. They looked and they listened and they smelled and they touched. In their minds they felt as many different colors and as many different sounds and smells and feelings as they could.

One day Paul was trying to gallop like a big brown horse, and he tripped and fell and ripped his shirt and hurt his arm. The strangest thing happened. Something wet started trickling down his cheek. It felt like water, but somehow it was different from water. It felt sad. A soft rabbit nearby asked him why he was crying, and Paul asked the rabbit what the word "crying" meant, because nobody ever cried on Planet Purple.

"When tears come trickling down your face, that's crying. Haven't you ever cried before?" asked the rabbit. The rabbit's name was Albert.

"No," said Paul, "I never have cried before."

"Then you've just started to live," said Albert.

When Pauline saw Paul's tears, she came close to him and put her arm around him and said, "All better." Albert smiled and hopped away. Then both Paul and Pauline thought about being on Planet Purple... and immediately they were back home.

When they arrived, the other Pauls and Paulines and Purple Pandas were still hiding behind their houses.

"Come out, everybody, we have something to tell you all!" shouted Paul.

The other Pauls and Paulines and Purple Pandas came out slowly at first, but then when they saw their friends who had gone away and come back, they rushed to greet them.

"Where did you go," they asked, "and what did you do?"

Paul and Pauline started by telling them about Lady Elaine Fairchilde and how they had gone to her neighborhood and what it was like there.

"Everything is so different and nobody is exactly the same as anyone else," Pauline explained.

"Do they eat Purple Pandas there?" one of the Purple Pandas asked.

"No, no," Pauline assured him.

"Well, then, why didn't Purple Panda come back with you?" another Purple Panda asked.

Pauline then told everybody about Purple Panda rocking on the rocking chair. Everyone knew the law about rocking on a rocking chair, so they all shouted, "Sixteen! Sixteen!" which meant bad, bad, for rocking on the rocking chair.

But Purple Panda was glad to stay in a place where it didn't matter if he sat on a rocking chair, a place where people liked you for being different.

"Do you know that there is not one other Purple Panda in that whole neighborhood?" said Pauline. The Purple Pandas were amazed and right then and there they started thinking some new thoughts, too.

Paul helped everyone imagine what the color blue was like. "It's a little like purple with red on vacation," he said.

And Pauline helped them imagine what the sound of a yellow canary, the smell of a green mint leaf, and the taste of a red tomato were like. Paul told them about crying and how tears feel like water, but they mean so much more than water. He told them what he felt like inside when his first tears came and how he talked to Albert about it. Suddenly one of the Purple Pandas started to cry. That Purple Panda said: "I miss Purple Panda, and I want to see him again."

And one Pauline said: "I want my house to be blue."

And another said: "I want my street to be yellow. I want my clothes to be red and my grass to be green and my dreams to be different from anyone else's dreams."

So they all set about changing their planet. Oh, it took them a long time to make all the decisions; and some people didn't like some things and other people didn't like other things, but everybody said that it was still better than being all the same all the time.

They even changed the law about rocking chairs so Purple Panda could come back any time he wanted.

The only things they didn't change were their sky and their skin, because that's the way they were and that was all right with them.

One day, as they all sat around in their circle singing lots of different songs, Pauline Blue House said: "I think we should do something nice for Lady Elaine Fairchilde. After all, she helped us to be different."

Paul Soft Green Grass spoke up and said: "How about adding her name on our planet? We could call it Planet Purple Fairchilde."

For the first time since the old days, everyone agreed. So Paul and Pauline, the ones who went to the other neighborhood first, went back and told Lady Elaine of their decision, and Lady Elaine and Purple Panda and his new friends all went to Planet Purple Fairchilde for the weekend to celebrate many different things.

CHAPTER 3:

A LITTLE
LATER ON

It's the "work" (the growth tasks) that children are doing beginning with the age of two that we've concentrated on most in *Mister Rogers' Neighborhood*. This work consists largely in children's figuring out who and what they are, in identifying and expressing their feelings, and in developing their own unique understandings of their places in their world. But of course these tasks have already been under way since birth. What the two-year-old brings to them is a budding *self*—a self that has begun to take shape out of a unique combination of genes, a unique set of early experiences in the world, and the unique organization of a particular mother who was just as unique herself when she was born.

Though we all grow to be different from one another, my work with children and with adults who know children well has convinced me that all children share certain growth tasks no matter where they are born or when. Those are the sorts of things we deal with in *Mister Rogers' Neighborhood*.

In case you're not familiar with our television series, I should tell you a little about what goes on there. To begin with, I don't think of our half-hours as "shows" or even "programs" as much as I consider them visits: television visits. I try to make them quiet and comfortable times with a caring neighbor, and each time I begin by coming into my television living room at the start of the visit singing, "Won't You Be My Neighbor?":

It's a beautiful day in this neighborhood,
A beautiful day for a neighbor.
Would you be mine?
Could you be mine?

It's a neighborly day in this beauty wood,
A neighborly day for a beauty,
Would you be mine?
Could you be mine?

I have always wanted to have a neighbor just like you!
I've always wanted to live in a neighborhood with you.
So let's make the most of this beautiful day;
Since we're together we might as well say,
Would you be mine?
Could you be mine?
Won't you be my neighbor?

Won't you please,
Won't you please?
Please won't you be my neighbor?

As I'm singing the song, I change into a comfortable sweater and sneakers. I almost always bring something along with me—a toy, a picture, an idea, something someone's made, or something people use—and that something is what I generally start talking about and continue to use one way or another throughout the visit. Often it will be the reason for going to another set in our television neighborhood: Don Brockett's bakery, Elsie Neal's craft shop, Joe Negri's music shop, François Clemmons's music studio, Betty Aberlin's theater, or the home of Mr. "Speedy Delivery" McFeely, who runs the neighborhood delivery service.

Whatever I bring in to talk about may also be the reason for a guest to drop by and talk about or demonstrate what he or she does. The list of guests who have generously made time in busy schedules to join us is too long to set out here. They have represented a rich variety of human creativity and achievement: sports greats like Lynn Swann, virtuoso musicians such as Van Cliburn, astronaut Al Worden, great entertainers like Rita Moreno, Marcel Marceau, and Tony Bennett, and superb artisans and performers of many kinds—stonecutters, cake decorators, gymnasts, dancers. With our guests' help, I have been able to show a wide diversity of self-expression, the extraordinary range of human potential. I want children and their families to know that there are many constructive ways to express who they are and how they feel.

Sometimes I show a short film on location about how something is made. It may be balloons or towels or dolls or robots. I want children to know that people make things, that things don't just make themselves. Some days we show children places they may be curious or apprehensive about. When we talked about divorce one week, we showed a visit to the inside of a commercial airliner, cockpit and all, because I knew that many young children fly alone on visits to their separated parents. We've gone into hospitals, doctors' and dentists' offices, and schools. Just like everybody, children like to be told what to expect.

And then there's the part of each "television visit" when, generally with the help of a little trolley that leaves my living room on a track and enters a tunnel in the wall, we pass into the Neighborhood of Make-Believe. I never appear on camera there (I'm behind the sets as puppeteer and voices). My "television friend" and I are part of the real world, where people can *pretend* about anything they want to.

We do pretend about real people—about Betty Aberlin, who becomes King Friday XIII's niece, Lady Aberlin; about Joe Negri, who becomes Handyman Negri and helps keep things running smoothly; about Mr. McFeely, who keeps on with his deliveries. But most of the neighbors in the Neighborhood of Make-Believe are puppets. They are small hand puppets for the most part, and it's usually the large human characters who help them talk about their joys and their worries, their work and their play. Naturally I hope that the small children who are watching—and who often identify with the puppet characters—are learning that there are also larger people in their real lives who can be trusted and who want to be helpful.

At the close of the program, we are back in my living room again. We think about some of the things we've seen and the places we've been to, and what we've pretended about. I often tell how I felt when I was a child and encountered some of the things we've brought up that day. And then I leave, changing back into my shoes and jacket, promising to visit again, and singing "It's Such a Good Feeling" (in the earliest broadcasts we used to sing a song called "Tomorrow"):

It's such a good feeling to know you're alive.
It's such a happy feeling: You're growing inside.
And when you wake up ready to say,
"I think I'll make a snappy new day,"
It's such a good feeling, a very good feeling,
The feeling you know you're alive.

And sometimes I add:

I'll be back when the day is new
And I'll have more ideas for you.
And you'll have things you'll want to talk about.
I will too.

Just before I go out the door (if I've timed it right!) I have a few seconds left to say something that means a lot to me, and, I've learned, means a lot to others (young and old alike). I say: "You've made this day a special day by just your being you. There's only one person in the whole world like you. That's you yourself; and, people can like you exactly as you are."

Everything on *Mister Rogers' Neighborhood* is done out of a concern for children's feelings—to encourage them to feel good about who they are, to help them understand themselves and their world, to enhance their healthy curiosity about that world, and to support in them an optimistic striving toward what they can become. That's what our play and our talk and our pretending are about. And because I am who I am—a person who sometimes finds it easier to say important things through songs—that's what I sing about, too. Here are some of the songs we sing most often on *Mister Rogers' Neighborhood*, along with some thoughts about why we sing them. (The complete words and the music for these songs begin on page 258.)

*   *   *

"You Are You"

You are you and I am I
And we will always be
Quite different to people who know us well
'Cause they're the ones who like us
To be different.

I eat and you do too.
You sleep and I do too.
I wake up and you do too.
So we two do so much the same,
But I'm Mister Rogers,
And you have your name. . . .

That's a song about the process of separation and being separate people, but it's also a song that lets children know that all human beings have some things in common. It's about the reassurance we can find in human kinship as well as the delight we can find in individual differences (see page 43).

As children learn they begin to sort and classify. Often, they do it by way of opposites—big/little, hard/soft, good/bad, black/white, night/day . . . and, of course, same/different. But not many things are all one way or all another, and certainly people aren't. We all know people who have grown up to dislike other people who are different—*because* they are different. I've often noticed that when someone feels that way, that person doesn't feel very good about his or her *own* differences. I think that's where it all begins for us parents: helping our children feel good about *their* differences so they can be accepting of, and open to, the differences in others. When we help them learn that, we help them build the foundation of compassion.

* * *

"Everything Grows Together"

Everything grows together
Because you're all one piece.
Your nose grows
As the rest of you grows
Because you're all one piece.

Everything grows together
Because you're all one piece.

Your ears grow
As your nose grows
As the rest of you grows
Because you're all one piece. . . .

As the song goes on, we add arms, hands, fingers, legs, feet, and toes—one each time, until we end up singing:

Everything grows together
Because you're all one piece.
Your toes grow
As your feet grow
As your legs grow
As your fingers grow
As your hands grow
As your arms grow
As your ears grow
As your nose grows
As the rest of you grows
Because you're all one piece

The process of self-discovery cannot be hurried, and it takes a long time. Even at five, children are still uncertain about how their bodies are put together. When a favorite toy is accidentally broken, or an ear comes off a much-loved teddy bear, a child might wonder if he or she can break like the toy did or wonder if part of his or her body could fall off. That sort of wondering can be very scary.

All children need to hear that they are not a lot of pieces stuck together, pieces that can break off or come unglued. Many children are even concerned about scrapes and cuts. When they see a little of their own blood, they may be afraid that it's *all* going to come out, just the way all the stuffing can come out of a stuffed animal when it gets torn (see page 208).

Not long ago we made a film to help explain emergency rooms to children in case they should ever have to visit one. There was a five-year-old boy in the emergency department where we were filming, and he started telling me what had happened to a friend of his. He began by explaining that he and his friend were both smart, but that his friend had fallen down and cut his head and nearly all of his brains had come out. He told me his friend wouldn't have been smart anymore if all his brains had come out. Children's fantasies about what might happen to them are often so much scarier than the reality.

Children need help in learning that people are all one piece, and that when they were born they had everything they needed to be who they are, and that every part of them goes on growing *together*.

*　　*　　*

"You Can Never
Go Down the Drain"

You can never go down
Can never go down
Can never go down the drain.
You can never go down
Can never go down
Can never go down the drain.

You're bigger than the water,
You're bigger than the soap,
You're much bigger than all the bubbles
And bigger than your telescope,

So, you see...

You can never go down
Can never go down
Can never go down the drain.

A lot of people ask me about that song and why on earth I wrote a song like that. It's a fact that there are many children who, when they see all the water and suds swirling down the bathtub drain, worry that maybe they might be carried down, too. Most people can't remember that feeling. I know I can't; nevertheless, I've heard of many very young children who scream and cry if they aren't taken out of the tub before the plug is pulled. And it's not only the tub that can be a problem. One parent wrote to tell me about her three-year-old: "He recently learned to toilet himself," she said, "and one of the things that kept him from doing it sooner was a fear he often expressed of falling into the toilet and being flushed away."

I don't think it's a coincidence that this common fear is likely to occur at the same time that children are working on toilet training. It's difficult to learn to hold on to and let go of something within us "on demand," particularly when we're still not quite sure what is really part of us and what isn't. When feces and urine are flushed away, it isn't so surprising that a child might worry that the rest of the body might go down a drain as well.

(I've been asked, too, about the words "And bigger than your telescope"—what's that all about? When I first started singing that song on *Mister Rogers' Neighborhood* I often used to look through a toy telescope as a way to travel imaginatively from my living room into the Neighborhood of Make-Believe. Telescopes can help us to focus on things we're trying hard to understand. I just included that familiar "prop" from the program in the song.)

*   *   *

MISTER ROGERS TALKS WITH PARENTS

"Children Can"

Who can crawl under a table?
Who can sit under a chair?
Who can fit their feet in little shoes
And sleep most anywhere?

Who can play very much longer,
Play much harder than grown-ups ever dare?
You're a child so you can do it.
You can do it anywhere.

Who can wake up every morning
And be ready right away?
Who can notice all the tiny things
That other people say?

Who can make the things they play with
Something different for every single day?
You're a child and you can do it.
Children do it any way.

Roll in the grass, squoosh in the mud.
Lick an ice cream cone,
Sing to a bass. Splash in a flood
By a stepping stone, all alone.

Who can put your hand in my hand
And be ready to feel all safe and strong?
You're a child so you can do it.
Children do it all life long.

As children come to be more and more aware of themselves and their world, they also become aware of how small they are compared to the people who look after them. It may seem to them that grown-ups get to do all the big and exciting things and make all the decisions too. But there are special things about childhood and being a child. I think it helps little children feel good about who they are when we adults put value on the many things children *can* do. It's a way for us to let them know that we don't want or expect them to be more grown-up than they're ready to be—that we really do like them just the way they are.

*   *   *

"I Did Too!"

Did you ever fall and hurt your hand or knee?
Did you ever bite your tongue?
Did you ever find the stinger of a bee
Stuck in your thumb?

Did you ever trip and fall down on the stairs?
Did you ever stub your toe?
Did you ever dream of great big grizzly bears
Who wouldn't go?

I did too.
It seems the things that you do,
I did too when I was very new.
I had lots of hurts and scares and worries
When I was growing up like you.

Have you noticed how delighted young children are to hear their parents tell stories of things they did when they were little? Part of that delight comes from shared moments of closeness with a person you love, and part of it comes from hearing that someone you love had the same kinds of feelings you now have, did some of the same things, was naughty, got dirty, got in trouble, laughed and cried and felt afraid. I've heard children say, very reassuringly, "Gramps got mad at Daddy just the way Daddy gets mad at me sometimes."

Stories of our childhoods tell our children something else: They let our children know, without our even having to put it into words, that being little and vulnerable doesn't last forever. Just as we grew from babies to children to who we are, so will they. That's important for children to know—important enough that I *did* put it into words in another song:

"You're Growing"

You used to creep and crawl real well
But then you learned to walk real well.
There was a time you'd coo and cry
But then you learned to talk and, my!
You almost always try.
You almost always do your best.
I like the way you're growing up.
It's fun, that's all.

Someday you'll be a grown-up, too
And have some children grow up, too.
Then you can love them in and out
And tell them stories all about
The times when you were their size,
The times when you found great surprise
In growing up. And they will sing
It's fun, that's all.

You're growing, you're growing,
You're growing in and out.
You're growing, you're growing,
You're growing all about.

Most of us can remember how long the summers used to seem and how long it was from birthday to birthday. When we were five, it seemed we'd never get to be ten, and at ten it seemed it would be forever until we were twenty. So often it is only by looking back at where they have been that children can see they are growing at all.

There are outward signs of growth that we can help children notice—clothes that get outgrown, pencil marks on a doorjamb that move up as they get taller. There are lots of things that they learn to do that we can remind them they wouldn't have been able to do a month or a year before—tying a shoe, riding a tricycle. But while these advances bring satisfaction to children and parents alike, it's children's *inside* growth we particularly need to help them appreciate. "Growing on the inside" are the words I use when I talk with children about such things as learning to wait, learning to keep on trying, being able to talk about their feelings, and to express those feelings in constructive ways. These signs of growth need at least as much notice and applause as the outward kind, and children need to feel proud of them—even more proud than they may feel when that line on the doorjamb goes up another inch.

*   *   *

"Sometimes People Are Good"

Sometimes people are good,
And they do just what they should.
But the very same people who are good sometimes
Are the very same people who are bad sometimes.
It's funny but it's true.
It's the same, isn't it, for me and...?

Sometimes people get wet,
And their parents get upset.
But the very same people who get wet sometimes
Are the very same people who are dry sometimes.
It's funny but it's true.
It's the same, isn't it, for me and...?

Sometimes people make noise,
And they break each other's toys.
But the very same people who are noisy sometimes
Are the very same people who are quiet sometimes.
It's funny but it's true.
It's the same, isn't it, for me and...?

Isn't it the same for you?

That song, and one called "Good People Sometimes Do Bad Things," are songs I sing to let children know that everyone does things that are naughty once in a while but that doing something bad doesn't make you a bad *person*. It may seem a small difference when it's written out like that, but the feelings we have as adults tell us what a big difference there really is.

It's so easy to say "Bad boy!" or "Bad girl!" to a child who spills or breaks or hits or bites or gets dirty. But the child is likely to hear "*I* am bad" rather than "What I *did* was bad," and a child who feels he or she is a bad person is also likely to feel unlovable. If we come to believe that we are unlovable, there's likely to be little motivation to avoid doing bad things.

* * *

"It's the People You Like the Most"

It's the people you like the most
Who can make you feel maddest.
It's the people you care for the most
Who manage to make you feel baddest.

It's the people you like the most
Who can make you feel happiest!
It's the people you care for the most, most likely,
Who manage to make you feel snappiest!

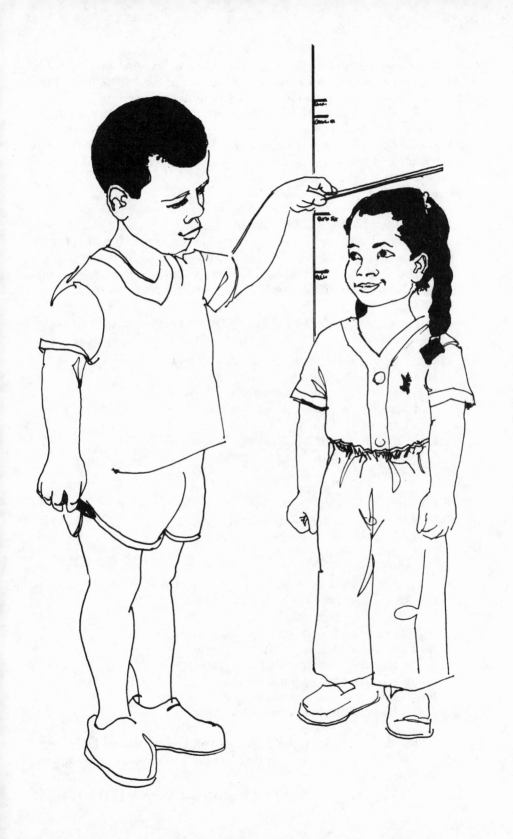

Love and anger are such a puzzle! You can imagine how puzzling they are for children. It's hard enough for us, as adults, to understand and manage our angry feelings toward parents, spouses, and children, or to keep their anger toward us in perspective. It's a different kind of anger from the kind we may feel toward strangers because it is so deeply intertwined with caring and attachment. Anger evokes old anxieties over separation and the loss of love from those we love and need to have love us. In the wake of that kind of anger can follow fear and guilt, and those feelings are hard to deal with, too.

It may be easier for us later on if, as children, we were allowed to have our angry feelings and if someone we loved let us know that those feelings were a normal part of loving and being loved. It will certainly have helped us if we learned to talk about those feelings and express them in healthy ways. Many people grow up afraid of their anger, afraid that it will make them lose control. That's why I sing this song:

"What Do You Do?"

What do you do with the mad that you feel
When you feel so mad you could bite?
When the whole wide world seems oh, so wrong
And nothing you do seems very right?
What do you do? Do you punch a bag?
Do you pound some clay or some dough?
Do you round up friends for a game of tag?
Or see how fast you go?

It's great to be able to stop
When you've planned a thing that's wrong.
And be able to do something else instead
And think this song:

I can stop when I want to,
Can stop when I wish,
Can stop, stop, stop anytime.
And what a good feeling to feel like this,
And know that the feeling is really mine.
Know that there's something deep inside
That helps us become what we can,
For a girl can be someday a woman
And a boy can be someday a man.

"What do you do with the mad that you feel when you feel so mad you could bite?" was a question that a child really did ask a doctor one day. When I heard it, it reminded me how intense children's anger can be—and how hard for them to cope with and understand. One of the most frightening things in the world is the fear of losing control—that you really might go out of control and hurt someone you love and then lose that person's love! On the other hand, how great it is to know that we can feel our feelings and still stop ourselves short of harming ourselves or others!

*   *   *

"Sometimes"

Sometimes I don't feel like combing my hair.
I don't feel like washing my face sometimes.
Sometimes I don't feel like saying "O.K."
But sometimes isn't always.

Sometimes I do feel like combing my hair.
I do feel like washing my face sometimes.
Sometimes I do feel like saying "O.K."
But sometimes isn't always.

Sometimes I don't feel like sometimes I do.
I feel like I don't like to feel sometimes.
Sometimes I don't and sometimes I do.
But sometimes isn't always.

Why at one time we feel like doing something and at another don't feel like doing it at all is a puzzle adults come to accept and seldom try to understand. It may not be so easy for children to accept their contradictory feelings. In fact, it's probably very hard for them to reconcile such different feelings with their new and uncertain sense of self. "Yesterday I wanted to go for a ride in the car. Today I don't. Have I become a different *me*?"

There are times, too, when we feel two ways about the same thing even at the same time. "I want to go for a ride in the car but I don't feel like it." That must be very confusing, too. Much later we learn that there's a word for that: ambivalence. In fact, I've noticed that "ambivalence" can often be a very interesting new word for children to learn at about ten. I remember once asking a ten-year-old how he felt about his older brother going off to boarding school. There were only the two boys in that family and they were competitive and fought a good deal. My young friend said, "It feels great not to have him around all the time...but I miss him." I told him I understood how he could feel both ways at the same time. "In fact," I said to him, "so many people feel two ways about the same things that our language even has a word for that." I printed the word "ambivalence" on a slip of paper and gave it to him. "That word is 'ambivalence,'" I told him. "People often feel ambivalent." His parents told me later that he carried that slip of paper in his pocket for a couple of weeks and that when they'd ask him how he felt about something, his stock answer for a while was, "Oh, ambivalent, I guess." Just knowing that people could feel like that and that there was even a name for it seemed to bring him some relief in his struggles with his conflicting feelings.

And then there are times, especially when children feel very sad or lonely, that they may think life is going to be sad forever. Young children haven't lived through enough of life's ups and downs to know that even if you feel deeply sad now you will be able to feel joy again at another time—that "the very same people who are sad sometimes are the very same people who are glad sometimes." Children don't learn that simply because we tell them, but it's important for us to let them know that that's the way life is. Someone can be very sad for a while but that while doesn't last forever. Each time they find out that what we say is true, they learn to trust us a little bit more about other difficult things.

*   *   *

"The Truth Will Make Me Free"

What if I were very, very sad
And all I did was smile?
I wonder after a while
What might become of my sadness?

What if I were very, very angry
And all I did was sit
And never think about it?
What might become of my anger?

Where would they go, and what would they do,
If I couldn't let them out?
Maybe I'd fall, maybe get sick
Or doubt.

But what if I could know the truth
And say just how I feel?
I think I'd learn a lot that's real
About freedom.

I'm learning to sing a sad song when I'm sad.
I'm learning to say I'm angry when I'm very mad.
I'm learning to shout, I'm getting it out!
I'm happy, learning exactly how I feel inside of me.
I'm learning to know the truth.
I'm learning to tell the truth.
Discovering truth will make me free.

That song means a great deal to me. Almost every day that I was at high school in Latrobe, Pennsylvania, I saw written in large gold letters over the auditorium's proscenium: "You shall know the truth and the truth shall make you free." It's part of a biblical quotation.

Freedom and truth are mighty large subjects for everyone, especially for young children, and I know it will be many years before children who are hearing that song today will understand what it all means. It took me many years to write it! But in our own ways we can begin thinking about what freedom and truth might mean to us personally. I know that I've thought about them a lot since high school days, and I believe they're closely related to love, no matter how old we are or how young.

When we're tiny infants, for instance, love and rage are fused—they're both just part of feeling. If a baby's needs are taken care of, he or she feels good, feels loving. If those needs are not provided for, the baby cries with anger and frustration. But babies aren't able to understand differences in feelings. They just *feel*. Little by little, though, we do grow to be able to tell the difference between our love and our rage. We can tell someone "I love you" and we can tell someone "I'm angry with you."

Adults have complex feelings toward children—even as children have complex feelings toward adults. When, for instance, one of our children does something dangerous despite our warnings and rules, we may be angry, frightened, frustrated, and disappointed all at once. It's our love for our children that gives rise to these different feelings, but that's not an easy relationship for young children to understand. In the heat of the moment, it's not easy for us, either, to keep in mind. At a time like that, our children are most likely to feel our anger, but even as we scold and punish, we need to help them learn where the roots of that anger lie. Trying to be honest with ourselves and our children about what we think and feel helps our own continued growing. Encouraging our children to be honest with us about what *they* think and feel helps them develop their capacity to love themselves and love others. Honesty in love is often very hard. The truth is often painful. But the freedom it can bring is worth the trying.

*　　*　　*

A LITTLE LATER ON

"Wishes Don't Make Things Come True"

One time I wished that a lion would come
And eat up my house and my street.
I was mad at the world and I wished that the beast
Would stomp everything with his big, heavy feet,
And eat everything with his big, sharp teeth,
And eat everything with his teeth.

But that wish certainly didn't come true
'Cause scary, mad wishes don't make things come true.

One time I wished that a dragon would come
And burn up my daddy's big store.
I was angry with him 'cause I wanted to play,
And my daddy just went to his store right away.
I wished that the dragon would burn his store.
I wished it would burn Daddy's store.

But that wish certainly didn't come true
'Cause scary, mad wishes don't make things come true.

I'm glad it's certainly that way, aren't you?
That scary, mad wishes don't make things come true.
No kinds of wishes can make things come true.

Most of us have at some time wished for "scary mad things" to happen to the people we love when they make us angry. Even adults may have sudden, almost inadvertent thoughts that can, if we're not careful to really understand them, bring in their wake a wave of guilt for even thinking such things.

Most of us are able to separate what we think from what we really feel. We know that an angry thought or wish is only that—something in the mind and nothing more. But young children don't know that for quite a while. They have the notion that thinking or wishing something can make it happen.

If coincidence makes a "scary mad wish" come true—for example, if a child in a momentary time of anger wishes that a parent would get sick or die and that parent does—that child may be left with a deep and long-lasting guilt, convinced that it was his or her wishing that caused the damage. The conscious memory of having had that wish may vanish along with other memories of childhood, but the feelings of guilt and badness may persist for a long, long time.

Helping children learn to separate fantasy from reality is a most important task of early childhood and one with which children need adult help. That's one reason I never appear in the make-believe segments of *Mister Rogers' Neighborhood*. In my living room and in other places in our television neighborhood, real things happen and we show them and talk about them as realistically as we can. In the Neighborhood of Make-Believe, we can make up anything we like and pretend anything we like and feel safe about it because it is only pretend. Each of our programs has something that is real and something that is pretend, and we try very hard not to confuse the two. All children need to pretend about their thoughts and their feelings, but healthy pretending means children knowing things like "no kinds of wishes can make things come true."

*   *   *

"You've Got to Do It"

You can make believe it happens,
   or pretend that something's true.
You can wish or hope or contemplate
   a thing you'd like to do.
But until you start to do it,
   you will never see it through
'Cause the make-believe pretending
   just won't do it for you.

You've got to do it. Every little bit,
You've got to do it, do it, do it, do it.
And when you're through, you can know who did it,
For you did it, you did it, you did it.

It's not easy to keep trying,
   but it's one good way to grow.
It's not easy to keep learning,
   but I know that this is so:
When you've tried and learned you're bigger
   than you were a day ago.
It's not easy to keep trying,
   but it's one way to grow.

That's another aspect of hoping and wishing and pretending and reality—it's *people* who make things happen, and to make a thing happen, you've got to work at it. You think of something first, but the doing is what makes it happen.

It's hard to know why some children seem naturally inclined to keep on trying to do something until they succeed and why others seem so ready to give up. It's possible that some are born more one way than the other; but, even if that's true, I don't think it's the only answer. It seems to me that feeling frustrated and discouraged is something that none of us can avoid, and that our different ways of coping with those feelings are among the many things we *learn*.

If, as little children, we are faced with tasks that are far beyond our capabilities, we may come to feel that trying is useless because it never works. On the other hand, if we are encouraged to work at small tasks that we can accomplish with a little effort, we may, very early in our lives, experience the pleasure and gratification that come with achievement and success. We may then grow up knowing that the trying always comes first but that it's worthwhile because trying is a path that *can* take us to where we want to go.

I think, too, that the capacity to try new things depends on how our earliest caregivers reacted to our natural curiosity. When our curiosity led us into places where we had no business going—like into dangerous situations or into other people's private possessions or private places—did we feel it was our curiosity that was being punished, or just that there were limits on the direction it was taking? It's very different to be told, "Don't be so nosy!" rather than, "I understand your interest in your daddy's tools, but they're his and if you want to use them you'll have to ask him." And when Daddy says yes or no, it will help for him to remember how he felt about his own father and his own father's tools...and tell his child about it.

Did we feel that those close to us put value on learning new things? Did we feel appreciated for our earliest achievements? Were those accomplishments celebrated? Or were they taken for granted and dismissed as the kinds of things all kids learn sooner or later?

Perhaps above all, I think that the willingness and the courage to keep on trying may develop best if there is someone we love close by who can lend us some of the strength we do not as yet have within ourselves. I don't mean someone who will do a task for us when we can't do it for ourselves, but rather someone who will share our times of trying by just being around and being supportive. Someone who can sustain a belief that we can succeed even when we doubt it ourselves. We all need people like that—grown-ups as well as children.

*   *   *

"Everybody's Fancy"

Some are fancy on the outside.
Some are fancy on the inside.
Everybody's fancy. Everybody's fine.
Your body's fancy and so is mine.

Boys are boys from the beginning.
Girls are girls right from the start.
Everybody's fancy. Everybody's fine.
Your body's fancy and so is mine.

As children begin to get a sense of what and who they are, it is only natural for them to compare themselves with the people around them. It is through trying to understand our relationship with others that we can learn about ourselves.

A child's awareness of body differences begins early in a family where opportunities abound to observe that a man is differently made from a woman and that children are made differently from adults.

Where children bring a lot of natural curiosity to talk about sex and sex differences, adults sometimes bring a lot of natural anxiety. Fortunately, the gulf between them is often lessened by natural humor.

It may be helpful to know that, most of the time, very young children are not curious about the things we're afraid they're going to be curious about. They're likely to be wondering why they are different, and worrying whether they're made the way they should be. Often, all they need to hear is the simple reassurance that their bodies are fine and exactly the way they're supposed to be: If you're born a boy baby you will grow up to be a big boy and then a man, and men are the ones who become the daddies—just as girl babies grow up to be big girls and then women and women are the ones who become the mommies. As time goes by, children will have new and more complex questions for us, which we should try to answer simply and truthfully. A lot of our anxiety, I think, comes from feeling we have to tell our children things we're sure they can't understand. We *don't* have to.

Chi va piano, va sano, va lontano is an old Italian proverb that means, "The person who goes quietly goes with health and goes far." I learned the proverb from the mother of John Costa, our music director for *Mister Rogers' Neighborhood*, one day while she was giving me a lesson on making bread and pizza. Mrs. Costa's point was that hurrying up and using a lot of shortcuts doesn't get us far at all—and that's not only true for baking, but also for many other things, including helping children learn. Some parents feel they must teach their children to spell and read c-a-t before their children have ever felt a cat or drawn a cat or played out how it might feel to *be* a cat. And while there are some parents who feel that sex should never be talked about at all, there are others who rush to explain to their very young children the biologically correct facts of reproduction and birth before their children are able to understand them or before they even really want to know.

Young children may have some very imaginative fantasies about how life begins, and these fantasies are likely to reflect their current understanding of their bodies. Whether it be the stork or the lily pad, I feel it's a disservice to them to dismiss quickly their explanations and replace them, instead, with graphic descriptions of intercourse and birth. It always makes me uncomfortable when children are deprived of the opportunity to play out their feelings and fantasies by adults who are overconcerned with technically correct answers to everything. I've always found that it's much more helpful to ask children about their fantasies than to try to squelch them. I've learned so much from them, and I've often discovered that at a certain level the children knew they were dealing in fantasy themselves. Shortcuts which interfere with a young human being's play and normal development may turn out to be very long and unhealthy ways around growing into adulthood.

Chi va piano, va sano, va lontano....

* * *

"Going to Marry Mom"

One day I said, "I'm really going to marry,
Really going to marry, really going to marry,"
One day I said, "I'm really going to marry,
Really going to marry my mom."

I told my mom, "I'm really going to marry,
Really going to marry, really going to marry,"
I told my mom, "I'm really going to marry,
Really going to marry you."

She smiled, didn't laugh, said, "I hope you will marry,
Hope you will marry, hope you will marry,"
She smiled, didn't laugh, said, "I hope you will marry
Maybe someone *like* me."

There are many more verses to that song, in which the mother explains that she is already married to Daddy and that as her boy grows up he will become more like Daddy and love someone who may become his wife and maybe the mother of his own children, who, in turn, will in some ways become like him (see page 106).

Wanting to marry Mom or wanting to be Dad's wife—desires known widely as "oedipal feelings"—are common to almost all children when they're about three or four. We adults need to take these feelings seriously and react to them lovingly because they create a lot of tension for a child over the issues of separateness and oneness, love and anger... and guilt. For a child begins to think thoughts like: "How on earth am I ever going to get to marry Mom unless I can find some way to get rid of Dad... but I *love* Dad... and yet I want Mom for my very own! But if Dad would go away I'd be very sad, and yet...."

There are many deeply disturbing times of this kind for young children. Such feelings are some of the hardest for them to cope with because, while these urges are strong, children at this age have not reached a level of development where they can even identify them—let alone talk about them, understand them, or comprehend the reactions they may evoke from parents. For our part, most of us have forgotten that we ever had such feelings toward our own parents when we were little. Since our children will probably be experiencing times like this they will need our help and understanding while they do so. It's *not* helpful to encourage a small daughter when she flirts with her father, as most little girls tend to do, or to encourage a little son's fantasies about being the "man of the house," even when his daddy is away. What probably *is* helpful to our children's growing is to aid them gently, lovingly, but firmly in learning what the real relationships are in a family and that they have a very special place of their own that no one else can have—just as Mommy and Daddy have. We needn't be upset by the anger children may feel for a while when they have to learn, as everyone does, that many of their wishes and fantasies can't ever come true. That's the healthy anger of growth, and so long as they feel that our love is greater than their anger, all kinds of experiences can help everyone in the family grow.

*　　*　　*

"When a Baby Comes"

When a baby comes to your house,
It's a girl or it's a boy.
It's a sister or a brother,
But it's never just a toy.

It can cry and it can holler.
It can wet and it can coo.
But there's one thing it can never...
It can never be like you.

The arrival of a baby brother or sister is bound to be a big event in the life of a firstborn child. From oneness with the mother, to twoness, and then to threeness with the father (but still the center of loving attention), that firstborn child now has to make sense of *four*ness. With all the attention the new baby is getting, it may seem to the firstborn that the family is still three... and that he or she has just been pushed out of the family triangle by the little newcomer. I know one child who said, "When the baby gets born and is really here, then who will be *my* mommy?" It's rare for the first child not to show *some* hostility or resentment, and most often that will come out in play, or in the child's drawings, or in dreams, or in anger directed toward us as parents. Sometimes a young child will seem to go backward in development— that is, once again he or she might start thumb sucking or bed-wetting or become extra-clinging. After all, those are the sorts of things babies do, and babies seem to get all the attention!

How much easier it would be if a child could say to us, "I'm really mad that you've brought home another baby. Wasn't I good enough for you? And now no one pays any attention to me anymore. No one loves me anymore. I *hate* you!" But young children aren't able to tell us that in this way. They can only feel it and then find some way to let that feeling out. When it does come out, it may not seem to have anything to do directly with the new baby, but when there are noticeable behavior changes just after a new baby's birth, we can be fairly sure they are in some way related.

What we need to do, of course, is to try to make enough time specially for our firstborns—time together when we can let them know in different ways, again and again, that no one can ever take their special place in the family, that they were there before the baby and they will always be the oldest—always be our children. At the same time that we reassure them of their *place* in the family, we can try to reassure them that no one can ever *be* like them either—not the new baby nor anyone else in this world, and no matter who else joins the family, we'll always go on loving them for who they are.

*   *   *

These, then, are some of the things I particularly like to sing and talk about on *Mister Rogers' Neighborhood* because I believe that they are important to all children in their early years: feelings about separateness and togetherness, sameness and difference; feelings about what's part of the body and what isn't, what's on the inside of the body and what's outside; feelings about what it's like to be small in a world of big people when you think you'll *never* grow up; feelings about being bad or good, angry or loving, or just plain not sure how you feel; feelings about telling people how you feel; feelings about wishing and pretending, about what's real and what's make-believe; feelings about how boys' and girls' bodies are different; and feelings about Mom and Dad and a new baby.

When you think about it, all these songs are really songs about how we feel about ourselves. How children feel about themselves *is* what I care about most. If we can help our children feel acceptable and valuable when they are small, they'll have a better chance of growing into adults who can feel good about who they are then, too. And so I often also sing songs like "You Are Special," "It's Such a Good Feeling," "Won't You Be My Neighbor," and one that, as I write down the words, I warmly offer not only to children but to you reading this book:

"It's You I Like"

It's you I like,
It's not the things you wear,
It's not the way you do your hair—
But it's you I like.

The way you are right now,
The way down deep inside you—
Not the things that hide you,
Not your toys—
They're just beside you.

But it's you I like,
Every part of you,
Your skin, your eyes, your feelings
Whether old or new.
I hope that you'll remember
Even when you're feeling blue
That it's you I like,
It's you yourself, it's you,
It's you...I...like!

CHAPTER 4:

DISABILITIES

When we began developing the story of Planet Purple, we were working under a grant from what was then the Bureau of Education for the Handicapped (of the Office of Education). It was a grant that continued for three years, and during that time all of us at Family Communications had the privilege of working closely with some remarkable teachers. There were consultants—professionals in many fields who had chosen to make their careers working with children and adults with disabilities—and then there were those adults and children themselves.

It's hard, just because of the way language works, to talk about disabilities without giving the impression that having a disability puts a person in a separate world, a separate culture, and that "they" are different from "us." How untrue that is, but how hard to move from knowing it's untrue to *feeling* it's untrue!

Part of the problem with *disabilities* is that the word immediately suggests an inability to see or hear or walk or do other things that many of us take for granted. But what of people who can't *feel*? Or talk about their feelings? Or manage their feelings in constructive ways? What of people who aren't able to form close and strong relationships? And people who cannot find fulfillment in their lives, or those who have lost hope, who live in disappointment and bitterness and find in life no joy, no love? These, it seems to me, are the truly crippling disabilities.

Our charter under the grant we received was "to help foster among children constructive attitudes toward handicaps whether the handicaps are in themselves or in others." Understandably, we were directed to concern ourselves with the more classifiable handicaps, such as orthopedic conditions, vision and hearing impairment, mental retardation, and emotional disturbance. To have broadened the range of possible handicapping conditions would have risked losing focus in our work and lessening its usefulness. As it was, we found the broadness of the range we were given quite challenging enough.

In addition to the new programming we produced for the daily *Mister Rogers' Neighborhood* series, we also produced video cassettes, audio cassettes, and books that, together, became called *I Am, I Can, I Will* because they dealt primarily with young children's self-concept, self-confidence, and motivation. As we began working on this project, it was easier for me to understand my own feelings toward people with handicaps than it was for me to imagine what it would be like to have such disabilities. I knew what it was like not to be able to do some things as well as other people did them; but, it was different trying to imagine what it would be like not to be able to walk or hear or see. We needed lots of help from people who knew what it was like. And what an abundance of joy and hope and love we have encountered among the many people with visible handicaps we have worked with.

Chrissie Thompson was one of our first helpers. She joined the cast of *Mister Rogers' Neighborhood* as the granddaughter of Mr. and Mrs. McFeely. Her sister and parents joined us, too. Chrissie was eight then. Her lower spine had never grown in completely—a condition called spina bifida—so she was paralyzed from the waist down and walked with the help of braces and crutches. When we first met, Chrissie could

sense my uncertainty about how and when to help her. But Chrissie had no hesitation in letting me know when she preferred to do something by herself or when she needed my help. She showed me in the most natural way how her leg braces strapped on and how the hinge worked that let her legs bend for kneeling or sitting. She talked about her feelings, too—even sad and angry ones.

After Chrissie had appeared on our program several times, we received a letter from a mother who showed us just how constructive television *can* be for performers and viewers alike. She told us that her daughter had also been born with spina bifida and had been through five operations. Though this little girl had been able to walk with braces and crutches before her last surgery, she had since developed large fears about trying to walk and would no longer do so. But several weeks after seeing Chrissie on our program, as this mother told us, her daughter once again asked for her crutches and said she would "walk for Mister Rogers."

Well, that letter from California arrived on a day when Chrissie was scheduled to tape with us in the afternoon. Chrissie had once expressed some strong feelings about the white orthopedic shoes she had to wear. "White's for babies," she had said disdainfully, and went on to say that she could hardly wait until she grew into a size that had a wider color selection. With that in mind, I'd decided to be on my porch, shining a pair of my shoes, when she dropped by. We had no preset script and were just going to see what kind of conversation developed between us. We talked about different kinds of shoes for a moment, and then our conversation went like this:

Mr. R: *How do you feel about your white shoes and the braces?*

Chrissie: *Well, there's this girl that I heard about once, and she didn't like her braces and crutches because she . . . well . . . because they caused her all these problems . . .*

Mr. R: *What kinds of problems, Chrissie?*

Chrissie: *Like having trouble with her legs and stuff. She always watched your show and she was mad at them and she said that she wouldn't wear them anymore, and so she put them back in the attic.*

Mr. R: *She put her braces and crutches in the attic?*

> *Chrissie: . . .and so then she said that her mother would have to carry her because she wasn't going to walk anymore. One time she was watching the show and she saw me, and when she saw me she noticed that I wore them, and then she said to her mother, "If that girl on television can walk as good as that, then I can, too." Then she went up to the attic, crawling, and she got out her braces and crutches and then she told her mother that she was going to walk again, and then she put her braces on and she started running and walking.*

> *Mr. R: And your television visit helped in that way. Does that make you proud?*

> *Chrissie: (nods).*

Our relationship with Chrissie helped us in many ways: all of us. One of life's joys is discovering that we can be open to new experiences that at first seem strange or even scary. It's always exhilarating to find, as happens so often, that the barriers that seem to separate us from other people are like mirages and vanish as we get closer to those people. Nowadays when I meet a person with an obvious physical handicap I try not to let much time go by before asking about it. That acknowledgment seems to clear the miragelike obstacles and open the way for us to accept every part of each other just as we are.

Another person who worked with us was a young man named Tim Scanlon. Tim is an exceptionally gifted actor and at one time was a star performer for the National Theater of the Deaf. He beguiled us all with his wit and inventiveness and generously shared with us the feelings he remembered having as a child when other children wouldn't play with him because he couldn't hear. He was often lonely and sad, but he obviously had the love and acceptance of important people around him, because he grew up feeling good about who he was and became someone of unusual creativity and achievement.

While he was working with us, Tim appeared as himself—an actor and amateur photographer—in those parts of the program that take place with me in the "real" neighborhood. In the Neighborhood of Make-Believe segments, he acted the part of a teacher who had been sent by the Owl Correspondence School to give lessons to X the Owl. X liked him right away, but Henrietta Pussycat was frightened of the strange-sounding way he talked. As for King Friday. . .well, he thought that Tim couldn't possibly be a good teacher because he couldn't hear and he didn't talk like everyone else. In the end, of course, all the neighbors in Make-Believe, King Friday leading the list, came to accept and like and admire Tim for who he is—just as did all of us at Family Communications.

It's tempting to marvel at how Tim "overcame his handicap"—a phrase we often hear—but there's something about that phrase that doesn't ring true to my understanding. Not being able to hear was part of who Tim was and may remain so all through his life. Rather than "overcoming" who he was, Tim, as he grew, "became" who he is, drawing on both his talents and his limitations and incorporating them into a whole and strong personality capable of giving great gifts to others. A disabled person? Not Tim!

Ted Lennox, another friend, couldn't see; he had been blind since he was a little baby. When he came to work with us, Ted had children of his own and, in addition to being a teacher in the Michigan public school system, was trying to market toys and books that he felt were particularly appropriate for young children. For one of our audio cassettes, Ted spent a lot of time with us reminiscing about his childhood and his growing up without sight. Many people—both with and without sight—have told us that Ted's experiences meant a great deal to them. Here is some of what Ted told us.

I was born in the big city, Detroit, but I spent most of my early life in the country, from the time I was about maybe one year old until I was around twelve years old. I had two brothers. Frank was a year younger than I am and Ces was two years younger than I am. So we were very close.

When you are close with somebody, there are times when you have arguments and misunderstandings. You hurt one another's feelings, and there were certainly periods as we were growing up when we fought with each other, either argued or even sometimes got right down and had a big fat battle. But I found that usually after the fight was over it cleared the air and things were even friendlier than they had been before.

I remember one wintry day. I might have been only four years old, perhaps, and it snowed, snowed, and snowed. After the snow was over we went outside and my mother showed my brothers and me how to roll the snow into a ball, and we rolled many, many snowballs and put them all together in a big circle. Then we put snowballs on top of snowballs, and when we were through we had a little snow house or a little fort that we could crawl inside. I think we dug a hole through, made a little tunnel we could crawl in. I remember building that snow house together with my two brothers and my mother, and sometimes my father would join in. That was a marvelous, exciting thing to do together as a family.

I can remember in our neighborhood we all used to like to play baseball. We had an empty lot on the corner of our block.

It was a half a block down and across the street. It was a great big area, just wide open. We played over there, and instead of hitting the ball in the air, the pitcher would roll the ball and I would hit it on the ground. We found ways that I could do things like that.

I think the things that scare me or have scared me, especially when I was little, were things that I didn't understand. I can remember a slide, for instance: What is a slide like? And what happened to you when you slid on something? The only way I could handle that was to climb up that slide and not be in any hurry, find out what was up at the top of that slide, and then carefully, but slowly, go down the slide.

Once I understood what that slide was, that took away the scare. Then, of course, it became fun.

I can remember my first time at the dentist's office. I didn't really know what was going to happen, and only when the dentist told me what he was going to do... and how he was going to do it... and then when he was going to do it... that helped me a lot, helped me not to be as scared.

There were times, when I was a boy, when I would get bullied or teased, mostly by boys who were older. Sometimes I didn't mind because I knew they weren't trying to hurt me, and they were really being quite friendly. Sometimes they kept it up so long that it did hurt me and made me feel very bad.

There were times when my brothers would run off and play, either leaving me home and not thinking of how I felt, or going off and playing and doing things that perhaps I couldn't do. That was very sad for me. I used to fill my hours doing many things. I can remember playing games in my living room. I think I can even remember back when I was very little. I had a soft rag doll that I guess I used to sort of have as a friend. And I can remember building cities in the living room. I used to use old shoes or boots or just about anything.

Many times I felt different. Sometimes people would come up and talk to my mother about me, and I'd be standing there, and they would say things like, "Oh, I'm sorry to see your little boy can't see," or they would say other things that made me feel embarrassed or ashamed because I couldn't see. They seemed to feel sorry for me. That made me feel very bad. It made me feel that maybe there was something wrong with not being able to see. But that's how they felt; that's not how I needed to feel. When I didn't feel badly about myself, when I was proud of what I could do, and what I did do, this seemed to make other people feel comfortable with me.

I remember having the opportunity to make my first sandwich. I was hungry and nobody was home and I went to the icebox and got out the materials. I remember spreading the peanut butter and so forth, and I'm sure I didn't do it as well as I do now. Or I'm sure I didn't do it as well as my mother could have, but that was a great-tasting peanut butter sandwich. I did it and I was proud of it and probably I'll never have another peanut butter sandwich ever taste so good!

One of the things I had to learn as a boy was what I could do myself and where was it that I needed help and was it okay to ask others to help if I really needed it. I also found out that there were things I could do that others couldn't do, simply because I had ability that others didn't have. For instance, I was very strong and I could do some things that the other kids couldn't do. I found that there were times that I would help them do things, and they would help me.

I began my schooling when I was five years old. At that time most blind children went away and lived where they went to school. I went through a period of time where I was very lonely and very sad. I can remember going to bed at night and lying in bed weeping, missing my family very much. But it passed and I became able and comfortable at school.

I remember very fondly my first teacher, my kindergarten teacher. Her name was Miss Hammond, and she didn't seem to mind the fact that I missed my family so much. I can still remember sitting with her, and I can remember her listening to me be very unhappy, and I probably cried a bit, and she allowed me to feel sad without making me feel that I shouldn't. She just accepted me.

There was a time in my life when I used to be worried a great deal about how I appeared to other people. How I did things. Did I do things well? Did I do things the right way? This used to make me feel very self-conscious. I'd want to do very well because I knew I was being watched. I found that I wanted to do so well that I would get tense and sort of frightened.

I still have these feelings to some extent at times when I know people are staring at me and wondering, "Will this man be able to do what he appears to be doing even though he's blind?" I try to relax and just forget it and not let myself be so frightened that I make mistakes. I would rather go ahead and do things the best I can. If I make a mistake, that's fine. If I don't, that's fine.

What did blindness mean to me when I was a little boy? What did that mean? All I knew was that other people could

see. There was something called sight and they could do things
with that sight that I couldn't do. Someone could walk in the
house and they could look up and see who it was. I might have
to wait until they said something. Or they could look way down
the road and see a car coming before I could hear it.

For instance, I can remember one time at school when the
lady in charge told me I would have to take time before I went
out to play to pick up my clothes. I wasn't too happy about this
because I really wanted to go out and play. But I went in the
closet and I got distracted with something in the closet and I
wasn't picking up my clothes. I was just sitting there on the
floor, playing. The lady in charge was way down the hallway.
She hollered down the hall, telling me to get to work and hang
my clothes up so I could go out to play. And I recall wondering
how she could see around corners into my room and around the
corner into my closet!

When I was a boy, and now as an adult, I experience all
kinds of feelings that I think all human beings do. Some feelings

are happy feelings and, of course, they're to be treasured. Other feelings are sad feelings, and maybe they're to be treasured, too. Sometimes we're angry. Sometimes we're jealous. Sometimes we're sad. Sometimes we get let down, and so forth. I think we shouldn't feel badly about our feelings. I think one of the things I always felt as a little boy was that when something happened that hurt me, or something happened that angered me, it was always a marvelous experience to go to another human being and say, "I feel this way," or "This has happened to me and it affects me this way."

It's important that you have some dreams, some goals for the future that you hope to see happen someday. What would we like to be? What kind of person? What kind of job would we like to have someday? I think dreams are part of the present, part of living in the present. The past...all we can do is learn from our past. We can't do anything about that. But we certainly can do something about our present, and we sure can dream and plan and think about our futures.

Parents' Feelings

At birth, a child cries out for care and acceptance. Without these a baby cannot survive. No matter how eagerly they have anticipated their baby's arrival or how carefully they have prepared, though, many first-time parents are surprised at how much care a newborn actually requires and sometimes bewildered by the strenuous physical and emotional demands a newborn makes. For all parents, the birth of a child means that life will never be the same again, and each new child forces changes and reorderings of old relationships. Our pleasures and pains are now bound up in yet someone else's life, someone else's needs, experiences, feelings, triumphs, and misfortunes, and bound more closely than they may ever have been before.

I believe very few parents come to parenthood without ambivalence. There are just some days when we'd like to be freed of the responsibility. How much harder it must be, though, for parents whose newborn child is clearly going to need a great deal of extra care and attention, or for parents whose once healthy and flourishing child suddenly develops these extra needs. How needful those parents suddenly become, and how sad and angry they can easily feel.

Through the years, I have encountered a very broad range of feelings among parents of children with disabilities. Some have told me that they felt they were being punished by God for something they had done in their own lives, while others expressed exactly the opposite feeling—

that they had been specially chosen to be the caretakers of one of God's specially needy children. I have talked with parents who felt overwhelmed by the prospect of a difficult and expensive future, who were angry and depressed, and who wondered again and again, "Why *us*?" Then there were those who were able to take a deep breath and rearrange their lives to include a handicapped child. They seemed to be looking ahead not only to the problems of the future, but also to that future's possible rewards.

There's certainly no way parents *should* feel about this or any other sad or difficult situation that comes with raising children. In fact, the beginning of our being able to cope with anything is in our acknowledging the feelings we *do* have and accepting them as part of being human. We may need help in learning to manage those feelings or even in learning to talk about them. But whether we do it by ourselves or with someone's help, dealing with our own feelings and our own needs is primary. I say that because I believe this is generally true: How other children feel toward a brother or sister with a handicap, and how the handicapped child feels about himself or herself, is going to have a lot to do with how the parents feel.

None of us is superhuman. Each of us can only accept and give what we are able. Often, under trying circumstances, we find that we are capable of more than we thought; but often, too, we find that we reach the limits of who we can be and what we can do. Not everyone can provide the physical and emotional home care a handicapped child may require. It takes a special kind of courage to accept our limitations when it means entrusting a family member to someone else's care, particularly when the kind of care we would ideally want is either not available or not affordable. There are heartbreaking decisions in everyone's life, times when there seem to be only poor choices and no perfect solutions. Doing "the best we can" in these situations may still fall short of what we would like to be able to do, but life isn't perfect—on any front—and doing what we can with what we have is the most we should expect of ourselves or anyone else.

We have received many letters from parents of children with disabilities. Most have reflected optimism and fulfillment and an abundance of caring. I'd like to offer you this one example from a parent in Illinois.

Thank you for a program last July that meant so much for our almost three-year-old son. I'm sure you sometimes weary of talking to a television camera lens that stares coldly back at you. Let me tell you about our little boy on the other end who needed your message of comfort one afternoon.

Jonathan had awakened from his nap after a discouraging morning.

He was sitting on his potty chair, rather sleepy yet, when you began. I stood by the television and noticed his expressions.

When you said you liked him, and you said it very slowly, he smiled first, then crossed his arms to hug his shoulders. When you said he was special, he touched the little eyeglasses he wears for "quite a bit of astigmatism." Looking up at me, he nodded that he was happy. But then he uncrossed his arms with a troubled expression on his face and touched his legs.

"Legs, Mommie?" he asked.

And you answered. You said that you liked him just the way he was. No different. Just the way he was, because he was a special person.

Jonathan rubbed his knees with his hands and sighed up at me, "Likes me."

I answered, "Yes, Mr. Rogers likes you just the way you are, Jonathan. We all do."

That didn't solve his problems, but that afternoon our little son was a tiger in the neighborhood, joining in play, crawling slowly up and down the sidewalk on legs spastic from brain damage.

On such brave days Jonathan says, "Bye, Mom," and opening the door by the low knob his father put for him, he goes out and backs down the steps on hands and knees. Then he visits up and down the sidewalk. His hands and knees have good calluses to protect them. But his little heart is open to hurt.

If he gets knocked over, ignored or hears a thoughtless remark, he comes inside, kneels on a chair by the window and simply watches.

I wish he were satisfied to be a loner, but he's the opposite. His gregarious personality practically explodes inside him. He's happiest in the midst of a wild group of kids.

Jonathan has cerebral palsy. At first it was diagnosed as quadriplegia, or involving his whole body. The pediatrician at the clinic for handicapped children said, "It would be going out on a limb to say that this child would ever walk."

Today he is diagnosed as the milder diplegia, or legs more involved than his arms. He can sit alone for short periods, pulls to standing, and crawls on hands and knees.

Jonathan gets frequent medical evaluations and prescriptions for eyeglasses (and eventual eye surgery), for medication to avoid convulsions, for short leg braces to avoid deformities, and for weekly physical therapy which we carry out daily. His physical well-being is attended to. What we worry about is his self-esteem, his happiness, his need for helping others.

Luckily Jonathan has four brothers and sisters, three of them adopted like him. He gets plenty of rough-and-tumble wrestling and toy snatching, in fair and unfair play. He needs it. When he fights back, sometimes he wins. When he is really having a hard time, he simply bites his opponent. This seems so funny to his brothers who are eight and six years old, and his sisters who are five and almost three years old, that they laugh and leave him alone.

Jonathan was a double adoption along with his sister, Marsha. He was six weeks old and Marsha was four weeks old when the nurse put them in our arms. They were perfect infants. At last we had five beautiful children.

We thought we had a full course in sensitivity as a black family handling the feelings of one natural and four adopted children along with our own emotions. We all "feel" for our children as they grow anyway, but with our handicapped child, the cup runneth over.

We have been astonished that Jonathan could realize so much about himself so young. Our other children seemed to grow like Topsy, with little self-consciousness.

At 14 months, a resident ophthalmologist questioned, "Does a child this young need to see?"

Looking through his eyeglasses for the first time, Jonathan stared at things around him and burst into laughter. He asks for his glasses first thing in the morning.

At 18 months Jonathan rubbed his legs with his fists and said, "Legs no go-go."

At two Jonathan told his father, "I can't walk."

Today (not one of his braver days) he sat beside me on the front porch and watched children running and scrambling after a ball. He told me, "I can't do that."

Today and other days I tell him, "That's true, Jonathan, but other people have handicaps too. And there are many things you can do."

(Most of us have handicaps. Jonathan's are just more clearly defined.)

Like all the family, Jonathan has jobs. Unlike the other kids, he's eager to do his work.

One job is to put hot-pads on the table for meal time. The pads are in a cabinet by the floor, and he crawls to get them one at a time, pulls up by his youth chair, and slowly pushes them onto the table. Sometimes he helps his oldest brother set the table, leaning over the table from the benches on each side.

Each morning Jonathan takes his father's shoes to him, pushing them in front of himself as he lumbers along. He also insists on putting away socks when I fold laundry. He carries one pair at a time in his hand, sometimes in his mouth like a puppy dog, and pulls slowly up to the dresser drawers where each kid's socks go.

He gets angry and hurt, but he bounces back more quickly than the others. When his almost-twin sister first roamed freely into the

neighborhood, leaving Jonathan behind, he came in and cried, "Make Marsha come back."

I had to tell him, "Marsha has to go and play. You will have to play here until she comes back."

Quite often his brothers give him rides in the wagon. But I have to explain that they can't always pull him around.

Our family word is comfort. When another child is crying, Jonathan is the first to hug and say, "Comfort." "Comfort" Jonathan gives; "comfort" Jonathan asks for.

On those days when he asks for "Comfort, Mommie," I sit with him and read books or look at pictures in magazines. I avoid giving him candy or food, and I won't let him sleep when he's sad. He has to learn to know his limitations and not be crushed by them. In a short time, he's a tiger again.

DISABILITIES

At his last evaluation the orthopedist said, "By gum, this kid might walk yet." Jonathan beamed at him. I'm sure some day with or without crutches, Jonathan will walk. I only worry about what kind of person he will be when he does walk.

Thank you, Mr. Rogers, for helping us with "comfort."

We all worry about who our children will become when they grow and set off on their own. What happens to them may often be beyond our control, but a great deal of how they face the events and circumstances of their lives, and what they make of them, will have been started in their years with us. When Jonathan does walk, I have a lot of confidence that he'll be headed toward many of life's satisfactions.

In *Mister Rogers' Neighborhood* we try very hard to encourage a child's pleasure in being unique. I hope that we were able, through our work for the Bureau of Education for the Handicapped, to help children and their caregivers put disabilities in a constructive perspective. We all can become more aware that a person has many, many characteristics, of which a disability is but one. It's the whole *person* who is capable of finding fulfillment in life—and capable of bringing joy to others.

*   *   *

Thoughts about our sameness and our differences, and what we can mean to one another, have been with me for a long time. When I was at Rollins College I began writing a musical story called "Josephine the Short-Neck Giraffe." It grew into a little "opera," which friends from the Neighborhood recorded, and most recently it took on another life as a short poem for an illustrated children's book.

Not all stories end as happily as does Josephine's; but happy endings tend to awaken hope, and the need for active hopeful striving is something healthy humans share. Here's the poem. It's something we'd like you to have for your children... and yourself.

Josephine
The Short-Neck Giraffe

The very next time that you go to the zoo,
You may be reminded of Josephine, who
Though a friendly giraffe, was a different sort:
She looked like the rest—but her neck was too short.

The animals teased her, and that made her cry.
Alone in the forest she'd wonder, "Oh why

Can't I reach the sweet buds at the top of the tree
And be like the others—instead of like me?"

Hazel the elephant, Josephine's friend,
Told her one day of a place that could end
All those sad feelings, mad feelings, and worse by far,
The feeling you don't really like who you are.

"It's a school," Hazel said, "and it helps you to grow."
"Hey! Just what I need for my neck, as you know,"
Josephine said. But then Hazel replied,
"Don't forget that there's growing both out and *inside.*"

So they went off to school—oh yes, Hazel went, too,
Just to help Josephine with the things that were new.
They were met at the door by a handsome giraffe
Who said not a word—didn't smile, didn't laugh...

Just looked at them shyly and showed them the way
To the part of the school where they both were to stay.
(J.R. was his name. He was miserably shy.
When Josephine spoke, he could never reply.)

Classes and classes and so much to learn!
And every day Josephine's only concern
Was the length of her neck. Had it started to grow?
But each time she asked, her friend, Hazel, said "No."

So after a month she decided to quit.
And the night before leaving she went off to sit
Alone in a small, secret place she had found.
But a shadow showed somebody else was around.

It was bashful J.R., and when Josephine spied
His lovely long neck in the moonlight she cried:
"This school doesn't work for me! What shall I try?
Oh tell me, J.R.!" All J.R. did was sigh...

And look up at the moon and look down at the ground.
"Oh J.R., when I met you I thought that I'd found
A friend I could talk to, to give me a hand."
Said Josephine sadly, "I don't understand."

DISABILITIES

J.R. listened hard to what Josephine said.
Still he couldn't reply. He coughed. He turned red.
"I need you," said Josephine, "need your advice,
Need someone to talk to because I'm so..."

"*Nice!*" said J.R. And he went on to say:
"You're smart and you're friendly. That very first day
That we met...just as soon as I saw you...I knew...
I'd like to...I'd try to...I need someone, too!"

"You *need* me?" asked Josephine, wiping her tears.
(She was having some trouble believing her ears.)
"That makes me so happy! And that isn't all—
Neck or no neck I feel *20 feet tall!*"

And so they both grew in their own special ways:
J.R. lost his shyness, and Josephine plays
With the other giraffes now and no longer cries
When the meaner ones make rude remarks on her size.

So Hazel and she and J.R., in that wood,
Live close by and talk often of times that are good
And times that are hard. They all say, "It's true,
The best times are times when you're glad to be you!"

CHAPTER 5:

PLAY

Most people have a sense that "play" is appropriate for children as "work" is appropriate for adults. However, the distinction we adults tend to make between "work" and "play" can be misleading, particularly when we use the words to apply to what preschoolers do. It can even be misleading when we apply those words to our own everyday activities, and that's something I'd like to think about first because it may help to shed some light on what play in early childhood is really all about.

If you ask an adult to define the difference between work and play, you're likely to get an answer such as, "Work is what I do for pay and play is what I do for fun." Or, "Work is hard and play is easy. You know, like something is 'hard work' or something is 'child's play'?" If you were to ask your friends the difference between work and play, what answers do you think you would get? It's not easy to come up with a definition that feels just right. And that's probably because something deep within all of us "knows" the immense value of play.

Many people work very hard at the things they do for fun. They may exert a large amount of mental energy learning new skills or they may expend a lot of physical energy in "letting off steam." It's certainly not "child's play" to learn how to work a lathe or play a better game of basketball. Or to master a sonata on the piano, or the movements for a dance, or to capture on paper a likeness of the human body, even if one of those may be your avocation. Some people find they can earn money with the things they do for fun. Does that mean their hobbies have become "work"? And there's no doubt that one person's work can be another's play—and the other way around. What are we to make of it all?

No one has the complete answer to the difference between play and work, or to the problem of when it is that one seems to turn into the other. Over the years, however, I have come to think of play in a way that makes it a very serious matter indeed. I think play is an expression of our creativity; and creativity, I believe, is at the very root of our ability to learn, to cope, and to become whatever we may be.

People whose work is creative self-expression of the most obvious kind—artists, writers, musicians, dancers—seem to be drawing heavily on play to do what they do. Artists play with shapes, colors, tones, values, materials, and tools; and, by constantly trying out different combinations of all these things, they come up with new kinds of expressions and often with new solutions to particular problems. Writers play with words to give their ideas new expression, combining and recombining words to give sentences new meanings. Musicians play with strings and keyboards and breath and notes and harmonies and melodies. Dancers play with body forms and rhythm, movement and music. What they all have in common is the urge to take what is known and rearrange it in new combinations. I'm not sure it's a coincidence that we say we "play"

music or write "plays." I know personally that doing either can be really hard work!

But of course it's not just "creative artists" who work like this. Mathematicians play with numbers and formulas, scientists play with hypotheses and experiments, taking elements of our known world and trying them out in new combinations to see what happens. Businesspeople play with corporate structures, trying out new combinations of all the many things that determine profit and loss. And what about ourselves when we take time off to play games? Almost all games are based on trying out new combinations—of cards, pieces on a board, dots on dice, strategies, formations of people... and all within set limits. Sometimes the limits are rules made by people, and sometimes the limits are rules set by the nature of the things we are playing with. But it would be very hard to play or invent a game that had *no* rules to work with. Or to be creative in a setting that had no limits to work within.

One way to think about play, then, is as the process of finding new combinations for known things—combinations that may yield new forms of expression, new inventions, new discoveries, and new solutions.

I like thinking about play in this way because it gives play the importance it deserves. It's also exactly what children's play seems to be about and explains why so many people have come to think that children's play is so important a part of childhood—and beyond. In fact, in childhood, work and play seem to come together. However we may think of the two words now that we're grown up, it's fair to say that for young children, their play *is* their work, and the more we can encourage children to play, the more we will be giving them a really important lifelong resource to draw on.

Some Uses of Children's Play

Children have to be problem solvers. From the moment they are born, the world presents itself as a huge set of puzzles, puzzles that always seem to be changing. At first, there's the puzzle of comfort and discomfort, the puzzle of what is "mother" and what is not, what is *me*, what is not, how to turn over, crawl, and walk, how to "communicate," how to fit things together and how to take them apart, what things can hurt and what things don't and on and on and on. Children can get help and clues from the people who take care of them, but they can't ask a lot of questions or look things up in books. For the most part, they have to try things out with their senses—try them out again and again and again. They have to play with what they know to be true in order to find out more, and then they can use what they learn in new forms of play.

Learning about the outside world, then, is one of the things that play makes possible. Here's a description I've always found helpful from Selma Fraiberg's *The Magic Years*:

Have you a six- or seven-month-old baby who snatches the glasses off your nose? If you do, you hardly need this piece of advice. Remove the glasses when the baby reaches for them, slip them in a pocket or behind a sofa pillow (and don't forget where *you* hid them!). Don't trouble to be sneaky about it, let the baby see you hide them. He will not go in search of them. He will stare at the place he last saw them—on your nose— then lose interest in the problem. He does not search for the glasses because he cannot imagine that they have an existence when he does not see them.

When the baby is around nine months old, don't rely on the old tricks. If he sees you remove your glasses and slip them behind a sofa pillow, he will move the pillow and pounce on your glasses. He has learned that an object can be hidden from sight, yet can still exist! He can follow its movements in your hand to the place of hiding and actively search for it there.... We still have some tricks up our sleeve. Let's try this: Let the baby see you slip your glasses behind the pillow. Let him find them, persuade him to give them to you, then hide the glasses under a second pillow. Now he is confused. He will search for the glasses under the *first* pillow, in the first hiding place, but he will not search for them in the second hiding place. This means that the baby can conceive of the glasses having an existence when hidden, but only in one place, the first hiding place where his search had earlier been successful.... An object can still vanish. In a few weeks he will extend his search from the first hiding place to the second one and he is on his way to the discovery that an object can be moved from place to place and still have a permanent existence....

During the first half of the second year, the baby is really pretty good at following an object from your hand to two suc- cessive hiding places, *if* he can follow your movements with his eyes. This means that you still have one trick up your sleeve but it's practically your last chance to be one up on the child in these games. Try this: Put your key-case in a purse and close it. Let the baby see you do it and let him find it. This is old stuff to him now. Now persuade the baby to give the key-case back to you. Put it back into the purse and move the purse with its concealed key-case behind a sofa pillow. Remove the key- case slyly, taking care that this operation is concealed from the eagle eye of your child, and slip the key-case behind the pillow. Bring the empty purse back into view. Now ask your child to find the key-case. He will examine the empty purse, search for the missing key-case in its emptiness. He will look confused and puzzled, but it will not occur to him to search for the key-case behind the pillow although he had followed your movements originally to that place. He does not search for the key-case there or any other place because he has not *seen* you remove it. In other words, he cannot yet imagine the object existing *some* place if he has lost track of its movements through his eyes.

But now he's almost ready for the final step in this process. Try your disappearing key-case trick for a few days and he's pretty certain to catch on. A few more experiments and he will fill in the visual gap with an imaginative reconstruction. He will establish the fact that a key-case can leave a purse without his perception of the process, but a key-case has a substantial existence some place and he will search for it in a fairly systematic way. He will find it and confirm for himself that an object has an existence independent of his perception of it. Your days as a magician are numbered and the child's era of magical belief is on the wane. This is an intellectual giant-step for the child in the second half of his second year...

So play and learning go hand in hand!

By the age of three and beyond, a child has acquired much more language to use in finding out about the world. There are new kinds of play going on in a child's head by this time—the combining and recombining of words, thoughts, concepts—as the child tries them out and experiments to see which will fit together. The four-year-old son of a friend of mine ran to the window one winter morning and shouted, "Look at all that snow pollution!" A five-year-old walking down a long airport corridor tugged on her mother's sleeve and asked, "Mommy, if I walked backwards could I get to yesterday?" (I wouldn't be surprised if Einstein played with an idea like that as he was working on the theory of relativity!)

Play gives children a chance to practice what they are learning. We all need to practice new things before we can feel comfortable with them. Children who are about a year old may spend a lot of time practicing about the inside and outside of things. It may surprise us to see how long a baby of this age can spend putting a block in a box... and taking it out again... and putting it back in... and taking it out again. Or a toddler may, over and over again, climb into a little cart and then climb out... in and out. It may seem odd play to us, but how else except through this kind of play is a child to understand the difference between the inside and outside of things? The relationship between larger and smaller? Part of the intensity of such practicing comes from the need to "work" on something more mysterious still: the difference between the inside and the outside of one's own body.

There are many, many times when a young child's play reflects a growing awareness and curiosity about his or her body parts and body functions. There is a time when things with holes seem particularly fascinating. That's not surprising. The baby's own mouth is an important source of information and comfort in the early weeks and months of life, and it isn't long before a child seems to discover his or her mother's mouth as well as other people's mouths, and then *things* that seem to have "mouths," such as cups and jars, drawers, rings of all kinds, concave shapes in furniture, and discs and blocks with drilled-out centers. It is only with lots of practicing through repetitive play that a child can begin to understand what holes are and what can be done with them.

Another source of great interest for toddlers is things that open and shut on hinges like doors and boxes with lids. Practicing with hinges is perhaps a way to better understand the "hinges" of the jaw or the opening and closing of the hand and fingers.

And there's all the practicing with water and sand that pour into things and fill them up and pour out of things and empty them. How can fluids be contained? How can you stop them overflowing? This kind of play seems such a direct expression of a child's wondering how body contents can be both contained and released.

These are not concepts we adults can explain to young children. What is important is for us to understand that inner urges do dictate much of children's play, much of all play, and that this is children's way to explore the whole inside world of feelings. That's been the part of play that has interested me most in the work we do with *Mister Rogers' Neighborhood*.

As children get a little older, they begin to include *pretending* in their play. In fact, pretending soon becomes the keystone of children's play, and I often sing a song about it on television to let children know that there are adults who understand just how important pretending is:

> Pretending you're a pilot or a princess!
> Pretending you're a doctor or a king!
> Pretending you're a mother or a father,
> By pretending you can be
> Most anything you want to think about
> By pretending... just pretending.

You can try out many things by pretending.
Your own make-up play can be different every day,
But it's your work, it's important, pretend.
You can try out life by pretending.
You can even say you're a baby today
By pretending...pretending.

Here's part of a letter from a parent who let me know about pretending in her family:

> My three-year-old son and I have a special pretend game we play. I've cut out different colored circles of construction paper and we set them in a circle on the floor. We sit in the middle and, one by one, we name a color, find something in the house that color, and then something outside of that color. Then we pretend we are the object. For example, green grass: How do we feel when it rains or when we're mowed? Or a green chair: How do we feel when people sit or jump on us? We have so much fun pretending, and we always decide that being a person is the best thing we could be.
>
> The game also helped us help our son get over a fear of darkness and black things in general. He was afraid of the dark, spiders and witches. All are black. So we pretend to be night, and spiders, and witches. We've convinced him that witches are pretend and shown him how we can pretend them any color or pretend them nice instead of mean. We also showed him that black doesn't mean bad because our piano is black and look at the beautiful sound it makes!

Pretending is what our Neighborhood of Make-Believe is all about—a place where, after talking about real things that may be puzzling or difficult to do or frightening to think about, we can go and try out our feelings about them. Our timid tame tiger, Daniel, has helped us try out sleeping away from home for the first time and having to go to the hospital. Our royal family—King Friday XIII, Queen Sara, and Prince Tuesday—has let us try out how a child might feel when parents quarrel and also when it's time to start school. When Henrietta Pussycat thought her best friend didn't want to be her best friend anymore, we practiced our feelings about that. And again and again, through many children's favorite puppet character, Lady Elaine Fairchilde, we have tried out how it feels to be a mischief maker who is unsure of the acceptance and approval of loved ones.

We've aired more than five hundred programs in *Mister Rogers' Neighborhood* and we have used our times of pretend in them for many, many different kinds of "tryouts"—ones that we felt were important for most children. In doing so, I hope we've encouraged children to try out the important feelings and events in their own lives and talk about them with the real-life grown-ups they trust.

Making and Building

The urge to make and build seems to be an almost universal human characteristic. Often that urge is a response to necessity—the need to

MISTER ROGERS TALKS WITH PARENTS

build shelters to live in, or the need to fashion tools and implements to work with. But the urge to make and build—whether a pastry or a pyramid—goes way beyond meeting our needs for survival and seems to be the expression of some deep-rooted part of being human. It isn't surprising, then, that these acts of creation should be such a large part of children's play.

I think that a large part of children's making and building play comes from the desire to feel in control of the outside world and the inner self. When children play with blocks, they are making the decisions about what form the blocks will take and what they will represent. Of course, these "decisions" aren't the kinds of decisions that we make— "Should I make a tower or should I make a fence?" The "decision" a child makes in putting blocks into a certain shape is really the outside expression of some inner feelings. "I feel like making a tower" or even "I feel like a tower" or maybe "How does it feel to be tall?" A child simply makes whatever he or she feels the need to make. In doing so, the child is in control of what takes place. Being able to express his or her feelings is a healthy part of a child's growing.

All of us, at one time or another, have been tempted to rearrange a child's block structure so that it conforms more to how *we* feel about things—"Look, why don't you put this block up here, and then it will look just like a chimney!" A child's play changes when we do this. Sometimes a child will go along with our suggestion but lose motivation to continue with the building. Other times, the child will look at us, perhaps a little puzzled, then knock the whole structure down and go off to do something else. The feeling of control and mastery has been lost. There may be times when children ask for your help as they build. "Just hold this right here till I tell you to let go," children have said to me. And of course I've done it, and it felt good to be useful. On those few occasions when I did more than I was asked to do, I quickly discovered how important it was to respect the architect within the child.

Even without any interference from an adult, children will spend a lot of time carefully piling blocks up into a tower only to push the building over once it's completed. That often-repeated game seems to be saying, "*I* can build up and *I* can knock down." We may be so pleased with what a child has managed to build that we are reluctant to see it destroyed. Or, sensing our child's delight in the knocking over, we may participate in the destruction. We don't always find ourselves welcome when we try to play with our children in this way. When our children show obvious displeasure, we may feel rejected, disappointed, or even a little bit "put down." We may feel irritated or a touch angry—"I was only trying to help," or "Okay, do it your own way!" Children will very quickly feel our negative mood, and if it happens over and over again, they may come to believe that by engaging in their own forms of play and controlling their own creations, they run the risk of losing the love of the people they love the most. But we want our children to learn, to be in control of their actions. If they are to do so, we need to let them control their play as much as they can, so long as their play remains within safe boundaries.

Therapists working with children who have special problems can often find clues to those problems and to children's feelings by observing the children at play. That's a real skill, of course, and most of us don't have the training and experience to see and hear what a therapist may see and hear. But we parents have one advantage that therapists lack—we know our children better than anyone else does, and so we have the opportunity to be particularly sensitive to changes in our children's play habits and behavior. We also are more familiar than any therapist can be with the world our children live in. Consequently, we are in a position to identify stressful situations that might be affecting our children and their play.

Many parents who look and listen carefully notice changes in their children's play at times—for instance, when there is a lot of sad and violent programming on television (see page 115). I'm thinking here of sad and violent real-life events like assassinations that get shown again and again with constant news-bulletin updates. There may be a lot of family television watching at times like this, and a child is exposed not only to the violence on the television set, but also to the shock, sadness, and fear that everyone in the family is feeling. At the time that Robert Kennedy was killed, we made a program in which I tried to help parents be alert to how their children might be using play to work through the anxious feelings that television's coverage of the assassination might be evoking.

I recounted the story of one boy here in Pittsburgh who was clearly upset by what he had seen. In his play at a child-care center he used his blocks to build a tall and very precarious structure. Sooner or later, the structure would collapse, and the teacher noticed that each time it did so, the boy would very intentionally get in the way of the falling pieces. After he made his building collapse on himself the first time, the teacher sat quietly down beside him, available to the boy but silent. The second time, the boy looked up at her and said, "I feel grumpy." "Why?" she asked. And he replied, "Somebody shot my head today." That was the opening she needed to talk with him about the scary things he was seeing at home on television and why his parents might seem sad and even angry for a while. That teacher was obviously looking and listening very carefully to the children in her care. She was aware that children often do need our quiet support as they work at their play. They need encouragement and our nonjudgmental acceptance. Sometimes they even need to borrow from our energy in order to keep on playing. But above all, they need us to let them stay in control of their play.

Artwork

As soon as young children begin to play with pencils and pens, crayons, chalk, paintbrushes, clay, and the like, they can begin to express their feelings in colors, forms, and shapes that are entirely of their own making. They are little interested in creating exact representations of what they see. For the most part, what we may consider crude symbols serve them just fine for giving visible expression to what they feel. Each child develops a "language" of his or her own. There's a lot we can learn from this language if we can resist the temptation to make our children's creative expressions conform to our notions of what "art" should be.

Art begins with feelings on the inside of the artist. Whatever it is that makes us want to express ourselves is something that is taking place within ourselves. Creativity doesn't wait until we're old enough to go to nursery school or elementary school. It isn't something that waits to be taught. Often the creative urge, once we express it, brings real relief in whatever form it takes. We have an inner sense that we can make what *is* into what we feel it could and should be.

It may seem strange to you at first, but when I think about the subject of creativity, I think of our first son, who was very slow to conform to our wishes for him to use the potty. When he finally did, there was great rejoicing in our house—both on our part and on his. "Come see what I've made!" was J's cry, and of course we would go and see and tell him how pleased and proud we were. The trouble was that he continued to want us to come and admire and exclaim after every single successful elimination.

After several evenings, I told J that I was proud of him and that he had mastered something very important and that I hoped he was proud of himself...but I couldn't be coming each time to compliment him about it. I think he understood, but shortly before Christmas he came to me excitedly and said, "Daddy, come quick! I made you a Christmas tree!" And sure enough, his product in the potty looked very much like a Christmas tree. Obviously he felt that it was a *new* creation, worth looking at.

As he grew, J became very clever in fashioning Play-doh and clay into things that were important to him at the moment. I've often wondered if it's because he was allowed to feel proud of the way he had learned to master something within himself. That pride carried over into a pleasure in learning to master materials outside himself. It seems to me that he grew with the confidence that he could make something worthwhile of the outer materials of his world.

Children who are encouraged in their own unique forms of artwork can come to use them as very reliable aids for understanding and coping with the stresses that accompany all their growing. The more serious the stresses, the more people need to be able to call on such a resource within themselves. I remember one day being very struck by a child's drawing in a school I was visiting. It was of a little girl with a large transparent oval at her midsection. In the oval was a baby. The drawing had been done by a five-year-old, and it turned out that the child's mother was pregnant. In making that drawing, the little girl, it seemed, had transferred the baby from her mother to herself, and I've often wondered since what inner feelings prompted that drawing—what kinds of wishes, or envy, or anticipation. Whatever the answer, it was certainly something that was very important in that five-year-old's life.

A good friend of mine, Dr. Jim Hughes, has set up a well-equipped play space for children in the visitors' area of the state penitentiary in Pittsburgh. Trusties, who are trained in child development, supervise the children in their play. It's a place I have often visited. On one visit I observed two boys at "work" in the play area. One was a six-year-old who was creating a building with blocks. His block building looked somewhat like the prison, and once he had built it, he proceeded to drive a wooden truck into it and knock it down. I wondered if that might have been his way of pretending to rescue his father whom he came to visit every week.

The other, a ten-year-old, was using crayons to draw a building with two lookout towers, an entrance door, and an iron fence, which looked exactly like the prison we were in. He filled the picture with Halloween creatures—bats in the sky and ghosts in the lookout towers and a torture chamber right in the middle of the building. I told him it looked like a scary place. He said that it was, and then he told me that it was this place where we were. Then he said, "I draw pictures a lot. I have one at home I did just like this one, only there are screams and yells and people crying 'Help!' in that one at home." As we talked, I thanked him for helping me understand more about the things children create, and on the way home I wondered what it must be like to be a child and to have someone you love locked in a prison. I thought, too, how essential it is to find safe ways of expressing how we feel about what is important to us.

If your child likes to draw, you might want to set aside a special place—a particular wall or the refrigerator door—where you can display his or her pictures. As your child keeps updating them, consider storing the old ones, marking them with the date they were done. When the two of you look back over several months of artwork, you may find that there is a lot to talk about.

MISTER ROGERS TALKS WITH PARENTS

Dottie was a little girl who had some really deep competitive feelings about her mother and father. One day, in an angry tone, she said accusingly to her mother: "You didn't even invite me to your wedding!"

Her mother replied good-naturedly, "Well, you weren't even born yet."

"But I'm going to marry Daddy!" Dottie insisted.

"Daddy's already married to me," her mother explained.

"Well," said Dottie, "don't tell me I have to marry Rob." (Rob was her younger brother.)

In a kindly way, Dottie's mother explained that when she grew up she might find somebody her own age whom she would like to marry.

That conversation was only the beginning, and Dottie took some of her feelings to the easel at her kindergarten. She drew a big face with dabs for the tears. "It's a big old ugly girl and she's crying," she explained. Then she drew a second picture of another girl—a blonde—and said, "This is a beautiful girl." Next, she drew a small, beautifully decorated Christmas tree, and beside it a tall, unadorned evergreen.

Just why Dottie settled on trees as her comfortable symbols is hard to say, but that was what her inner urgencies led her to do. She began a whole series of drawings and paintings of many different kinds of trees—colorful trees, barren trees that looked sad—but all her pictures contained one small and one large tree. She continued these tree drawings for several years.

One day, when Dottie was twelve, she made a drawing that anyone who was familiar with her "portfolio" could see was dramatically different. She drew a single colorful tree, all by itself, and she drew it upside down. When asked about her drawing, Dottie said, "It's a girl and she's talking on the telephone"—the first time she had ever suggested her trees were anything but trees.

A little conversation brought out the information that in her tree drawings Dottie had suddenly included a Bell Telephone ad that was seen in a lot of different places at that time: an ad picturing a girl lying on the floor with her feet up in the air, talking on the telephone. The flare of the girl's skirt and her feet sticking out of it did, indeed, suggest an upside-down tree.

Now, there might be many different ways to read a picture like that single tree coming at the end of a long series of other tree drawings. Nevertheless, one strong suggestion it contained was that Dottie had begun to be able to declare that she was an individual, that she had worked through her urgent competitive feelings about her mom and dad, and that she could now take these feelings beyond the immediate family and into the outside world.

There's something else that's important about Dottie's story. All through those years, her family and her teachers had let her go on drawing trees in sad and angry ways when she felt like it. It would have been so easy to encourage her, or even (yes, it often happens!) *tell* her to draw something else and make it pretty and happy. If she hadn't been allowed to draw what she felt, what would have happened to those feelings? I often wonder about that in my own case. My earliest care-givers must have permitted me to play on the piano whatever I was feeling. If they hadn't, if they had said, "Oh, don't play that loud, ugly stuff, play something pretty and happy" all the time, I might have given up "the musical way" of dealing with my feelings.

Children are likely to try different ways of expressing who they are and what they are feeling. Some may dance or make up songs. (I once had a six-year-old send me an "opera"!) Others may make up stories or build pretend spaceships. Whatever they find that seems appropriate for them, we can encourage. Why one child chooses one thing and another child another may be a mystery to us parents; nevertheless, it's important for us not to pass value judgments on young children's creative products. On the one hand, criticism of a child's work because it isn't "good" by our standards can certainly dampen the urge to create, while on the other, lavish praise for everything children do isn't healthy en-couragement, either; it can lead them to develop such unreal expec-tations for themselves that they end up casualties in the real world. In the early years, it's the *doing* that needs to be encouraged. When our children show us one of their creations, they are usually trying to *tell* us something, not create a work of art, and they will get the most encouragement to go on trying when we show them that we care about what they are trying to say. Angry blobs on a page, even if they are done in "beautiful" colors, are not attempts to create beauty. If we ask them, our children are often willing to tell us what their pictures mean to them, and we, in return, can tell our children how their pictures make us feel. If the artwork our children create does result in such moments of closeness and sharing, then our children are likely to want to do more.

Honesty linked with love is the most important response in any relationship. Our children take our opinions seriously. What they may need most when they come to show us something they have done (and are proud of) is a big hug, along with, "I really like that, and I'm proud of you for doing it!"

Dramatic Play

As a child I always liked puppets. They were important to me then, they were important to me when I first started working with children, and of course they're still important to me now in the work I do with television. Some puppets are very easy to make—out of old socks, paper bags, plastic bottles, or paper plates on sticks—and with willing hands, they can easily take on personalities of their own. Usually, of course, these personalities are really parts of our own personalities. Often, our puppets allow us to express those parts of our personalities that we might not be quite comfortable expressing all by ourselves. There seems to be a feeling of safety created by the distance between our heads and the puppets on the ends of our hands. When we talk to someone through a puppet, that person can never be quite sure whether what the puppet says is what we really feel, or whether it's just something such a puppet character might feel. That allows us to take risks.

When children meet a puppet for the first time, particularly if the puppet is on an adult's hand, they may feel as shy as if they were meeting a new friend. I've found it helpful first to talk *about* the puppet without it being on the hand at all—what it's made of, how it looks, what sort of character it might have. Once you talk about the puppet with a child, then you can slip the puppet on your hand and start talking *to* the puppet. You can tell the puppet what's been happening before it "arrived." Your talking to the puppet shows the child that that's an acceptable thing to do. Already you may see the child becoming absorbed in the puppet and its little movements rather than in you and what you're saying. The puppet has started taking on a life of its own. Finally, you can begin talking *for* the puppet, and at that point it seems the most natural thing in the world for the puppet to start speaking back to you and turning to include the child.

I often take the Neighborhood puppets with me when I go visiting with children. Most of the time the children I see are already familiar with these puppet characters from our television series, so they know their different characteristics, how they talk, and how they behave. Almost always, each child has a particular favorite that represents most directly how that child feels at the moment—the authoritarian King Friday, the kind and understanding Queen Sara, shy Daniel, or mischievous Lady Elaine.

I had some of our puppets with me one day when I visited a new ten-year-old friend, Erik Renlund, at his home in California. We were filming a program for *Old Friends...New Friends*, a television series for adults that we produced for three seasons. Its main purpose was to document some remarkable people whose lives had made a significant difference in the lives of others. At the time Erik, who had cancer, was under the care of Dr. Gerald Jampolsky at his Center for Attitudinal Healing in Tiburon. Erik, naturally, was receiving a lot of special attention both at the center and at home. When I arrived to see him, he was playing with his younger brother, Brett, and two friends. They were delighted to be able to play with their puppet "friends," but both Erik

and Brett wanted to play with Daniel Tiger. Erik got him first.

I asked "Daniel" how he was feeling.

"Scared," Erik replied in Daniel's little shy voice.

"Can you tell me why you're scared?" I asked.

"I don't like all the noise," Daniel replied.

At this point Brett became determined to get Daniel to play with, and he asked me to take King Friday and command Erik, in King Friday's gruff voice, to give him Daniel. I suggested that he could make the king talk if he felt like it, and Brett did.

"Erik Renlund," said Brett as the king, "I want you to know . . . give me Daniel . . . okay?"

But Erik still wouldn't yield, and Brett threw the king on the floor with a disgusted, "Oh, rats!"

Putting the king on my hand, I said in a kingly voice, "Sometimes there are disappointments in my castle."

"And sometimes," said Brett, pointing to Daniel, who was still on Erik's hand, "I want *him.*"

"Sometimes you want Daniel Tiger?" the king asked. "Can you tell me why?"

Quite agitated, Brett complained about Erik. "He gets control of every darned thing! Every darned time we play he gets it [meaning Daniel]! So I think it's fair for me to have it one time!"

"What shall we do about that, Erik?" asked the king.

"Well," Erik said after a pause, "I think it's really up to Daniel."

So the king turned to Daniel. "Daniel," he said, "Brett is anxious to have you with him for a moment. Do you think you could pass over to him?"

Daniel's little voice said, "Yes, I think so."

"You think you could?"

"Yes."

"Do you think he'd take good care of you?"

"Yes, I think so."

"Do you think you could come back to Erik another time?"

"Yes."

"Well," said the king, "you do what you like."

So Daniel finally went to Brett for a time, and Brett took him behind a chair and talked to him about how hard it is when you're shy and you have to meet new people. Daniel firmly agreed.

Meanwhile, Erik had become the king. He commanded Lady Elaine, who was on the hand of one of the friends, to appear before him. When she obediently did, he commanded her to stop doing magic with her magic boomerang.

"Why don't you like magic?" I asked the king (who was still on Erik's hand).

"She buckles up the whole place," the king replied. "*I just want this to be an ordinary neighborhood.*"

Well, I'll bet Erik certainly did want to live in an ordinary neighborhood and live an ordinary life without periodic traumatic bouts with cancer. And Brett had strong feelings, too, about himself and his brother and people who were intrusive in their world. Many feelings were played out in that impromptu puppet activity, and I've often thought how privileged I was to have been there.

Children's dramatic or fantasy play may be as simple as their dressing up and pretending to be other people or as complicated as their construction of a whole little world inhabited by animal and doll figures who go through elaborate rituals and adventures. For many children, dramatic play is one of their most important tools for dealing with everyday problems.

It can also be a tool for parents, a way to learn what is uppermost in a child's mind at the moment. If you observe your child's play, you may be able to pick up echoes of something that has happened, like a recent move to a new home, the sickness of a sibling, or the death of a pet. You might see your child practicing for something that is going to happen, like a trip you're going to take together or a time when you're going to be away. Frequently children play about their sense of family relationships and where they belong. You may find your child taking charge of the family as the play mother or father, acting out angry feelings about brothers or sisters, or trying out what it's going to mean when that new baby arrives. If you pay some careful attention to your child's play, you may find that you and your child have some very important things to talk about.

Some children spend so much time in fantasy play that their parents become concerned that something is wrong. While it is true that children have been known to lose touch with reality to the point where professional help is needed, it's also rare. We make great use of fantasy in our Neighborhood of Make-Believe in *Mister Rogers' Neighborhood*, but we are also very careful to keep the difference between reality and fantasy as clear as we can. Parents can do that, too, by encouraging their children to engage in make-believe play as much as they want to, but by reinforcing, at the same time, that some things are *only* pretend.

Drs. Jerome and Dorothy Singer, Yale Child Study Center psychologists who have done such extensive research on the effects of television on children, had this to say about the benefits of children's pretend play in the March 1979 issue of *Psychology Today*:

> Our research on imaginative play in early childhood suggests that private fantasy has significant benefits for a growing child. Children of three or four who engage in pretending or make-believe play not only appear to be happier, but also are more fluent verbally and show more cooperation and sharing behavior. They can wait quietly or delay gratification, can concentrate better and seem to be more empathic and less aggressive, thanks to their use of private fantasy.

Janie was a six-year-old girl who had to be hospitalized for rheumatic fever. Her doctors were very worried because she was so listless and refused to eat. She would simply lie in her bed and shift from one helpless position to another. One day a family friend suggested making a nurse's outfit for Janie. That little uniform and cap turned out to be one of the biggest helps of all. When Janie was given the outfit, she wore it every day and began sitting upright in her bed. Somehow in that costume she didn't feel so helpless anymore. In fact, she became quite assertive, giving orders to everyone who came near. To be sure, she was much more difficult to deal with in that nurse's uniform, but she had a much better chance of getting well. It seemed that playing the part of someone in charge allowed Janie to feel less a victim.

Times like hospitalization (see Chapter 9) when a person may feel frightened and helpless can bring out a lot of anger. All children, as they grow, need to find acceptable ways to deal with those angry feelings—ways that give those feelings expression without risking the loss of love from the people they love the most. Destroying block buildings, pounding clay creations, scribbling over drawings—all these aggressive acts can vent anger in permissible ways. In fantasy play, dolls can be scolded and punished . . . and then sometimes forgiven. Often, as children find ways to dramatize their feelings, their play can show us what big strides they are making in accomplishing such childhood tasks as gaining self-control.

One little girl used to pretend that her stuffed animals were so wild that she had to keep them in cages. She'd say that no one could ever open the cages because "you just can't trust those wild animals if they aren't locked in." Little by little, though, as she came to master her own angry wishes, her feelings about those animals changed. One day she said, "I don't have to have the cages locked today because the animals aren't going to bite the people." Whereupon she took some little doll figures and put them up close to the animals with the cage doors open. "You see," she said to the dolls, "they didn't hurt you."

MISTER ROGERS TALKS WITH PARENTS

What a wonderful thing it is to see children dealing with their own inner struggles in their own creative ways!

Imaginary Friends

Some parents feel their children's fantasies have reached uncomfortable limits when their children suddenly turn up with imaginary friends who have a way of moving into family life just like real people. It may even seem that family life would be simpler if the friends *were* real. Then, at least, parents might be able to exercise some control over those friends. With imaginary friends, though, it seems that only the child is in control.

Many children have imaginary friends. I think that's because when a young child wishes for something that he or she doesn't have, that child will often create it by imagining it. That's a normal part of childhood.

I asked a friend of mine whether his two boys had ever had imaginary friends. It turned out that one had and one hadn't. When his younger son was about four, he explained, he'd had two constant imaginary friends—"Puckino" and "Juicy." They kept his son company for about a year, and then they disappeared. Puckino and Juicy settled in just after the family had moved east from the West Coast. In making that move, the boy had had to leave his real friends, and his family had had to give away their two dogs that had been with the boy since his birth. That child was moving to a strange new place and living among strange new people. My hunch is that Puckino and Juicy were trusted comrades who showed up at just the right time when that boy was having to deal with a lot of lost companionship.

Most of the children I've talked with about "imaginary friends" have said that they did have such a friend at one time or another, but for many of them, these friends were either too unformed to talk about or had already become faint memories. That wasn't so, however, in the case of "Santaweena."

Santaweena turned out to be a very special friend of a girl named Ashley. Ashley explained to me that a long time ago she'd wanted to have an imaginary friend and that now she had two—Santaweena and Hunka. Hunka, said Ashley, was Santaweena's little brother. Ashley went on to tell me what Santaweena looked like.

"Santaweena has blond hair with bangs," she said, "and she mostly wears a pink shirt and a pink sweater and her striped pants are pink and blue and yellow and her wings are pink and blue and yellow."

I told her I thought Santaweena must be a beautiful make-believe friend.

"Hunka," she added, "is mostly shy and doesn't go outside too much." Santaweena, on the other hand, stayed with Ashley all the time, wherever she went.

Naturally, I wanted to talk to Ashley's parents about this imaginary friendship, and I asked Betsy, Ashley's mother, if she remembered when Santaweena had begun.

"Ashley was in nursery school," Betsy explained. "We didn't know that Santaweena was make-believe in the beginning. We thought there was somebody new at nursery school. I told Ashley she could have Santaweena—I thought maybe her name was Sandy or something—over for lunch sometime. But Santaweena was always busy. She was always going somewhere with her mother, or visiting her grandmother, or going on vacation. Then I figured out who Santaweena really was. And then Santaweena started coming all the time. She had dinner at our table with us. We set a place for her."

Jim, Ashley's father, thought Santaweena might have been created because Ashley was by far the youngest of their four children. It was particularly hard for Ashley, he thought, to go to bed a lot earlier than everyone else. "I think Ashley just decided: 'I'm going to have myself a friend.'"

Like most children, Ashley used her imaginary friends as scapegoats. When her room was messy, she'd tell her mother that Hunka had been over and *he'd* made the mess. In that case, Betsy would tell Ashley that she and Santaweena and Hunka would all have to go upstairs and clean up the room together. When there was a mess left on the breakfast table, Ashley would say that *she'd* left it clean when she finished, but that Hunka and Santaweena came down later and they weren't used to tidying up after themselves.

When I left Ashley, it looked like there was going to be a new addition to the imaginary family. Santaweena had just received a dog as an early present for her birthday, which fell on the following day.

"Is Santaweena's birthday always on the thirtieth?" I asked.

"No," Ashley told me, and she went on to explain that her imaginary friends had different kinds of birthdays: "Like when they're five, and then they get to be five and a half, and then six."

I was very impressed by the completeness and detail of Ashley's imaginary world. But I'm sure that Santaweena and her brother and her dog will go away someday when Ashley doesn't need them anymore. I was impressed, too, by the way Jim and Betsy allowed their daughter's fantasy to develop, by the way they made room for it in their family life, and by the way they managed all the same to keep firm boundaries between what was real and what was not. Perhaps this was partly because Betsy herself could remember having an imaginary horse friend when she was little—a friend she would ride to school and tie up to the bicycle rack. Both Jim and Betsy were aware that Ashley's friends were important and valuable to her at that particular time in her growing.

Monsters and Superheroes

There have always been times when children wished for superhuman powers. Cave children probably pretended to be superhunters, just as children today pretend about being superstrong or superfast. Fairy tales and other stories for children abound in characters with magical abilities confronting giants and monsters. That kind of story is part of a long, long tradition—and a healthy one, reflecting, as it does, children's age-old need to imagine and play about being big and strong in a world where they may often feel little and vulnerable.

Recently, though, I became concerned about the shape many children's play seemed to be taking under the influence of televised versions of Superman, Batman, Spider-Man, Wonder Woman, the Incredible Hulk, etc. I wondered if it was television's particular ability to make the unreal look real, coupled with children's hours and hours of watching these simulations, that was making their fantasy play different. But whatever the cause, the mail we were receiving from parents told me that I wasn't the only person who was worried.

One mother of four children, who is also a preschool teacher, wrote us a letter that includes this most important point:

> I agree that children often feel small and inadequate and that they have feelings of anger and hostility that frighten them. Their dramatic pretend-play reflects these feelings and is one of the ways they learn to deal with these feelings. I also agree that if monsters and superheroes did not exist, children would create something similar. But there is a vast difference between what children would create and imagine for themselves and what adults create for them. What adults imagine and then depict is more terrifying, more out-of-bounds, and at the same time, determines or structures the child's imagination. What children depict for themselves may be scary, but it is scary within their own range of experience and frame of reference.

Further confirmation of my feelings came from a psychologist friend, Dr. Robert Abramovitz, who had singled out children's superhero play for observation. He noted that pretend fights between superheroes and "bad guys" frequently turned into real punching and kicking. He also concluded that these children's own creativity was being dampened by their constant mirroring of situations they remembered from superhero stories they had seen. Their play was not only less original than usual, but it also seemed a response to excess stimulation.

And then I began to read and hear stories of children being injured by believing that their pretending could give them real superpowers. Some children's play ended up by their even needing stitches. In one extreme instance a little boy playing Superman tried to fly out a window and was seriously injured.

Well, we decided to make a week of Neighborhood programs about monsters and superheroes, and we also produced a special for parents that aired just before that week of programming began. (We had a studio audience of parents, and we had parents call in from all across the country. Parents' concerns about superhero play in their households turned out to be real; their anecdotes echoed the many I had already heard.)

The Museum of Natural History at Pittsburgh's Carnegie Institute gave us an opportunity to let children know what real monsters—dinosaurs—had been like, *but that they did not exist anymore.* In a film segment at the museum, Dr. Mary Dawson, the curator, told some visiting children about how these prehistoric creatures lived when they inhabited the earth millions of years ago. She made it quite clear that there are none alive today, and added: "The only place dinosaurs are ever found now is in people's dreams."

That was the theme we picked up in the Neighborhood of Make-Believe: Prince Tuesday, bothered by a nightmare about a dinosaur, talks about his scary dream with the people he trusts. The prince comes to understand that while people sometimes do have dreams about frightening things, those things are imaginary.

Here is a real-life parallel we learned about in a letter from a concerned (and resourceful!) mother:

> As I watched my son and his playmates at their monster and superhero games, it seemed that two quite different things were going on. Superheroes express wishes and an unbounded sense of "me." Monsters express fears, particularly nightmares. So I made Carl a Superman cape and a series of grocery-bag monster masks.
>
> The masks proved very helpful in his struggle to overcome fear of the dark. The morning after a bad dream, I'd have him describe the scary face, then draw it on a mask. Then he'd chase me around, while we laughed and treated the whole thing as a big joke. At the end of the game, we would ceremoniously tear up the mask and stuff it in the garbage can, as I explained that the dream was as pretend as the paper. After a few mask games, he voluntarily gave up his nightlight.

In another film sequence during that week of programming I took my "television friends" to California to visit the set of *The Incredible Hulk.* That series' stars, Bill Bixby and Lou Ferrigno, made it possible for us to show children how makeup, fake props, stunt men, and television technology could make it look as though superhuman things were actually happening—things that could *never* happen in real life.

In addition to being an actor, Bill Bixby has been known to be a concerned parent. He told me how he had helped his preschool son, Christopher, understand that his dad was just part of a pretend story—that Bill was his dad and only his dad, and couldn't ever turn into a scary monster, even when he got mad:

> We did not allow Christopher to see *The Incredible Hulk*, not because we disapproved of his seeing it, but because in this unique instance I was his real father. To see me go through a transformation, with the white eyes, into Lou Ferrigno, and to separate the reality and fantasy, could be very difficult for him. So we brought him down to the set many times and he met Lou and saw the makeup, and saw me put in the white eyes, and finally he saw the show and he had no fear of it at all.

Bill believes, as I do, that talking with children is often the best way to reach them. As he put it, "If you don't talk, you don't touch."

We need to talk with our children about all sorts of things, the things that concern them and the things that concern us. We need to let them know how *we* feel about their play as well as listen carefully to hear how *they* feel. When our children's play makes us uncomfortable, we don't have to pussyfoot about it—or worry about setting limits on that play.

Children's fantasies can become very frightening for them when the make-believe becomes too real or when their imaginings threaten to get out of control. Children need to know, deep down inside, that the people who love them will keep them safe, even while they play.

There's something else that we need to help our children learn: It's not an imaginary superself, but each person's *real* self that does the really important things in life. As we give importance to what they're learning to do when they're little, we can also assure them that as they grow, they will be able to accomplish other important things, too.

Gun Play

Often parents find, to their dismay, that at a certain age young children turn almost everything they pick up into a "gun," and that if there isn't anything to pick up, a cocked thumb and forefinger will do just as well. "Bang! Bang!" or "Gotcha!" resound both indoors and out, and one dramatic death scene after another takes place on the living room rug or in the shrubbery.

This is how one mother described her dilemma:

I do not know how to deal with violent play in my three-and-a-half-year-old son, especially the "bang-bang-you're-dead" kind. Violence, and especially killing, is so repugnant to me that I hurt inside when, for example, he grabs a handy toy, points it, and walks around the house saying, "Kill...kill...kill." On the other hand, I am aware that children need to work all kinds of things out for themselves through play. I feel caught in the middle and don't know what to do.

What a familiar parental feeling that is! There are many reasons "violent play" of this kind becomes so compelling for our children. That they need to feel powerful and in control is certainly a large part of it. The person with the gun literally "calls the shots." If a child has cooperative playmates, they may act afraid of the gunslinger. They may even let themselves be ordered around, or fall down and lie still when they're "shot."

Guns seem to confer a kind of superpower because they can make things happen at a distance, as though your arms were enormously long. Perhaps for this same reason, remote-control toys like train sets or battery-driven cars often have a powerful attraction for young children. Certainly water pistols confer *real* power, and many of us can remember how hard it was not to squirt someone with the garden hose when we were meant to be watering the flowers or washing the car. Even flashlights have this power, and are reassuring to children who are afraid of the dark.

Almost anything that extends our children's control over the world around them is bound to have a strong lure for them, and that will be true all their lives. In itself, that urge is a tremendous motivation for creativity and invention, for learning how to control disease or for finding ways to make deserts bloom. But, of course, it's also the same urge that leads some people to find ways to control others through fear of physical harm or death. How to make this urge a constructive force in our children's lives is a problem all parents face. Certainly television and comics and real-life events all seem to conspire against us by emphasizing negative models of people who want to be in control through violent acts. Again and again we learn from killers or would-be assassins in the news that their motivation was, at least in part, the desire "to show the world that I'm not just a nobody."

I don't think many of us believe that when our children play with pretend guns it means that they are likely to grow up to use real ones. But even so, that form of play can be very painful to us because it touches our own deep feelings about death, loss, love, and the value of human life. *Those of us who are made uncomfortable by gun play need to let our children know it and let them know in as many ways as we know how that they are very valuable to us.* Even though we can never stop our children from engaging in some form of gun play when they are out of our sight, we can certainly refuse to buy gun toys for them; and, as one family I know did, we can have a firm rule against gun play in the house. In that family, all guns of any kind were "checked at the door." We can also discuss with our children the use of guns and other forms of violence that they see in comics or on television (see page 178).

What is important is not so much whether our children engage in gun play, but whether they know how we feel about it—or about anything else they do. Our children need us to be able to make rules that express our values and help ensure their safety. Children may sometimes find the reasons for these rules hard to understand or may consider the rules unreasonable. "But Johnny's parents let him stay up till ten" is something we may hear; I think the answer is a simple one that children, in their own way, can comprehend: "But you're not growing up in Johnny's family, and we feel differently about it." It is from the people they love the most that children acquire so many of their values.

Electronic Games

My concern over children playing more and more with preprogrammed machines goes back far beyond the current spate of electronic video games that has now inundated the country. It began some years ago when I became aware that very young children were spending an increasing amount of time with toys that, by their design, determined how children should play with them. Sometimes they were battery operated and had buttons that had to be pushed in a "correct" sequence in order to get a "correct" result. Others had metallic voices that would say the "correct" thing in response to "correct" manipulation. These toys appealed to children's delight in achievement and mastery. Indeed, at their best and used selectively, they could help children learn and memorize. Those machines all had one thing in common, however: They made children conform to them; they were not objects that children could make conform to their own fantasies and feelings. The time spent making them work, added to hours of watching television, meant less time spent in the kind of play that young children need most—play of their own invention.

The state of the electronic art has now brought preprogrammed video games to a level of sophistication that makes them remarkably fascinating and challenging. There may be studies some day that show they can increase a child's eye-hand coordination, as well as certain kinds of concentration. So much the better. Often these games are touted as introductions to "computer literacy," but there is no way that I myself could include computer literacy on a list of priorities for early childhood development. The work through play that children need to do in their early years is work about self, feelings, and relationships to others. It is this kind of play that will help determine whether the grown-up child programs a computer for bridge building or for body counts.

This game technology proves once again that there is almost no technology that is good or bad in itself—only in how it is used. Video games, like television, are only "wires and lights in a box" until someone puts a quarter in to make them work. That is still a human decision, not a mechanical one. For young children, it needs to be a parental decision. How much these games are used in the home as attachments to a television set is clearly a parental decision, too. From what I read and hear and see, I have no doubt that millions of children of all ages are getting an overdose of mechanical entertainment and suffering a deficiency in healthier forms of *play*. Although I don't know what the consequences will be, I feel sure they will be measurable and specific and will affect the quality of human relationships and an individual's capacity for self-development.

There is another kind of game that children have been playing for some time now and that seems to have a powerful fascination for them. These games are played in children's heads and the players make up what happens as they go along. The games may be set in old-time dungeons inhabited by mythological creatures or they may be set in some far-off future. They do have rules, but these rules are guidelines that children can adapt and alter as they see fit. The games have to be played with other human beings. Children can learn how from one another. They don't have to buy anything or spend any money to make the games work. A friend of mine told me that his son was on a long bus journey recently and found himself sitting next to an older child who was also familiar with this kind of game. That's how they whiled away the time; but, more than making time pass, they made friends.

I find it interesting that there should be two such completely different kinds of game playing attracting children's attention right now—almost as if the one sought to make up for what the other lacked. In any event, the comparison pointed up for me the contrast between noncreative and creative play.

Play as Problem Solving

As I look back over what I have written here about play, it occurs to me that almost all play involves problem solving, whether it's balancing blocks on top of one another or trying to maneuver a video spaceship to outwit alien invaders. At the same time, I think there is a really important distinction to be made between play in which the problems are of our own choosing and the solutions of our own making, and play in which the problems are set by someone else as well. There is also a big difference between toys that we can adapt to our inner needs and toys that make us adapt to them.

Play can continue to be a valuable tool for creative problem solving all of our lives if we have been encouraged to develop our creative capacities when we were very young. Those capacities are the ones that are most helpful in bringing us unexpected and satisfying answers to the great puzzle of who we are becoming as we grow. There's so much we can't do for our children even though we'd like to, but letting our children know how we feel about them, their play, and the world they're growing into is something we *can* do—and that's a lot!

*　　*　　*

It's easy to overlook the importance of play in children's lives and in the lives of adults, too. Even wise and kindly kings have been known to do so—in make-believe, at least. Here's the *beginning* of another story you and your children could talk about together. You'll find the *conclusion* at the end of Chapter 6.

The Day No Child Could Play
Part 1

Once upon a playful day in the Neighborhood of Make-Believe, everywhere you looked someone was playing. At the platypus mound, little Anna, Prince Tuesday, and Daniel Striped Tiger were making up a play about being grown-ups. Mrs. Platypus was helping them by writing down the words they wanted to say.

At the Museum-Go-Round, Lady Elaine Fairchilde was playing the piano.

X the Owl and Henrietta Pussycat were playing ball in the tree where they lived. Sometimes they tossed the ball back and forth, and sometimes they would take turns throwing it high up in the air and seeing how many times they could clap their wings and paws before catching it again.

No one in the neighborhood was sick that day, so even Dr. Bill was sitting in the sun outside his office in the Eiffel Tower playing cards with Grandpère. "It's a bill bill beautiful day," Dr. Bill was saying, "and sometimes play is the bill bill best medicine of all."

And high in the sky, the sun was playing, too, playing down through the clouds and making shadows skim across the grass in front of the castle where Bob Dog was frisking about with Queen Sara.

"Now, don't get near the ladder, Bob Dog," Queen Sara was saying as Bob Dog woofed and rolled and jumped. "We don't want Handyman Negri to fall."

"We certainly don't!" said Handyman Negri from the top of the ladder, where he was cleaning a turret.

"Owwwowwwoww!" howled Bob Dog, looking up at Handyman Negri. "Haven't you finished yet? I'll bet you're about the only person in this whole neighborhood who isn't playing right now!"

"I'll be finished in a minute. I promised the King I'd clean this turret this morning," Handyman Negri said, "and then I'll play, too."

Just then the telephone on the castle wall began to ring.

"Dear Bob Dog," said Queen Sara, "would you answer that telephone for me?"

Bob Dog bounded over to the phone.

"Hello," he said, "this is the castle where lives the king who married the queen who played with the dog who answered the phone and said: 'Hello, this is the castle where lives the king who married the queen. . . .' Oh, it's you, X!"

"Yes," said X, who was calling from his tree. "We've got a problem over here."

"Owwwowwww," said Bob Dog. "I hope it's a playful problem."

"It is sort of a playful problem," said X. "You see, Henrietta and I were playing ball, and the ball's got stuck up in the branches of our tree and I can't get it down. Is there anyone over there at the castle who could give us a hand?"

"Well," said Bob Dog, "I'd be glad to give you a paw. And Handyman Negri's here with a ladder and I could just borrow that when he's finished and come right over."

"Thank you, Bob Dog," said X. "You're a real friend."

Bob Dog hung up the phone and told Queen Sara about X's problem. "It's okay if I borrow the ladder, isn't it?" he asked.

"You'll have to ask Handyman Negri about that," she said. "After all, it's his ladder."

So Bob Dog told Handyman Negri about X's problem and asked if he could borrow the ladder.

"Don't you want me to go over and get the ball down for you?" asked Handyman Negri.

"No thanks, Handy," said Bob Dog, "I'd like to get it. Myself."

"Okay," said Handyman Negri. "I'm finished here. But please be careful. You really have to keep your balance when you're up on a ladder."

Bob Dog was so happy to be going somewhere and doing something that he hardly heard what Handyman was saying.

While X and Henrietta had been waiting for Bob Dog to arrive, they had been making up a nonsense poem to pass the time. This is what Bob Dog heard as he came over to the tree:

"Lidderdy ladder."

"Meowderdy madder."

"Sowderdy sadder."

"Sadderdy Sunday, meow!"

"Sunder I wonderdy."

"Meow feeling gladder, meow!"

"Here comes the ladder now!"

"One two three."

"Here I am," said Bob Dog, setting the ladder up against the tree. "Now, where's the ball?"

"Right above Henrietta's house," said X.

"Meow can see it, meow," said Henrietta as Bob Dog climbed the ladder.

"Can ya see it?" asked X.

"Not yet," said Bob Dog, climbing a little higher. "Yup! There it is!" He was so excited as he reached it that he turned around to show X and Henrietta, quite forgetting where he was. The ladder slipped from underneath him and he came crashing down through the branches and landed on the ground.

"Owwwowwwowww!" howled Bob Dog.

"Are you hurt?" said X. But all Bob Dog could do was howl.

"Meow think we'd better meow Dr. Bill right away!" said Henrietta. "Meow meow office meow meow Eiffel Tower!"

"You're right, Hen. I'll go get him," said X. "And Handyman Negri, too. We're going to need somebody big. You stay here and I'll be right back."

"Meow getting help," Henrietta said to Bob Dog. "Meow okay?"

But all Bob Dog could do was go on howling.

That's how all the trouble started one playful day in the Neighborhood of Make-Believe.

* * *

MISTER ROGERS TALKS WITH PARENTS

When Dr. Bill got to the scene of the accident, he didn't think Bob Dog was badly hurt, but he wanted to take him to the hospital just to make sure.

By then, Handyman Negri was there and so was Mr. McFeely. Someone had the idea to use a hammock to carry Bob Dog, and that's what they did.

The news of Bob Dog's fall from the ladder had already reached the castle, and King Friday and Queen Sara were out on the balcony when Handyman Negri and Mr. McFeely approached carrying Bob Dog in the hammock.

"I'm so sorry for poor Bob Dog," said Queen Sara.

"There was a lot of playing going on today, was there not?" asked the King.

"Everyone was having such a good time, too," said the Queen sadly.

"It didn't end up that way, however," said the King in a stern voice. When Bob Dog's helpers came past, the King ordered them to stop.

"Mr. McFeely, Handyman Negri, and Bob Dog, I presume?" he said in his most kingly tone.

"Correct as usual," everyone replied. Everyone, that is, except Bob Dog, who let out another howl.

"Oh, poor Bob Dog," said the Queen. "I'm so sorry you're hurt."

Bob Dog howled a little louder.

"Of course," said the Queen. "I understand. But we'll take good care of you."

"And I," said the King, "am going to see that there will be no further accidents. You may all hear a new rule." After a loud fanfare of trumpets, King Friday declared his new rule: *There will be no more play in this Neighborhood of Make-Believe.*

"No more play?" everyone asked in disbelief.

"No more play," said the King. "Nobody may play anything anymore."

"But Friday," said the Queen, "that will be just impossible."

"It will be quite possible, as you shall see," said the King. "From now on we are going to play it safe, and that means there will be *no* play in this neighborhood. I will not have any more foolishness causing accidents. Is that understood?"

"Yes, King Friday," everyone said slowly.

"But right now we'd better get Bob Dog to the hospital," said Handyman Negri.

"Very well," said the King, "you may go. But remember the rule: *no more play.*"

Just as they were leaving, the Neighborhood Trolley came along the tracks in front of the castle. It stopped before the King, jiggling back and forth and dinging its bell as if to ask what was going on.

"Not so playful with your running and ringing, Trolley," commanded the King. "No one's allowed to play anymore in this neighborhood, *and that includes you!*"

* * *

MISTER ROGERS TALKS WITH PARENTS

The next day, King Friday ordered his niece, Lady Aberlin, to appear before him.

"Lady Aberlin, I presume?" he said when she came to the castle.

"Correct as usual, Uncle Friday," said Lady Aberlin.

"Niece Aberlin," said the King, "I have some signs here for you, and I want you to put them up all over the neighborhood."

"What do they say, Uncle Friday," Lady Aberlin asked.

"They say No Play Allowed," said the King.

"Oh, Uncle Friday," said Lady Aberlin, "are you sure you want to keep this new rule?"

"Very sure," said the King. "I will not have other people hurt in this neighborhood."

"But stopping play is no way to stop people from getting hurt, Uncle Friday," Lady Aberlin argued.

"It is *one* way," said the King, "and you can get to work putting up the signs right now."

"All right, Uncle Friday," said Lady Aberlin, "but I don't approve at all."

"You may begin right here on the castle wall," said the King.

And so Lady Aberlin took the first sign and started nailing it up on the castle wall. Tap, tap...tap, tap, tap...tap, tap...tap, tap, tap went her hammer. It sounded like drum music.

"That hammering sounds like play to me," warned King Friday.

"Oh, Uncle Friday," Lady Aberlin complained, "you're making everything so dull."

"Dull, perhaps, but *safe*," answered the King. "When you've finished with that sign you may take the rest to the outskirts. Farewell."

CHAPTER 6:

EVERYDAY FAMILY LIFE

"I hear you're writing a book about parenting," many friends have said to me lately. I've found it hard to give them a simple yes in reply because I haven't yet become comfortable with that word *parenting*. Something about it suggests that it's an art to be learned or a science to be understood, and that there are clear answers to the everyday problems and uncertainties of being one of the major caregiving adults in a young child's life. I know from my own experience that there aren't.

I remember the principal of a local high school once saying to me, "You have no idea, Mr. Rogers, how many parents have just given up on their kids. Many parents feel they've tried and tried and still they've failed. They just don't have the energy to try again." How sad for parents to have to think of their children as some kind of exam that they either pass or fail—and how sad that these parents are abandoning in despair one of their own greatest opportunities to grow.

There's another problem with the word *parenting*: It doesn't suggest that being a parent *is* a process of continuing mutual growth, growth of the father and mother as well as of the child. It's a time of growth and change for everyone, whether we want it or not. Many of us find change threatening or upsetting—change in the world around us or change in ourselves. In fact, I imagine that most of us can remember times when we wished for things to stay just as they were, or when, for a little while, everything seemed to be more or less in balance. But of course those times don't last forever, and least of all in the hectic round of everyday family life. I think of how I've grown through my twenty-plus years of being a father—how I not only learned to change a diaper, but to listen for the cry that told me the diaper needed changing. I learned about child safety and nutrition and what it was like to feel proud and sad and angry and delighted at my own relationship with my very own child. I even learned to appreciate parents more—my own parents included. I realized that it wasn't all that easy to be one. And all along the way, I've been discovering many things about myself—what I was like when I was the different ages of our sons. Their growing evoked memories of my growing and I've had another chance to work out some things I thought I'd finished and forgotten. So much of this occurred not by my conscious effort but just by my being present and available to my children—just "being there" for them. "Being there" is what everyday family life is about.

Being There

Parents who expect change in themselves as well as in their children, who accept it and find in it the joy as well as the pains of growth, are likely to be the happiest and most confident parents. Just "being there" as a willing participant in the process of change is an important part of parenthood. Focusing on ways to encourage mutual growth rather than on some supposedly right and wrong ways to raise children day by day is more likely to produce the outcomes we want in the end. In fact, I doubt that we can ever successfully impose values or attitudes or behaviors on our children—certainly not by threat, guilt, or punishment. But I do believe they can be induced through relationships where parents and children are growing together. Such relationships are, I believe, built on trust, example, talk, and caring.

As I was writing this I was thinking how much easier it would be—easier for me and easier for you—if I would just jot down simple rules like:

Buy your baby a 4.75-inch teddy bear and present it the day of the first full moon after the baby's birth.

But there are no simple rules for parenting and you can't buy the skills that you need. Like anything that really becomes a part of who you are, parenting develops by practice, by "being there."

One thing being there can mean is *listening*.

More and more, I have come to feel that listening is one of the most important things that we can do for another person, whether that someone is an adult or a child. Our commitment to listen to who that person is can often be our greatest gift to that person. Whether he or she is speaking or playing or dancing, building or singing or painting, if we care, we can be attempting to listen.

We all have different gifts, so we all have different ways of telling the world who we are. Part of me is a songwriter. I made up music long before I knew the alphabet. My five-year-old fingers pounded and patted the keys of my piano according to the way I felt inside. Since I had no brothers or sisters until I was eleven, my piano was my only daily playmate, and I used it and used it. And my parents, with understanding and patience, listened. (Of course, there were times when I didn't want anybody to hear how I was feeling, so I'd shut the door to the room where the piano was.)

Listening takes practice. I found this out when I first started working with children at a family and child-care center. Under the supervision of gifted specialists, I made myself available to children as an adult counterpart in therapeutic puppet play as well as in music. Often I would feel that a play session just hadn't gotten anywhere. After one particularly difficult session with a child I told my supervisor I thought I had managed dreadfully, and my supervisor said to me: "Fred, an hour with a child in which you've given your attention and tried to understand that child as well as you know how—that hour is never wasted." That turned out to be true, especially after I came to learn and to *feel* that it was the relationship that was growing, not just the child or myself.

As time went on, I spent hours and hours observing and listening, and little by little something wonderful began to happen: I remembered how it felt to be a child myself. I remembered the bewilderments, the sadnesses, the joys, the lonely times, the angers. Having remembered these things, I found that I could make *myself* more available to the children I was with. I could take the time to listen to these children's needs before deciding what their needs were. Once we've listened to our children, we don't have to impose our own notions of what an experience means—whether the experience is sad, happy, or angry. Instead, we can help them develop their own expressions of the events, people, places, and things of their lives. We can help them develop their own inner natures.

A few years ago, during an open house in Chicago's public television station, I was singing and talking with a large group of children. At the conclusion of the visit I asked if anyone wanted to tell me anything else. One three-year-old boy said, "I do," and when I encouraged him, he spoke out in a most trusting way. "Mister Rogers," he said, "I wear diapers just at night now." There was a hush over the whole room. I could tell some people were wondering if others would laugh, and others were hoping someone else would say something quickly so that the awkward moment would pass. I didn't answer quickly because I was listening. In doing so, I realized that the most important news in that little boy's life at that very moment was that he was getting by without diapers in the daytime. I told him I was proud of the way he was growing and that he would be the one to decide when he wanted to stop wearing his diapers at night. The little boy smiled, and the room breathed a sigh of relief.

I was proud of that little boy... but I was proud of his caregivers, too. They must have been good listeners for him to have been able to speak out to me like that... to tell me what was of prime importance to him right then and there.

Being there can mean *waiting.*

Healthy human babies grow from one phase to another in a predictable way—from lying still to turning over, from crawling and toddling to walking and talking. Once we start to work on something, we'll be insistent about it. When we're ready to crawl we'll find every chance we can to crawl and crawl and crawl, and we don't want people to stop us from crawling. And we don't want people to hurry us to walk; we'll walk when we feel ready and not before.

The progression of our emotional phases is just as well defined. There is an inner rhythm that sets the normal beat for human physical and emotional growth, and we need to respect that rhythm in ourselves and our children. It's tempting to push our children faster than they're ready to go. One reason is that we often want for them the pleasures that we know await in standing or walking, in learning to read or riding a bicycle. Sometimes, of course, we push our children for our own convenience and try to get them potty trained or able to feed themselves, brush their teeth, or dress themselves sooner than they're really able. Sometimes we can feel very frustrated and even worried when our children aren't developing as fast as we'd like them to. We may think that in some way our children's "slow" growth means that we're being poor parents, and that if we could only find the book with all the "right" answers we would be able to move our children along more quickly.

But the truth of the matter is that each child is an individual and moves according to a unique inner timetable. We do know within what general age boundaries children as a whole may become ready to learn certain tasks, but those boundaries are wide and there's no way to figure out a formula for any particular child. I've heard of children who didn't begin to talk until they were three years old or more, and then began speaking in complete sentences. Or a nine-month-old infant who seemed very slow in physical development—and then, in four days, mastered sitting, crawling, and turning around. It's common, too, for children to seem to go backward in their development for a while. They may have learned to walk—but seem to prefer crawling nonetheless. A child who has finally given up thumb sucking may suddenly go back to it for a time. But the chances are that these are temporary regressions; often they reflect the child's need for a little more readiness before taking on something new once and for all. It's during stressful times that children are particularly likely to regress. When there's something urgent and difficult to deal with, a child may need to go back to some earlier, more comfortable way of doing things until the stress has passed.

One thing is certain: Children need lots of free, quiet time to get used to all that's developing within them. Have you noticed that an unhurried time by yourself or with someone you really trust can be the best setting for your own personal growth? It's no different for children.

This kind of waiting on a parent's part is *active* waiting. We need to be there with quiet surveillance and a sense of partnership in the growing process.

One of the most vivid examples of this partnership in action is also one of the earliest. If you watch a mother with an infant in her arms at a quiet time, you are almost certain to see moments when, although there is nothing particular going on, the mother becomes totally preoccupied with her child. It is almost as though she has "tuned out" from everything else around her. She will gaze fixedly at her baby, and all her other senses, too, are turned in the same direction. She may rock her body ever so slightly. When you speak to her, she may appear to be coming out of a daydream.

These are moments of intense and active waiting, waiting to be responsive to little signs and signals from her baby. She is acutely aware of changes in her baby's state, alert to the flutterings under those small eyelids that may indicate formless infant dreams, or the frowns and twitches of the mouth that may reflect sensations within that new body. It is as if she is saying by her complete absorption, "You are safe, all is well. Go on getting used to who and what you are. I am waiting here."

As her baby grows into a creeper, a crawler, and then a toddler, the same very specific and noticeable kind of waiting continues. The mother will sit on the floor with her child and watch intently as her

EVERYDAY FAMILY LIFE

budding explorer leaves her lap to roam and investigate, to practice being a separate person. Now, instead of surrounding her child with her arms, she uses her voice to send messages of encouragement or caution or reassurance. She is saying, "Everything's okay. Go on finding out about your world. I am waiting here."

If you doubt the baby's *need* for this kind of waiting, just watch a little longer. Regularly and predictably, the exploring child will look to his or her mother, checking back to make sure she is there. Periodically, as the tension of being apart grows, the child will toddle back to Mom for a hug and a squeeze, and then think about things awhile before setting off again. It's as if that child is saying, "Wow, was that ever an adventure being out there! But boy, am I glad you're right here where I can find you!"

These are good times for the growth of trust as our children learn that they can count on us to give them time, to keep them protected, and to help them move along in their development when they are ready.

Being there can also mean *standing firm*.

It is we, after all, who have to define and organize our children's worlds before they can do so for themselves. They need structure. So do we all.

Some of the boundaries we draw for our children are necessary for any child—boundaries that keep them out of danger. Others, though, are ones that we draw because they reflect the way we were brought up ourselves and express the values we have come to hold important (see page 150). This second kind of boundary varies from family to family and from person to person. In fact, many husbands and wives have to work hard at reshaping these boundaries when they get married so that both partners are reasonably comfortable within the shared limits they have chosen.

I think it's important to stand firm behind the boundaries we set for our children's actions and behaviors. But when our children challenge those limits they need to know their opinions will be respected, too. Their rebellions in early childhood and in adolescence are all a healthy part of their unique growing. It's tough for us and for them, extremely tough at times, but they must try out who they are and who we are in an effort to know who they will be. There's tension—just like the tension of a bud about to burst into bloom—but these challenges are most important times and not times to "give up."

Privacy

I've mentioned how small and vulnerable little children can feel in an adult world and how much of children's play reflects their need to feel in control of their world and themselves. So much of growth is involved in gaining mastery over things—one's own body functions, one's own feelings, and events in the world outside ourselves. That sense of mastery has a lot to do with our sense of self all during our lives.

For a long time a small child must wonder if he or she is in control of anything at all. Parents make up the daily schedule, the whats and whens of eating, the hows and wheres of elimination. They determine what to wear and where to go. Doctors and dentists prod and poke into the body, barbers cut off hair, and so on (see Chapter 8). Grown-ups, particularly parents, seem all-powerful and all-knowing. I can imagine a small child wondering something like, "Is there really no part of me that's all mine? That belongs to me alone? That is safe from intruders? Over which I, and only I, have control?"

Even if a child isn't able to *think* that kind of thought yet, he or she might be able to *feel* something like it. Maybe it's out of that discomfort that human beings develop the need for privacy. Like all feelings, the need for privacy is different in each person, but I believe it's always there—a need for both inside and outside privacy.

There's no inside privacy that's more important than the privacy of our own thoughts. As we grow up, we come to take the security of that private world in our heads for granted. Knowing that we can think what we want to think, imagine, fantasize, dream, and daydream without anyone else being able to eavesdrop is important to anyone's emotional and mental stability.

Yet finding a way to get inside someone else's head has always held a powerful attraction for human beings. Have you noticed the popularity of books and lectures on extrasensory perception and mind reading? I've even heard that one of the reasons we can be so captivated by novels is that they give us a chance to do just that—get inside someone else's head. We can get to know a character in a book in a way we can never know a real human being because the writer can take us inside that character's mind. On the other hand, the possibility that someone might be able to read our thoughts is a very frightening notion. Terms like *thought control* and *brainwashing* are threatening and sinister.

From the time our children are very young, we need to help them develop a sense of security about their private inside worlds. Part of that security comes from the knowledge that there's no magic in our minds that can actually make something happen in the real world. For children, the phrase "wishing won't make things come true" has two sides. One side is that children have to learn that to make something good happen, an event they want, they have to *do* something about it. Sitting around and wishing won't make it happen (see page 65). The other side (and this is extremely important for children's sense of security!) is that they have to learn that wishing for something *bad* can't make that happen either (see page 64). To be comfortable with our thoughts and feelings we have to know that they are safely a part of our inside private worlds and that it is up to us—under our control—how we give them expression in the world around us.

Another part of giving children security in their privacy is letting them know that no one can spy on their thoughts. Children's play is often a private time because they are frequently giving their thoughts expression. That's a reason we have to be so careful when we feel like joining in or reorganizing their play in some way. We may be intruding in something very personal and private.

With parents and other adults seeming so all-powerful in so many ways, it's hardly surprising that children may believe that adults are "mind readers" as well—like my friend Ted Lennox (see page 79), who grew up without sight and who thought for a while that sighted people could see around corners and through walls. Children may even believe that the doctor who is peering with a little flashlight into the nose and ears, or listening with a stethoscope to the heart, is really eavesdropping on what's going on in the mind.

You may have noticed how frightened a small child can be at the sight of a department-store Santa Claus. There are so many stories and so much lore that our culture has built up around the figure of Santa Claus. How he became a symbol for rewarding "good" children and punishing "bad" children no one seems to be completely sure, but he certainly touches children and families very widely and deeply. Part of the Santa lore is that he spies on you when you're asleep and knows when you're being bad or good, and I don't think that's helpful for children, whose feelings about Santa are rooted in their view of their parents' omnipotence. It can only reinforce a fear that there *are* adults who see all, hear all, and know all.

A healthy child grows up with the sense of being a whole person— a unique person separate and distinct from any other, with an inner privacy that can be shared or not shared as he or she sees fit. There is no one on this earth who sees all, hears all, and knows all about any one of us. Who we are inside and what we do alone is our own business. What we choose to tell and to whom we choose to tell it is our own business, too.

In an effort to dispel children's feelings that adults are omnipotent, we used the Santa Claus myth in *Mister Rogers' Neighborhood*. When we did so, we raised quite a ruckus, and one community even refused to air the programs at the time of their distribution. Some people seemed to think that we were setting out to debunk Santa altogether. As one critic wrote:

This time, by Donder and Blitzen, they have gone too far: The traditional image of Santa Claus is going to be dented next week...on the kiddie program of *Mister Rogers*, of all places....

I think Rogers—himself the father of two sons—is way off base with this one. I think his reasoning is intellectually pretentious. I think he is the biggest Christmas party pooper since Ebenezer Scrooge.

Well, of course, that's not what we were setting out to do at all, and we later heard that that critic hadn't even seen the programs when he wrote his column. There is much that is both fun and fine about the Santa Claus story, and families for years have been finding their own ways to include Santa in their holiday celebrations. Here, in fact, is what happens in our programs:

In my television "living room" I try on a Santa Claus suit, explaining that during the holiday season people sometimes like to dress up as Santa. But the suit is much too big for me, so I take it over to Chef Brockett's bakery and ask Don Brockett if he'd like to try it on. It fits him fine.

In the Neighborhood of Make-Believe there is general excitement because Lady Aberlin brings the news that Santa is going to pay the neighbors a visit. One neighbor, Daniel Striped Tiger, isn't excited at all. He's plain scared.

"What's he going to do to us?" he asks Lady Aberlin.

She replies that it will probably be something nice, but Daniel isn't reassured at all. "I try to be good, but I'm not always good," he says. "I think I'm afraid of Santa Claus. I wish he weren't coming here."

Lady Aberlin is surprised until Daniel explains that he has heard that Santa sees you when you're sleeping and knows when you're good and bad. Lady Aberlin suggests to Daniel that he talk with Santa about that when he comes. It's a scary prospect for Daniel, but he agrees to try.

When Santa stops by the clock where Daniel lives, the first thing Daniel blurts is: "Oh, my! You did come! I'm Daniel Striped Tiger and I'm not always good!"

To which Santa replies: "Well, I'm Santa Claus and I'm not always good, either." And he adds, "Good people aren't always good. They just *try* to be."

As Santa is about to leave, Daniel screws up his courage to pose the big question that's been on his mind.

"Can you see people when they're sleeping and do you know when everybody's bad or good?" he asks.

"Of course not," says Santa. "Somebody made that up about me. I'm not a spy and I can't see people when they're asleep."

EVERYDAY FAMILY LIFE

"You can't?" asks Daniel.

"Of course not," Santa replies, "and I know that everybody's good sometimes and everybody's bad sometimes."

Daniel tells Santa that he's decided he likes him after all.

"I like you, too," says Santa, "and I'm glad you asked me that."

What we were trying to do in that television episode was to encourage children's strivings for wholeness. I believe that we were being honest, and therefore freeing, in declaring the inner privacy of self.

Outer privacy is important, too. Many of us feel the need from time to time to have a place where we can go alone and shut a door and be sure of being by ourselves for a while. For the members of a large and busy family living in a small house, such solitude can be really hard to come by. Children show their need for outer as well as inner privacy very early on in their lives. When they take delight in a special box or container in which to keep their treasures, they are showing a need for privacy. They are also adept at finding special places to keep themselves when they feel like it—a tent in the backyard, a space under the stairs or in the back of a cupboard, or under a blanket draped over a table or chairs. In that sense, children may be more fortunate than adults, because in almost any home there is room for a child to make at least a small special place of his or her own.

Protecting our children's needs for privacy is one of the best ways to help children learn to respect the needs for privacy that parents have, too. It might seem that our adult needs for privacy are sure to run head-on into our children's healthy curiosity about bodies and beds and bathrooms. Those issues will certainly come up, but I don't think there need be painful collisions. If we are clear about what our needs for privacy are, we can make the limits of physical curiosity quite plain in a loving but firm manner. I think that these issues of privacy become most difficult to handle in families where there is too little talk. I don't believe that any question asked by a child invades our privacy. It may not be easy to find the most appropriate answer on the spur of the moment, in which case we can promise to talk about it in a little while—a promise that's of course important to keep. But nurturing our children's trust in us as the people they *can* ask about their uncertainties is one of the most important tasks in all of parenting. Privacy and secrecy are *not* the same thing, and I've come to believe that the presence or absence of trust is exactly what makes the difference.

Competition

It's a word that makes many of us very edgy, and it's a situation that we have probably been living with since we were very small. For some people competition is a thrill, a stimulation, a challenge. For others it's a source of sadness and anger and apprehension. For still others, it's a mixture of all those things.

It's not possible to go through life without competing. As one woman told me, "Competition is a part of our everyday life, whether we're competing for a job, or on the soccer field, or for love." Some people make professional competition their life's work—like Lynn Swann, the all-time-great wide receiver for the Pittsburgh Steelers. "In the game of football," Lynn told me, "competition is what it's all about—wanting to be first because a lot of us think people love winners best."

There are many kinds of competition, to be sure. But I think that love does have something to do with them all. In fact, I believe that if we've ever wanted someone's love, then we've known what competition really means.

For many children, their first intensely competitive situation occurs with a baby brother or sister (see page 70). Suddenly there's a new baby in the house and everyone seems preoccupied with the newcomer's needs. There's not so much time anymore for "me" in Mommy's or Daddy's arms or laps. All the special looks and sounds and gestures and even smells that have been telling me that I'm the loved child aren't just all mine anymore. Who *is* that baby, anyway? And what's it doing here?

Even older children secure in the many relationships within a family may have some strong and conflicting feelings about such a rival. One four-and-a-half-year-old I know greeted his baby brother's return from the hospital with true joy. He hugged his mother and said, "Oh, Mom!

Now we're a *real* family!" A few days later, though, while he and his father were looking at the sleeping infant, he said, "If Andrew died, he'd sure make a small skeleton, wouldn't he?"

In many families the arrival of a new baby brings out downright hostility and aggression in the older child, and that behavior can be scary for parents. In the course of making a television program about competition in families, I talked with many parents. Some of what they said may sound familiar to you.

One mother described life in her family like this:

I have a three-month-old baby and a two-and-a-half-year-old baby. After the baby had been at home about two weeks, the older one bit her finger and tried to take it off. I said, "What are you doing?!" She said, "Her finger gone." She knew she'd bit it, and then she wanted to go to her room and she went to bed. After that it kind of eased off.

Just recently she started again. She's been taking her little sister's feet and bending them backwards while she's in the infant seat. Yesterday she knelt on her head and laughed. I told her, "We don't do this to Michelle, you know. We don't do that to your sister." Later on in the afternoon she gave her a quick kick in the head as she walked past. She is just on that baby constantly. She'll hug her, you know, and pat her on the head. And then slap her.

Now, this is a really nice little girl, a real sweet little angel of a girl, and there she is beating up on her little three-month-old sister.

I read one time where if your child is doing that to a younger baby you tell them, "Why don't you do that to your baby doll? If you feel like taking out your anger, do it with your baby doll." I tried it with her. She said, "I don't want to hurt my doll. I'll do it to Michelle." Her dolls have their place on her bed. They are never hurt. But Michelle puts up with all this abuse. I don't know where it's going to end.

I could certainly sympathize with that mother's concern. Here was her little girl, "a real sweet little angel of a girl," with such intense feelings of wanting to be the only one for her mother to love. I thought, too, how scared that little girl must feel when she does all those things to her baby sister...how scared those feelings of rage must make her. It's absolutely essential for that little girl to know that if she finds it too hard to stop hurting the baby, *someone*—Mommy—will help her stop. She may complain bitterly if she's limited in her times with the baby; nevertheless, way down deep she'll be grateful to know that when her feelings get beyond her control, they won't be beyond her parents' help.

I talked with another mother who was having similar problems. She had a two-and-a-half-year-old son and year-old twin boys. The oldest bit and kicked his little brothers to the point where that mother said she really feared for their lives. Then she realized something: Whenever her oldest boy was being friendly, she left him alone, thankful for the peace and quiet. Whenever he was aggressive, he got her full attention. As soon as that mother began putting special times aside just for her and her firstborn, and as soon as she was careful to appreciate his times of cooperative behavior, the situation eased up. Rivalry among the brothers continued and probably will continue for years, but at least the older boy's aggression became more manageable as he came to feel more secure about still being his mother's loved child.

I've learned so much from parents and children who have trusted me enough to share what's important to them in their lives. There is a lot to think about in what those mothers told me—the importance of keeping curbs on unacceptable behavior in firm but loving ways; the importance of talking; the need to find special times for the older child; the need for reassurance; and how painful our own feelings of guilt can be when our anger gets the best of us or when we feel we aren't being all we should be to our children.

Some of the struggles these mothers and children are going through will probably continue. It's not easy for any child to give up cherished fantasies. Anybody would like to be his or her parents' sole loved child...but often can't be. It's a fantasy that many have to let go. And parents can't be all they would like to be to their children. That's hard to accept, but often in the struggles and confrontations, there can be a positive side to what may seem a negative response on our part. For instance, when we tell an older child that the baby is *not* going to be taken back or given away no matter what anyone says, we are telling that older child that he or she would never be taken back or given away either. When we say, "I will not let you hurt your little brother," we are also saying that we will protect the older child, too, not only from being hurt by other people, but also from acting out their own scary wishes.

Even a child who doesn't have a brother or a sister is likely to meet competition early in life. Around the age of four, almost every child feels some rivalry with the parent of the same sex. There is a time when it is perfectly normal and natural for a boy to have fantasies of growing up and marrying his mother, and for a girl to decide that she's going to be her daddy's wife (see page 69). We may never know that our children are having such feelings. On the other hand, it may be fairly clear from the way a boy becomes unusually protective of his mother and angry and cantankerous with his father, or from the way a girl becomes overtly flirtatious with her father and hostile toward her mother. There's nothing unhealthy going on here, and we need to know that. In fact, in terms of the way children grow, there's probably something healthy happening. But how should we respond?

Well, we certainly *don't* need to encourage these fantasies, and we *do* need to help our children understand what the real future does and does not hold for them. I like the way Dottie's mother (see page 106) responded. Matter-of-factly, she let her daughter know the truth. "Daddy's already married to me," she said, and then went on to tell Dottie that when she grew up she wouldn't marry her father but she might find someone her own age whom she would like to marry. We can show our children that we love them as our sons and daughters, that we need them to be who they are in order for us to be mothers and fathers, and that that's a truly special kind of love. Of course, one isolated conversation like that won't settle our children's competitive feelings, but if we stick to it and help them to understand it, sooner or later they can come to be more comfortable with their real place in the family. The fantasies will become part of their dim past—to the point where few adults can even remember having had them.

A child's quest for love and approval doesn't stay just within the family for very long. Soon, most all of us find ourselves feeling in competition for the love and approval of the world beyond—teachers, friends, and spectators. Many of the games we play are structured around winning and losing, and whatever the actual goal of the game may be, a little voice within us often says it's all a matter of winning or losing *love*.

It can be hard when one child in a family is a strong competitor and a frequent winner while another is not. One mother told me of a problem that many families have to deal with.

> *We have two sons in our family, and the nine-year-old boy is very involved in competitive swimming. The six-year-old, his younger brother, resents going to swim meets every weekend and having to structure the family evenings around swim practice. The older one has his ribbons hanging all over his room and his brother sees this. And we say, "We have to go to another swim meet."*
>
> *The six-year-old hasn't got into any of that sort of thing. But he has his own talents, definitely. I guess we have to nurture them more. He would rather be with his books and his reading and his records.*

That mother sounded very wise to me—we do need to nurture our children's unique talents and interests. She went on to tell me how either she or her husband sometimes stays home with the younger boy while the other parent goes to the swim meet. That way they are placing value on what both boys like to do. All the same, she said, it was proving hard to get her younger boy to enjoy his brother's success. It will stay hard, too, both for the parents and for that six-year-old. It may not be easy for the nine-year-old swimmer, either, when he loses in a swim meet. But both of those boys know that their parents try because they care, and, no matter what, that's the best message we can give to anybody.

There's probably no way we can keep our children from feeling sad or angry when they lose, any more than we can keep ourselves from feeling that way. What we can help them understand, though, is that though we appreciate them for what they *do*, we love them even more for who they are. We can let them know, too, that win or lose, we will always be proud of them for doing the best they can. In the disappointment of a defeat, a child may seem to find little comfort in our saying, "But you really tried hard and I'm proud of you." It takes time to get over a disappointment. For those children who have learned to feel valued and loved by the people they love, these disappointments do pass. It's the children who are less fortunate, the ones who feel they have to bank everything on their performance, who come to believe that losing in a competition means being one of life's unloved "losers."

A man with whom I worked closely while we were making our programs about competition is Tom Cottle, a Boston-based psychologist, writer, and television personality. We agreed that competition isn't always destructive—only some of the forms it takes and the way it makes some of us feel about ourselves can be unhealthy. In fact, healthy competition among people who have healthy feelings about themselves can be a fine way for them to stretch themselves to new limits. As Tom put it, competition can be "constructive fuel."

MISTER ROGERS TALKS WITH PARENTS

He said something else, too, that I'd like to share with you:

We must be loved and we must be valued. We must feel
that we have some sense of worth, that we matter to somebody,
that there's a reason that we're here, that there's a justification
for our very being. And sometimes the competitive sense, the
sense of gaining competence and accomplishment, helps that.
My feeling is the people who feel loved and also feel they have
worth are the people who have really heard life's music.

Pets

When I was little and as yet had no sister or brother, I had a dog named
Mitzi. She was a brown wire-haired mongrel, and for a long time I think
she was *really* my best friend. We learned a lot about the world in each
other's company. We explored our neighborhood and beyond, and I
remember feeling a little braver whenever she was with me. She made
her own discoveries and I mine; but often we shared them with each
other—just as, it seemed to me, we shared times of particular excitement, joy, and sadness. We got scared together when there was thunder
and lightning. Sometimes, together, we even got in trouble with my
parents. When Mitzi died, I was very sad. For a long time I played
with a stuffed toy dog, pretending it would die and then come back to
life, over and over again. Only little by little did I stop playing that
game.

My friendship with Mitzi was like the friendship that so many children have with their pets. Like so many parents, I'm sure my mother
and father thought it was "good for me" to have a companion such as
she. Well, it *was* good for me, but it was only many years after she died
that I began to understand just how good it was... and why.

No one can really predict exactly what changes will take place when
a pet joins the family group, but it's fairly certain that changes will
occur—some of them pleasant and some unpleasant. There are good
reasons for petless families—especially families with very young children—to begin with simpler and smaller animals such as fish, birds,
gerbils, hamsters, guinea pigs, and rabbits. For one thing, these animals
are likely to be easier on the parents because their care is less demanding. But it also may be useful to introduce children to animals that
are largely for watching rather than handling, so that they can begin
learning in a simple way about the capacities and limitations of animals,
about differences between various kinds of animals, and about the differences between animals and humans. They can learn about animals'
basic needs and they can practice sharing the responsibility for meeting

these needs. They can learn how carefully some animals have to be handled, and they can come to understand to what extent animals do have feelings. Even these small animals offer opportunities for talk about sex differences and about the basic facts of procreation. Being shorter-lived and less robust than the larger animals, they are almost certain to provide the chance to talk about sickness and death. When you think about it, that's a great deal of learning for a small child to do, and it may seem easier for children to learn some of these things through pets that evoke shallower rather than deeper levels of emotional attachment. It seems that the more physical interaction there is between child and pet, and the more directly responsive the pet is, the deeper that emotional attachment is likely to be.

Larger animals seem to bring larger problems. Schedules and responsibilities become more urgent, and the disciplinary problems surrounding them tend to become greater. Parental patience seems to get put to greater strain. Issues of ownership among brothers and sisters, as well as rivalries and jealousies over the pet's affections, are often more intense. Safety problems are greater—both for the child and for the pet—and the upset over a larger pet's death is almost certain to be greater as well.

When any of us comes to a new experience, we bring many feelings from the past and from the present. These feelings will significantly determine what we make of that experience. Even a very young child is likely to bring deep feelings to a relationship with a pet—feelings that may go way back into infancy. One little girl we know had, by the time she was a year old, a really important friend in "Lambie," a small soft stuffed lamb. She slept with it, loved it, and could make it do whatever she wanted. Lambie often acted as her comforter. That toy lamb was a real part of her feelings, and for quite some time, this little girl felt that Lambie was really a part of *her*.

Stuffed animal toys can help older children with their growing, too. "Feedme" was an important playmate for one three-year-old boy. This companion was a teddy bear whose mouth opened and closed on a hinge. On the bottom of the mouth there was a tube leading to a pouch that unzipped from the back. This boy slept with Feedme, talked to Feedme, and made Feedme talk back. He could spend hours giving that toy bear things to eat, taking them out, putting them back through the mouth, and taking them out of the pouch again. He seemed to need to play a lot about feelings of feeding and being fed, and about his ideas of where food went when it was eaten.

Both these children were forming deep and close associations with an animal "friend."

Young children have—and need—a rich fantasy life that they can call on while they begin to sort out the complex world of reality and their place within it. Our culture, like so many others, makes representations of animals play a very large part in our children's early years. With the Neighborhood of Make-Believe segments in *Mister Rogers' Neighborhood*, we are certainly part of this cultural tradition. Our pretend neighborhood, inhabited largely by animal puppets, is, we think, a safe place to "play" about the important and sometimes scary feelings that accompany growing—a pretend place to practice real feelings. Our mail tells us, not surprisingly, that many viewing children identify very closely with one or more of these animal characters.

Most of us can think of many animal "neighborhoods" in nursery rhymes, fairy tales, puppet shows, newspaper cartoons, comic books, books, films, and other television programs. These animals are almost always given human characteristics—speech, humor, a limited range of human emotions, and even human clothes. They are shown as kind or wicked, brave or cowardly, sad, happy, mad, jealous, lonely. Sometimes animals are magically turned into people and people into animals. When a child looks at a live pet, it may seem quite reasonable to him or her to think that there is really a little *person* inside that bright-eyed, alert, responsive, and affectionate animal companion.

Just recently, the five-year-old daughter of a friend of mine asked her mother quite seriously whether Barney, their dog, was her older brother!

So, it may be that when you bring home a pet, your child may be bringing a lot of already animal-related feelings to that pet. You may find the pet at a "tea party" with your child, or tucked up on a baby carriage ready to go out for a walk, or dressed up in a T-shirt, or being scolded in words that are your own, or being read to, or fed with a baby bottle.

Pets can help children in so many ways! One of the most important ways is helping them clarify the difference between fantasy and reality. A child may do a lot of pretending with a pet, but there is only just so far that any pet will cooperate in a pretend situation. Pets, when they wriggle out of an embrace, or pull off a piece of human clothing, or won't sit still for a lengthy conversation, or refuse some kind of inappropriate feeding, remind children in their own ways that they are real animals and only animals. When a child is working through angry feelings in a pretend situation or thoughtlessly causing pain, many pets are capable of setting limits very clearly.

A pet often serves as a trustworthy repository for a child's feelings of loneliness, sadness, or fear. When adults and friends don't seem to have time to play, a child can usually count on a pet to be a partner in a game. When a child is sad, a pet can usually be counted on to "listen." When a child has been scolded and feels bad, a pet will still wag its tail nonjudgmentally and remind the child that he or she is still loved. A pet may help a child cope with simple fears such as a fear of the dark or a fear that there are monsters lurking under the bed. When something really scary happens, like a thunderstorm, pets and children (like my dog and I) may find comfort in comforting each other.

Parents need to be closely involved in the relationship between children and their pets—more closely, perhaps, than many parents foresee when they decide to introduce a pet into the family. A major reason for this involvement is to ensure the health and safety of both pet and child. Young children cannot be expected to know what they need to know about beaks and claws and teeth, nor can they be expected to learn all that overnight. They, too, are learning such things as where it's safe to play and where it's not; so, naturally, they are not yet able to make those decisions for their pets all by themselves.

Nor can young children be expected to take full responsibility for the feeding and cleaning needs of their pets—any more than they can take full responsibility for those things for themselves. But as we parents encourage and teach our children to *share* in the responsibility of taking care of their pets, we can, at the same time, be helping them learn how to take good care of themselves and understand a little more why we do the things we do out of concern for their own well-being. Pets need to eat regularly and to eat only what's good for them, so we control when and what they eat. We try to keep them safe, and so we restrain them from running loose in dangerous places. We may get angry and scold them for tracking across the kitchen floor with dirty feet or for jumping on the furniture. Cats and kittens learn to use their litter boxes, and we train puppies to use newspaper until they learn to ask to go outdoors. When pets play with things that are not toys and could get damaged, we stop them.

When we chastise our children's pets, it's not at all unusual to find our children acting as their comforters. You may even have heard your child explaining patiently, in *your* own words, the reason for a punishment: "You've got to learn not to run out into the street 'cause you could get really hurt and we'd be so sad if something happened to you!" Hearing that might come as the first indication that your child actually understands what you've been saying over and over again—and that your child is beginning to put together the relationship between discipline and care.

When pets have accidents, get ill, grow old, or die, we can use these difficult times to help our children discover some very important things, one of them being that a great many sad things happen in life that they are not able to prevent and which they didn't cause. The death of a pet, particularly, gives us the chance to help our children confront one of the most difficult facts of life—that all living things do die. It's a fact that remains hard for many of us to face, all of our lives. Children need a lot of help understanding death, and, like all of us, need time to grieve. When a pet dies, the understanding of what death means will come only little by little—as will a child's readiness to accept a replacement.

EVERYDAY FAMILY LIFE

My children grew up with a succession of pets, both small and large. Perhaps it was in watching them do so that I began to realize what Mitzi had meant to me. My younger son, John, had a dog called Frisky who would sleep on his bed. At night my wife and I could sometimes hear John telling Frisky about his troubles. It was only last year that Frisky died after a very full and long life, and that sad occasion made me think back once again on all the growing up Mitzi and I had shared.

No doubt, in time, John will have another dog. Perhaps that next one will someday help *his* children grow.

Discipline

As I talk with parents and colleagues, and as I look back over my own years of parenthood, I realize that more time than most people think goes into the "disciplining" of children. I have also become aware of how uncertain and uneasy most of us are when, in everyday family life, we have to confront what we think of as "the discipline problem." Perplexed parents so often ask, "How can I stop my child...?" or "How can I get my child to...?" or "Is it wrong to spank my child when...?"

Well, first of all, one thing I've learned for sure is that discipline and punishment are different. We may believe that discipline is what happens when rules are broken. But while discipline and rules and punishment certainly have something to do with one another, they are far from being the same.

I now think of discipline as the continual everyday process of helping a child learn *self*-discipline. No child is born with self-discipline, any more than he or she is born independent and self-sustaining. We feed our children, and as we do so, we help them feed themselves. We keep them clean and warm, and we try to keep them healthy, until they learn to do those things for themselves, too. And in the same way, we provide our children with the discipline they need until they learn to exercise it for themselves.

Disciplining a child—that is, giving them *our* discipline while they need it—is a loving gift and can be one of the great satisfactions of parenting. Time and again, for instance, we may have to stop our child snacking just before mealtime because it "will spoil your appetite." Then one day we may see our child take the top off the cookie jar, pause, ask "How long till dinner?" and then put the top back on. Disciplining includes comfort, care, and nurture. It includes passing on the traditions and values of our unique families and cultures. It includes praise for achievement, and it most certainly includes *examples*, from which young children learn so much. ("Character is caught, not taught.") That chores have to be done before play; that patient persistence is often the only road to mastery; that anger can be expressed through words and non-destructive activities; that promises are intended to be kept; that cleanliness and good eating habits are aspects of self-esteem; that compassion is an attribute to be prized—all these lessons are ones children can learn far more readily through the living example of their parents than they ever can through formal instruction.

Discipline is a teaching-learning kind of relationship, as the similarity to the word "disciple" suggests. By helping our children learn to be self-disciplined, we are also helping them learn how to become independent of us. We are also helping them learn, in their turn, how to be loving parents to children of their own.

Discipline depends less on distance and authority than it does on intimacy and trust.

Disciplining a child includes making rules. Personally, I prefer to think of this parenting task as "setting limits." We all need to observe limits, all life long. Many of the limits we now choose to set on our own behavior were gifts from our parents. We may have tested those limits, as most healthy children do, but the ones we found valuable became part of our growing self-discipline.

Children, when they're young, need a lot of limits. Many are for their health and safety, such as what can be touched and what cannot, what is good to eat and what is not, .where it's safe to play and where it's not. Other limits are set to help children move comfortably among other people—what they can say to whom, what they can do and where. Happy and healthy family life depends on limits, some that keep family life moving on schedule, others that serve to protect privacy and property.

In our family, for instance, my wife and I always made a practice of knocking on our boys' bedroom doors before entering. I can remember what a pleasure it was when J, our elder son, first knocked on *our* door. We had never *said* that knocking was a rule. J just started knocking because that was what had happened to him. One little girl I know started to put her toys away once she learned, with surprise, that the rule wasn't only for her mother's convenience: Her mother explained one day that the rule was there out of concern for *her*—so that people wouldn't fall over the toys and hurt either themselves or her *toys*.

Children feel safer when they know what the rules are—when they've been told by people they love what to do, especially in new or exciting situations. While children do need the permission to feel their feelings, they often need limits on the expression of them. It can be very frightening for a child *not* to have limits. Not only can the world outside be frightening, but the world inside, the world of feelings, can also be scary when you're not sure you can manage those feelings by yourself.

Call them rules or call them limits, good ones, I believe, have this in common: They serve reasonable purposes; they are practical and within a child's capability; they are consistent; and they are an expression of loving concern.

But what do we do when the limits are ignored, the rules broken? Even though punishment is often less effective than the continual showing of appreciation of limits that *are* observed, there come times for all parents when nothing but punishment seems called for. But what kind? And how much is enough?

Once again, there are no recipes for punishment, just as there are no recipes for child raising in general: The appropriateness of a punishment depends on the unique personality and experiences of each individual parent and each child, and, above all, on the unique quality of the relationship between them. Often, the way we choose to punish our children reflects the way we were punished by our parents. Character-istics of parenting do tend to carry over from generation to generation. Punishment, too, has a lot to do with cultural traditions and values— as does the decision of what kinds of actions require punishment.

There is a real difference, though, between what we might call "power" punishment and "loving" punishment. Power punishment, I think, tends to be a reaction to something that is seen as a personal challenge or a response to something that threatens a parent's sense of security. Power punishments might be accompanied by angry state-ments like "You broke *my* rule and this will show you who's in charge here!" or "Don't you dare talk to me like that. This will teach you!" Power punishments are more likely to include physical punishments such as spankings.

Loving punishments, on the other hand, tend to be firm reminders to the child that there are some limits that, for health, safety, or practical reasons, *have* to be observed. These punishments have a different sound: "You know you're not supposed to leave the yard because you might get hurt in the street. You'll have to stay indoors now, where I can keep an eye on you." Or, "I can understand that you're angry, but no one wants to hear all that noise. You can go to your room until you find a quieter way to be mad." Loving punishments are more likely to include restrictions on activity, the curtailing of pleasures, and the revoking of privileges.

It's a rare parent who hasn't lost his or her temper and reacted, verbally or physically, with a power punishment. No one, even adults, can observe his or her limits all the time. Young children can learn a lot from us when, after the heat of the moment has passed, we can apologize for something we did that was inappropriate. It's good dis-cipline (for us as well as for our children) to be able to say, "I'm sorry I got angry, and I shouldn't have slapped you. I was really scared you were going to get hurt. But you do have to learn not to touch sharp knives, because they can cut you." Having said that, you may then find a loving punishment that will help your child observe the necessary limits that you have set.

What kinds of punishments make for the most healthy kinds of discipline? I think there are some common characteristics regardless of what the specific punishment is. A constructive punishment:

- should follow closely on the heels of the offense. Depriving a child of a privilege or a pleasure that will come three days after the incident took place is confusing for a child and may well trigger another incident when the time for the punishment comes.

- should be within the scope of a child's understanding. If you send your child to his or her room, it should be for a period of time—like ten minutes—that your child can comprehend. Young children's understanding of cause and effect is still limited; during a long stretch of time in their rooms they may forget what both the punishment and the incident were all about.

- should keep a firm distinction between the behavior and the person. It's easy to say, "You're a bad boy," but that's exactly what a child may understand—that *he's* bad, rather than his particular behavior. On *Mister Rogers' Neighborhood*, I sing a song called "Good People Sometimes Do Bad Things," (see page 278) and it's true. Children need the most help in learning to feel good about themselves. Giving them that help is an essential part of being able to give them the self-discipline they need for checking the "bad" things they, like all children, may feel like doing.

Love, I feel quite certain, is at the root of all healthy discipline. The desire to be loved is a powerful motivation for children to behave in ways that give their parents pleasure rather than displeasure. It may even be our own long-ago fear of losing our parents' love that now sometimes makes us uneasy about setting and maintaining limits. We're afraid we'll lose the love of our children when we don't let them have their way.

So we parents need to try to find the security within ourselves to accept the fact that we and our children won't always like one another's actions, that there will be times when we and our children won't be able to be "friends," and that there will be times of real anger within the family. But we need to know just the same that we love our children and they love us. It is our continuing love for our children that makes us want them to become all they can be, and their continuing love for us that helps them accept healthy discipline—from us and eventually from themselves. When I recently asked one of our colleagues, "What is discipline?" she replied: "Discipline is the gift of *responsible* love." I think it's hard to improve on that description.

*   *   *

At the end of the last chapter, we began the story, "The Day No Child Could Play." Here is how it ends—with some thoughts about both rule breakers and rule makers.

The Day No Child Could Play
Part 2

No one except the King was happy with the new rule. Everyplace that Lady Aberlin went with her signs, people felt sad and angry. Angriest of all was Lady Elaine Fairchilde, who refused to have one of the signs—NO PLAY ALLOWED—on her Museum-Go-Round.

"You can take Friday's old signs and put them in the streets," she told Lady Aberlin. "That's where people shouldn't be allowed to play!"

"I have to put them everywhere," Lady Aberlin explained with a sigh. "Uncle Friday said so."

"Well, I won't have one of those signs on *my* place. I do what I want here. What's more, I'm going to talk to Friday about this nonsense myself," said Lady Elaine, and off she went to the castle.

"Get out here, Friday," she called when she got there. "I need to speak to you!"

"What's going on?" asked the King, coming out onto the balcony.

"I don't like your new rule, that's what!" said Lady Elaine.

"It's for everyone's safety," said the King.

"You can't just cut out play," Lady Elaine protested. "Practically everything in my Museum-Go-Round is play, and I'm not going to cut it out."

"There will be *no play allowed in this neighborhood*," insisted the King.

"You're sure about that?" asked Lady Elaine one last time.

"Absolutely sure," said the King.

"Well, then," said Lady Elaine, "I'm leaving."

"What do you mean, Fairchilde?" asked the King.

"I mean I can't live where there's no play," said Lady Elaine.

"Do you mean you're just going to take off?" asked the King.

"That's it," said Lady Elaine. "I'm leaving, Museum-Go-Round and all. If you ever have play here again, I'll be back. Toot toot, Toots," said Lady Elaine, and she was gone from the castle even before the King had a chance to tell her she was allowed or not allowed to go.

Back at the Museum-Go-Round, Lady Elaine told Lady Aberlin what had happened at the castle.

"But where will you go?" asked Lady Aberlin.

"I'm not sure, but I'm *going*," said Lady Elaine.

"But you can't just pick up and leave in two minutes like that!" exclaimed Lady Aberlin.

"That's what you think," said Lady Elaine. "Just you watch." She ducked into the Museum-Go-Round for a moment and came back with her hat and coat and her magic boomerang. "I don't stay in a neighborhood where there is no play. Here's a sign for Friday when you see him. Boomerang, toomerang, soomerang," she said, and with that she and her Museum-Go-Round vanished.

Lady Aberlin looked at the sign Lady Elaine had given her for the King. No Play—No Stay! is what it said. She shook her head. "Lady Elaine said she was going," Lady Aberlin thought, "and sure enough, she's gone. We're certainly going to miss her around here. There's nobody who speaks to the King the way she does!"

*   *   *

Bob Dog got better quickly after his fall. His leg was bruised and scraped, but it wasn't broken. He didn't have to stay in the hospital, but Dr. Bill did tell him that he'd better not walk or run too far on his leg for several days.

But even after Bob Dog was all better, King Friday still refused to change his rule about no play in the neighborhood. Bob Dog himself asked the King to change his mind. He told the King that his leg felt fine, and showed him he could even dance on it. All the King said was, "Stop that, Bob Dog. Stop that right now. Dancing is play!"

One thing that bothered the King, though, was not knowing where Lady Elaine Fairchilde had gone. He sent for Officer Clemmons and told him to search everywhere, and everywhere else, too, until he found her. "And when you do find her, then come straight back here and give me the news." Officer Clemmons set off on his search.

So time went by and nobody in the neighborhood played, and everybody in the neighborhood felt sad that Lady Elaine and her Museum-Go-Round weren't there anymore.

One day, Lady Aberlin and Bob Dog were walking through the neighborhood when they heard strange sounds coming from the place where Lady Elaine's Museum-Go-Round used to be. Going over to investigate, they found Anna Platypus, Prince Tuesday, and Daniel Striped Tiger laughing and running and jumping, and playing peekaboo and hide-and-seek. In fact, they had turned the Museum-Go-Round's old place into a playground!

"Children!" exclaimed Lady Aberlin. "What would the King say if he ever found out?"

"I'm afraid he'd be mad," said Prince Tuesday. "Lots of Daddy's rules are okay, but this one isn't good for anybody."

"Prince Tuesday's right," added Anna. "I nearly got sick from not playing for two whole days. We just *have* to play, Lady Aberlin."

Daniel agreed. "Do you want to play with us for a while, Lady Aberlin and Bob Dog?"

"I feel like singing," said Bob Dog.

"And I feel like dancing," said Lady Aberlin. So, singing and dancing, they joined the children in their play. One of the games they played was like ring-around-the-rosy; they all held hands and skipped around in a circle pretending to be the Museum-Go-Round. Anna pretended to be Lady Elaine.

What they didn't know was that King Friday was out making a tour of the neighborhood. He wanted to be sure nobody was breaking his no-play rule. When he heard the singing and saw the dancing and playing that was going on where the Museum-Go-Round had once been, he was angry.

"Lady and gentleman *players*, I presume?" he said in a loud and angry voice.

"Correct as usual, King Friday," everyone said in little small voices.

Then Prince Tuesday spoke up in a voice louder than the rest: "I'll handle this, everyone," he said.

"And what do you have to say for yourself, Son?" asked the King.

"What I have to say isn't just for myself, Daddy," said the Prince, "it's for all of us."

"And what might that be?" asked the King.

"Well," said the Prince, "most of your rules are very good rules, and we know you make them to help us. But this rule about not allowing anyone to play is not a good rule. We all *need* to play. Everyone needs to play, Daddy, we really do! And if you won't change your rule, we're going to have to find some way to play no matter what."

"Why, Prince Tuesday, how dare you?" said the King.

"I dare, Daddy, because I know that we're right," said the Prince.

The King was silent for a moment. Then he asked: "Do you all agree with the Prince?"

Everyone said that they did.

"I see," said the King. "I shall have to consider this carefully and decide what to do about breakers of rules. Farewell."

Scowling, the King left to go back to the castle.

"That was mighty brave of you, Cousin Tuesday," Lady Aberlin said when the King had gone.

"Do you suppose Daddy's very mad?" asked the Prince.

EVERYDAY FAMILY LIFE   157

"Owwwowww," said Bob Dog. "*I* think he's mad!"

"I guess he'll be mad for a while," said Lady Aberlin, "but I think maybe he's proud of you, too, Cousin Tuesday. I think we *all* are," she added. Everyone agreed, and they all sang the neighborhood proud song:

We're proud of you,
We're proud of you.
We hope that you are proud as we are
Proud of you. We're proud of you.
We hope that you are proud of you, too.

When King Friday arrived back at the castle, he found Officer Clemmons waiting for him.

"Aha!" said the King. "You've found that runaway Fairchilde?"

"I have Your Majesty," Officer Clemmons replied.

"Well," said the King, "at least *something* is going right today in this neighborhood. Where is she?"

"She has set up her Museum-Go-Round in a playground over beyond Some Place Else. She said to tell you she's having the time of her life, playing all day."

"I see," said the King. "And did you tell her to return at once?"

"Not exactly, Sire. I said everyone here missed her and wished she'd come back."

"And what did she say to that?"

"Well, Your Majesty...ummmm...."

"Her exact words, Clemmons, if you please," ordered the King.

Officer Clemmons cleared his throat. "'No way, Toots! Not until Friday comes to his senses about this play business!' That's what she said, Your Majesty."

"I see I have something more to think about," said the King. "Very well, Officer, you may go and tell the neighbors in the neighborhood that I shall give them a report tomorrow. Meanwhile, I shall go into the P room and ponder."

*   *   *

The following day, King Friday ordered everyone in the neighborhood to come to the castle for an important announcement. When he was sure everybody was there, he walked out onto the balcony. Usually, at times like this, the Court Musicians would play a fanfare on their trumpets, but this time there was silence.

The King turned to the Leader of the Court Musicians in surprise. "Well?" he asked. "And where is the fanfare announcing my announcement?"

"Fanfares are forbidden now, Your Majesty," said the Leader of the Court Musicians.

"And who had the nerve to forbid my fanfares?" asked the King. "*I'm* the King of this neighborhood."

"Why, you did, Sire," replied the Leader of the Court Musicians. "We have to *play* our trumpets to make a fanfare, and you have forbidden all play."

"*Play* your trumpets.... Of course. I never thought of that," said the King. "That's terrible. Oh, that rule! It's getting in everybody's way! Very well, then, here is my announcement: I, King Friday XIII of the Neighborhood of Make-Believe, do hereby announce that there will be play again in this neighborhood. My son was right. You all were right. Everyone needs play. But I also announce that whatever you decide to play, play *carefully*."

With that, the Court Musicians played the longest and loudest and brightest fanfare anyone could remember, and all the neighbors clapped and cheered the wisdom of their King.

"But what about Auntie Lady Elaine?" asked Anna Platypus when all the noise had settled down. "Will she ever come back?"

"Ah, yes," said the King. "We must tell Fairchilde she may return.

Miss Paulifficate," he said, turning to the castle telephone operator, "I should like to talk to Lady Elaine Fairchilde. I believe Officer Clemmons may be able to give you her number."

In a moment, Lady Elaine was on the line. "Hello, Friday," she said, "what's going on in that dull neighborhood of yours? Nothing much, I'll bet!"

"Fairchilde," said the King, "I am calling to tell you that I and Queen Sara and all your other friends in this neighborhood are asking you please to return..."

"In that case, Friday," interrupted Lady Elaine, "let's talk turkey."

"Fairchilde!" said the King. "I am *not* a turkey!"

"Never said you were, Friday," said Lady Elaine. "I said let's *talk* turkey. That means let's talk truth."

"Very well," said the King, "the truth is that I have learned that everyone needs to play, and I have just ordered that play may begin again in this neighborhood. Careful play, that is."

"You're sure about that, Friday? I mean, you're not just giving me a snow job?" asked Lady Elaine at her end of the telephone. "I'm having a pretty good time right here where I am!"

"It's the truth, Fairchilde," said the King, and he held the telephone away from his ear so that Lady Elaine could hear all the neighbors shouting, "It's true, Lady Elaine, please come back. We miss you!"

"Oh, sweet music to my ears," said Lady Elaine, and then King Friday could hear her saying, "Boomerang, toomerang, soomerang!"

No sooner had she said the magic words and waved her magic boomerang than she and the Museum-Go-Round were right back in the Neighborhood of Make-Believe where they belonged.

The King ordered another fanfare to celebrate her return and then said, "It gives me great pleasure to welcome back the Museum-Go-Round and its curator, Lady Elaine Fairchilde, who knows so well how to talk eagle...."

"It's *turkey*, Friday," corrected Lady Elaine.

"Oh, yes," said the King. "Turkey. Let's always talk turkey, Fairchilde."

"You bet, Toots," said Lady Elaine, and as the neighbors crowded around the Museum-Go-Round to welcome her back, she added:

"And let's always be able to play!"

CHAPTER 7:

TELEVISION

When I first started sketching out this book, I planned to talk about television as one of the things under the heading of Everyday Family Life. But the more I thought about it, the more it seemed to need a whole chapter to itself. Part of the reason, I'm sure, is that television has been a large part of my life's work, but another part is that television plays such an enormous role in our children's growing up and in shaping many adults' value systems. Of course, it's adults, first and foremost, who shape children's values.

It's now more than twenty-five years that I've been working in television, and although I've experienced a lot of disappointments and disillusionments with television in that time, I've never lost my belief in its great potential for good. Fortunately, I find it confirmed again and again when I see the many excellent programs on both public and commercial stations, programs that help us all better understand our environment and our place within it, or that enable us all to share the cultural heritage of the arts—music, dance, drama, painting, sculpture—things that once were available only to the privileged few. There is encouragement toward creative self-expression on television, just as there are examples of individual strivings toward excellence.

But there is an awful lot of other stuff, too, much of which is at best a waste of time and at worst can be downright destructive. In fact, television programmers' casual and often cynical attitude toward childhood played a large part in my decision to work in television and has much to do with my intention to keep on trying to provide alternatives.

My first job in television was working at NBC in New York City on *The Voice of Firestone* and *The NBC Opera Theatre* and *The Kate Smith Hour*. I had just graduated from Rollins College, having majored in music composition, and working with creative people in music through television was exciting because television then was a very new, challenging instrument. In 1954 I left New York to return to my home state of Pennsylvania to help launch this country's first community television station—WQED in Pittsburgh. My assignment was to produce a local children's program called *The Children's Corner*, hosted by a very creative Pittsburgher named Josie Carey. Our budget was thirty dollars per program, and we were on the air, live, telling stories and improvising with puppets and music for an hour each day. Daniel Striped Tiger and King Friday XIII were already part of our cast. Henrietta Pussycat was there, too, but in those days she was a teacher—of seventeen nice mice. In a cluttered attic set, Josie would sit and chat with Lydia Lamp, Lawrence Light, Phil and Rhoda Dendron, Gramma Phone, and other whimsical characters. In addition to producing the programs, my job included manipulating and voicing the puppets, composing the music, playing the organ, and occasionally appearing on camera as a mysterious prince, complete with mask and cape, who joined Josie for a dance.

It was about at that time, too, that I started attending seminary during my lunch hours. (It took me eight years to graduate!) One of my courses was in pastoral counseling and I was required to work closely with one person under professional psychological supervision. I asked if I could work with a child. The professor told me I could, on the condition that I would be supervised by Dr. Margaret McFarland, who was then the director of the Arsenal Family and Children's Center of the University of Pittsburgh. And so I was introduced to someone who knows as much as (or more than) anyone in this world about families with young children. For the past twenty years I've continued to consult Dr. McFarland at least twice a month. She and I go over scripts, words to songs, and concepts for future program themes. Most of the time we talk about children, children we have each known and worked with, children who have helped us understand childhood. Margaret Mc-Farland is one of those people who demonstrate that wisdom is closely associated with compassion. She is truly a caring person. That's one major reason that this book is dedicated to her.

In 1962, when I graduated from Pittsburgh Theological Seminary, I joined the Canadian Broadcasting Corporation in Toronto, where Dr. Frederick B. Rainsberry (head of CBC children's programs) told me, "Fred, I've seen you talk with children. I want you to translate that to television." I doubt if I would ever have "faced" a camera if it hadn't been for his encouragement. (I had stayed "behind the set" my first eight years of "being on television.") So I looked at the camera, remembered Mr. Hayes telling me about "one little buckaroo" (page 9), and I've been communicating directly to families with growing children ever since.

(It was also Fred Rainsberry's idea that the program should be called *Misterogers*. When I returned to Pittsburgh, we called the program *Misterogers' Neighborhood* and then later changed it to the present form, *Mister Rogers' Neighborhood*, out of a concern for viewers who were learning to read.)

I knew that I wanted to use television the way I had used the piano and puppet play as a child: to communicate some things that I felt were important in our world. Since one can't be a communicator with equal impact on all segments of society, I guess I made an early decision somewhere inside of me to communicate with children—a decision I haven't regretted. With the help and counsel and support of many people, I've tried to help children feel good about being children and hopeful about who they can become. And I've tried to show them the wide range of artistry and feeling that make up a varied culture like ours. I've wanted to help children learn to discover worth in little things, in things that had no price tag, in people who might have outer handicaps and great inner strengths. We've wanted every child to know that he or she was unique, valuable, and lovable, that everyone has limits as well as possibilities. We've wanted to engender feelings of responsibility toward the care of oneself as well as others.

My associates and I have been more fortunate than most people in the world of television programming because we have had the luxury of time—time to grow in our work, and time for our work to grow into what it has become. But was time to develop really a "luxury"? I think it's been a *necessity*. It seems that all living things need time if they are to grow in a healthy way. They need to pass through certain stages before they can move on to the next stages of their growth. This is certainly true for human beings, and I think it may be true for any work that human beings do together—from running a government to producing a television program. Something else that humans need for healthy individual growth and worthwhile joint enterprise is caring relationships. We have been greatly fortunate in being surrounded by these, too.

If we were setting out today to do what we started more than twenty-five years ago, I wonder if we'd find a place on a national broadcast network. *Mister Rogers' Neighborhood* has a slow pace compared to most other programs, and I think we would have a very difficult time justifying that pace and explaining the series' content to many network executives. Even a passionate plea that a little bit of television time be devoted to young children's emotional growth would most likely work against us: A West Coast writer-producer told me you must never show that you care about an idea you're presenting because if you do, management decision makers will be afraid you'll expend too much effort on content and not enough on demographics and ratings. Consequently, they'll turn you down.

There has been some improvement in children's programming over the past decade, but most of the improvement has come about through outside pressures rather than from the deep conviction of programmers themselves. Until change comes from within the industry, television will continue to have a negative effect on children, family life, and human relationships in general. Often, the kindest thing one can say about a television program these days is that it is a waste of time. Much of television, though, is degrading, reducing important human feelings to the status of caricature or trivia. Some of it, in my opinion, even encourages pathology. Yet here it is, for hours a day, part of the intimacy of family life, an influence on family values, a growing part of family tradition, and an accessory of family education. We parents need to think hard about how television is affecting our children and, in turn, our grandchildren to come. We need to think harder still about what to do about it.

Television and the "Inner Drama"

I've wondered for a long time what it is that makes television so fascinating. That fascination may begin very early in our lives, and it may have to do with the first very important relationship we make in this world—our relationship with the person who feeds us and cares for us and loves us.

Have you noticed how intently a baby looks at its mother's face when nursing or being fed? It's as though the baby were learning to "read" that face, to puzzle out the meanings of frowns and smiles, to interpret the sights and sounds of love, and all in a context that brings warmth, nurture, the relief of discomfort, and the sense of satisfaction and pleasurable fullness. I wonder if the young child's attachment to that first face is somehow transferred to close-ups of other faces on the television screen. In other words, could the television screen be analogous to the mother's face in infancy?

We have had many, many people tell us of a pattern their children followed when watching *Mister Rogers' Neighborhood*. The younger they were, the more likely they were to be interested in the parts of the program where I was on the screen—often in close-up. In fact, if they were very young, their attention would wander during the parts when I *wasn't* seen. As they grew to be four or five, they watched the whole program and came to understand how the parts related to one another. As they grew older still and were beginning to take a greater interest in their play and in the outside world, their major attention shifted to the adventures of the characters in the Neighborhood of Make-Believe, the section of the program where I stay behind the set voicing the puppets.

We have heard, too, that many two-year-olds are fascinated with Julia Child. As soon as her program, *The French Chef*, came on, children all over the country would run to the kitchen, pull out some pots and pans, and then sit for thirty minutes, watching intently all that Julia was doing. Why? The program was full of unfamiliar words and French phrases and certainly lacked the suspense of a strong story line. Do you suppose that it was because here was another close-up face talking warmly and conversationally, in direct eye-to-eye contact? A person deeply involved in an activity that was already associated with both nurture and mother? It could be so. And if this conjecture—that television viewing is somehow analogous to viewing the mother's face in infancy—is by any means valid, then television viewing could be considered as having its roots at the very core of human development.

(I can even see this association continuing later, as older children curl up in a corner of the couch and watch television while sucking their fingers or eating and drinking.)

There's obviously a lot of difference between nourishment from human mothers and nourishment from a television set, but one of the biggest differences is that a loving human caregiver can respond to how the baby or young child is feeling. That caretaker can try to *understand* when a child is upset, can provide reassurance and comfort from the outside while helping a child learn to find his or her own reassurance and comfort from within. And a television set? It certainly provides stimulations, but when those stimulations touch a child's inner feelings,

MISTER ROGERS TALKS WITH PARENTS

television just goes on stimulating, often in a way that is far beyond the young child's ability to manage.

We all carry "inner dramas" within us, all our lives. We bring them to everything we see and do. For instance, if we've been bitten by a dog when we were very young, we may have anxious feelings—at some level of our being—whenever we see a dog. Most of us, though, as we grow older, find our own ways of coping with stressful feelings like that. In fact, one of the important tasks in growing up is to develop these ways to cope.

If you've watched *Mister Rogers' Neighborhood*, you probably know that our programs do not try to avoid anxiety-arousing situations. We have dealt with the beginnings of life, as well as with its end, and with many of the feelings in between. We do try, though, to keep anxiety within a child's manageable limits and then *to deal with it*. We talk about those feelings and, in simple ways, try to show models for coping with them as well as models of trustworthy, caring, and available adults.

Television programs can so easily play into children's "inner dramas" and spark very anxious feelings. Unaware of what they have done, programmers take no steps to resolve the anxieties they have aroused. The song I wrote assuring children they could never go down a drain (page 53) was an attempt to be responsive to a widely shared "inner drama" of early childhood. It was certainly a quite different approach from that of a cartoon I remember seeing on a children's television program one time in which a deep sea diver went down to the bottom of the sea and pulled out a great big plug. Down the drain went all the water from the sea, all the fish, all the boats, and all the people, even the houses from the shore—all were sucked down the hole. Sure, the notion might have been "funny"—to adults, maybe—but it certainly showed little understanding of what many children might be bringing to that small piece of animation. Now, I'm sure no one set out to make that cartoon frightening, but I know children who talked about it fearfully for months. It just goes to show how careful we have to be and how much we all have to learn.

I remember one instance when we dealt with fire in the Neighborhood of Make-Believe. There was a fire in Corney's factory. It was a tiny fire, and no one was hurt. Even so, I knew it could be anxiety producing, and my child-development consultants had cautioned me that young children's concerns about fire often have to do with concerns about the direction and control of body fluids. So, a whole week before introducing the control of fire, we dealt with damming up streams, pouring water from one container into another, putting just enough water into an aquarium, and many other methods of showing how people can control fluids. For some children, that wasn't enough. One man from Boston called and said, "My child just won't watch your program anymore because of that fire episode." As we talked, I discovered that his little daughter had terrible urinary difficulties and was going through all kinds of painful procedures. Here again my consultants were helpful in explaining that the burning sensation that sometimes occurs in urination can easily be transferred to the burning from fire. The longer that Boston father and I talked, the more we both understood the anxiety of an "inner drama" that was very important to his little girl right then.

I remember, too, another father telling me that his daughter had cried and become very upset after an episode of *Little House on the Prairie*. In the story of that particular episode there was a threat that a man would have to give up his land and go somewhere else. The little girl who was upset as she watched that program had just learned that her family was going to have to move to another city, and when she saw others in a similar plight, even though it was "just on TV," she cried.

I've heard it said that for many teachers the worst day of the year is the day after *The Wizard of Oz* appears on television. Why would that be? It might be that all the negative things about all the important women figures in children's lives suddenly become concentrated in the form of the Wicked Witch of the West. It could be overwhelming for children to have so many negative feelings bound up in one character—and they might break loose through the negative feelings children have about their teachers. (If you're a good teacher, you're bound to evoke *some* negative feelings!) A person who helped us with this particular "inner drama" was that grand actress, Margaret Hamilton. When she made a guest appearance on *Mister Rogers' Neighborhood* she brought her *Wizard of Oz* witch costume with her and, as she dressed up on camera, made it very clear that no witches—not even the Wicked Witch of the West—were real.

The problem of aggression on television is really serious. I think the urge to bite is something virtually all children, at one time or another, have to deal with. As you watch programs for children, you might find it interesting to watch for scary mouths and scary teeth, for things that are mouthlike, and for the many incidents where things and animals and people are bitten or gobbled up. Biting and eating things up are made out to be funny and acceptable. But are they acceptable in *your* family? Watching television models of this form of aggression can be frightening for a child who, wanting to be loved, is trying so hard to control this urge to bite. (Incidentally, electronic games use many of these "biting" themes, too!)

If you want to know more about your own inner dramas when you're watching television, think about why some programs move you and others don't. Or think about why you and your friends may have such different reactions to the very same program. A producer-director who came to work with us several years ago told me that he had watched *The Adams Chronicles* every week and that when John Adams died, he just sat there and wept. Obviously there were things about John Adams's life that touched him very deeply. Who knows whether my friend cried because he had just moved from Washington to Pittsburgh and had to be separated from his wife and little boy for five days out of the week? Or whether he was feeling powerful memories of the death of his own father? Or any number of other things. In another family I know, where the father is British and the mother French, both parents were appalled when their two children became totally delighted with and absorbed in the series *Hogan's Heroes*. For the parents, both of whom had relatives in prisoner-of-war camps during the Second World War, the series was offensive and upsetting in its broad slapstick portrayal of both the prisoners and Nazi guards. Their children, having no such inner dramas of their own, reveled in the humor.

It seems obvious that a person struggling with cancer or alcohol addiction or loss of a spouse is going to have very strong reactions to a program that includes such themes. Often, though, our inner dramas are less clearly definable, unknown to others and even, consciously, to ourselves. Because every member of a family is unique, he or she will have unique inner dramas, and sometimes we may be truly surprised at another family member's reaction to a television program. What one family member may find "a dumb old program" may have real and unsuspected meaning for another. Sometimes a family member may want—and need—to be alone with the television set for a while. One way television can be used constructively is to help different family members become sensitive to one another's inner dramas. A television program can offer an opportunity to talk about a lot of different feelings, and by talking about them we may be able to help one another make them more manageable.

I remember many people sitting for hours in front of their television screens, waiting for the moment when the Iranian hostages would step out of the airplane that was bringing them to freedom. And when they finally did appear many viewers began to cry. I think it was because there is something in us all that longs to be freed (freed from the constraints of a certain race or class or disability or pain), and when we saw those hostages (who somehow represented what we wanted freed), the tears that we cried were tears of personal understanding... of real empathy. At least, this is how I understood my own feelings and the feelings of a lot of people around me at that time.

The inner dramas of early childhood are perhaps the hardest for us adults to understand. They are subtle and deep; and, of course, young children do not have the concepts or words yet to talk very clearly about them. For our part, we are so far from them that most of us can't remember what they were. But they are there, a part of every child, and, somewhere, a part of us. That's why I feel that those of us who make television programs—for adults *or* for children—have a responsibility to do our work with the greatest of care. Those of us who are parents have an equally great responsibility for knowing what our children are watching and for helping them cope with the inner dramas those programs may arouse.

Television and Learning Readiness

There's been a lot of research over the years on how children learn from television, what they can learn, and how fast. There have been several programs that have addressed themselves not only to helping children learn letters and numbers, but also to helping them learn concepts. A few programs have even tried to help children better understand and express their feelings and to become more adept at managing relationships and coping with stressful situations.

Much research on the effects of television is contradictory or inconclusive, but the fact that it is doesn't make the research useless, wasteful, or futile. We do need to know as much as we can about how children learn, and conscientious research of any kind can help teach us, if nothing else, how to do *better* research.

As far as children and learning goes, I've come to believe a very simple statement: Children can learn almost anything both easily and well so long as they are *ready* to learn. That does sound simple. What's not simple about it, of course, is just what it means for a child to be "ready." And that's where my concern lies with television's role in the learning process. Does it help children become ready to learn (even from material presented on television) or does most television programming in fact sabotage the development of a child's readiness to learn?

When I think of what "readiness" means, there are six fundamentals that come immediately to my mind. They may not be everything a child needs to learn, but they certainly seem to me to be basic necessities. They are (1) a sense of self-worth, (2) a sense of trust, (3) curiosity, (4) the capacity to look and listen carefully, (5) the capacity to play, and (6) times of solitude. To what extent is television likely to help or hinder a child in acquiring these learning tools?

To me, the most important of the six is the one I listed first—*a sense of self-worth*. In order for children to have a strong sense of self-worth, part of what they need to feel is that each human being is unique (there never has been another person exactly like you and there never will be; you're it; you're the only *you* ever) and that uniqueness has value. But in the largest area of the television world, people are stereotyped: They come out of set molds, and what's more, it is *things*, not people, that seem to be presented as having the most value. Advertised products and material possessions that dramatic characters have, want, steal, or kill for—those are things that television often says have value. As for the people who are given value, they are usually beautiful or handsome, strong, aggressive, athletic, sexy, smart, and affluent. Then there are the people who aren't. Usually they're the "bad guys." (Yes, there are exceptions, and, I'm glad to say, more than there used to be.) In the world that I know and the one I think is helpful for children to see and understand, each person seems to have both strengths and weaknesses, abilities and limitations, times of courage and times of fear, blemishes, and a whole gamut of human emotions.

Feeling lovable and capable of loving is another part of what a child needs for self-esteem. I think television makes this very hard for young children because so many programs insist that doing something bad makes you a bad person. When children feel *they* are bad, they may become very fearful of losing the love of their loved adults—and even get to be doubtful of their capacity to love in return. That can have serious repercussions. Is it any wonder that reminding people of how lovable they can be, and often *are*, is one of our programs' goals?

Another part of healthy self-esteem is feeling that you're able to learn and knowing that learning is worthwhile. That's certainly a major part of "readiness to learn"! That feeling about being able to learn is something a child gets or doesn't get, through experiences at home, at day-care centers, or in school. But as for feeling that learning is worthwhile...well, television often speaks to that in very negative ways. Three years ago *Newsweek* reported that nine of the ten most-watched television programs in this country were situation comedies which shared the common theme that *being dumb was best and that being smart was square.* In one of these series, the heroine had a collection of moldy sandwiches. Heroes in other series staged Jell-O fights and stuffed putrid halibut into their college's ventilating system. In contrast to these models of behavior there were the "four-eyed fruits" who were interested in such things as books. These programs consistently made fun of achievement and dedication and hard work.

The good feeling of self-control is yet another facet of self-esteem. It feels really good when we can stop before doing something we shouldn't do or when we can direct our anger from destructive into constructive outcomes (see page 60). That's hard enough for adults to do, let alone for very young children to learn. I just don't believe that spending hours and hours looking in on a world where people are routinely losing their self-control (as though that were the way all people behave) is any help to children living in a real world.

I'm convinced that children learn best from real live caring adults—adults they have learned to *trust*. Trust is important for all of the strivings of young children, but nowhere is it more important than in helping a child learn to talk about feelings. We really have to trust someone to be able to talk about our feelings with that person. But on television not only are there a lot of untrustworthy adults, but a major message about feelings seems to be this: When you talk about your feelings, most people don't want to listen to you. Or if they do, then you can easily get into trouble and even provoke violence.

When trust is absent fear can take its place, and fear makes it very hard for anyone to learn. I've worked with children suffering great deprivations, who have been terribly frightened by the conditions they live in. They've seen people shot, they've seen their mothers raped, they've been told they mustn't go beyond the locked door because they might never come back in again. They've seen and heard so much that is scary that they just begin to tune out. And the conditions of their real lives are the repetitive story lines in the world of television which they end up watching much of the time. There is a lot on television to frighten *all* children, even those who live in "safe" places. I don't believe that any educational gimmicks can be very helpful in teaching children who are burdened with overwhelming anxieties. For them, learning readiness really means the reestablishment of trust.

Curiosity. We have talked before about the early development of curiosity (see page 67) and how, toward the end of the first year of life, healthy babies seem to become engaged in a "love affair with the world." This strong urge to explore, to try out, and to understand has grown out of the infant's first relationship—that with the beloved mother or other primary caregiver. We may not usually think of curiosity as having deep emotional roots, but it does. If it is nurtured and it flourishes, it is one of the most valuable tools a child can bring not only to the early learning process but also to all learning throughout life.

The best of television can be a very powerful and constructive stimulus to a young child's curiosity. Even before children are capable of actually learning from programs that show how the body works, or how animals behave, or how machines work, or how the different parts of the environment fit together, or what the stars and planets are about, or human accomplishments in athletics and the arts, children can begin to feel an excitement in discovery. They can gain a sense that they and their world are wondrous creations and see that people are indeed capable of creating and doing wonderful things.

Precisely because curiosity does have deep emotional roots, the worst of television may be very damaging to a child's urge to explore, try out, and understand. The reasons are those I've mentioned earlier: the effects that programming may have on a child's self-worth, ability to trust, and willingness to engage in a world that television has made to seem a very frightening place.

I think that a fear of the world has a lot to do, too, with some children's difficulty in *looking carefully and listening carefully*. I'm thinking of those children who grow up amidst deprivation and in surroundings where so much of what there is to look at and listen to is painful and scary. A human being can take only so much frightening stimulation, and then he or she is likely to shut off the desire to look or listen to *anything* carefully. If a child is confronted with murder, rape, and other kinds of destructive aggression in daily life, it doesn't surprise me if that child "turns off" looking and listening carefully. I even feel that this may be one of the most frequent causes of trouble for children who cannot learn to read. If you can't look carefully, you can't learn to read. Might terribly frightening programming on television add to the illiteracy of a nation? I wonder.

Certainly the quick pace and fragmentation of television cannot help children develop the capacity for careful looking and listening. There just isn't time amidst the constant changes in focus and subject matter. Perhaps you've noticed it yourself as you've watched television: By the time you start to reflect on something you've seen and heard, there's a new barrage. Whatever you were starting to think about must either wait or be forgotten.

Sustained attention to things tends to foster deliberate thought. What the hectic pace of television may foster, I'm not sure. I remember one parent telling me how irritated he used to get with his six-year-old son, who would regularly flick back and forth every few seconds between two programs he wanted to watch that were on at the same time. The father said that he himself actually winced with discomfort every time the channel changed, and he finally made a rule against channel switching like that. A few days later he found his son watching two programs simultaneously—one on the family's little portable set, which the boy had placed right beside the living room set. He told me his son seemed to be perfectly at ease looking and listening to both programs at once. I don't think my mind could do that without a lot of retraining. Perhaps that boy was learning to do something that he will find useful sometime in his life, but I wonder if he was helping himself to get ready for the long years of concentrated learning that lay ahead of him.

"Deliberate thought" isn't something we expect of young children. That capacity develops later. But readiness to develop that capacity does begin growing very early as children engage in their own kind of thinking—daydreaming, fantasizing, and making up all kinds of activities that we call *play* (see Chapter 5). Most healthy children *are* capable of times of very deliberate and sustained play—sometimes hours of it. They can become deeply engrossed in what they are doing. It can often be highly creative and imaginative. As they work with blocks and crayons and miniature figures and trucks, or maybe just a variety of odds and ends, they are putting together images of family relationships, of their feelings, and of the complex puzzle that is the world around them. A lot of work goes into a child's play—and a lot of thought, too. Imaginative play is an essential part of any child's growth.

There's excellent research that suggests that, quite apart from their content, most television programs are put together in ways that hamper both imagination and learning. Drs. Dorothy and Jerome Singer, psychologists and codirectors of the Family Television Research and Consultation Center at Yale University, wrote the following in an article for *The Chronicle of Higher Education* (April 23, 1979):

Is television changing human consciousness? Is it possible that the rapid pace of presentation, the quick shifts of focus, the speeded-up blend of visual, musical, and verbal material that characterize American TV may actually be impeding our capacities for sustained attention, deliberate thought, and private imagery? . . .

In recent years we have been studying how television viewing in pre-school children relates to their emerging capacity for imagination and playfulness. We are struck by the fact that much of the programming to which these children are exposed is characterized by the fast paced, rapid shifts of scene with numerous distortions of time and space sequences. . . . Our research evidence suggests that while children may indeed pay attention and keep their eyes glued to the television screen, the rapid pace and constant intrusion of new material seems to interfere with effective learning. . . .

If, at such an early age, we can already see the impact of television's format on children, think of the substantial influence the medium must be having on our attention and information-processing capacities in the 15,000 hours of accumulated viewing by the time of high school graduation. . . .

We need slower-moving programs, more sustained images, less frenetic activity. The trend toward electronic games and motorized, computerized, and robot-like toys suggests a danger that even more of our children's and our own capacities for imposing and practicing private imagery will be preempted [see page 120]. . . .

The human imagination is one of the great miracles of evolution. We dare not let it go down the tube.

Parents sometimes ask, "How much television is it okay for my child to watch?" There's no specific amount of time that is the right amount for all children. It depends on what the child is like, what television means to him or her, and what's on television. Each child is unique, lives in a unique family, and is surrounded by a unique combination of other stimulations. There are some children whose life experience is so restricted that television is enormously enhancing. These children would never have a chance to learn much about the world or about many kinds of creative human expression if it weren't for television. There are others who might be using television as a detachment from life, as encouragement to live in television's unreal world all the time. That could be very restrictive to their development. Figuring out how much television is appropriate for a child is a little like making sure that our children have balanced diets. The best of television programming can be a nourishing part of a diet that also includes time with parents, time with other children, time for active play, time for quiet play, and, of course, enough time for sleep. If television watching is taking over a child's waking hours, though, we can be sure that's too much television.

Finally, *solitude*. Solitude may seem like a grown-up concept to use for little children, but it's an important ingredient for helping children's readiness to learn.

When I think of solitude I think of an anecdote from *With the Door Open: My Experience* by the late Danish religious philosopher, Johannes Anker-Larsen:

> The most comprehensive formula for human culture which I know was given by the old peasant who, on his death bed, obtained from his son this one promise: to sit every day for half an hour ALONE in the best room. The son did this and became a model for the whole district. This father's command had taken thought for everything, for Eternity, soul-deepening, refinement, history.

I like to think about that story. Like many parables, the more you think about it the more meanings you can find—some, no doubt, that were never intended, and that's because of the unique inner dramas in each of us that they touch. For instance, the confident and trusting way the old peasant spoke to his son suggests to me that the peasant had to have trusted *himself* as well as his son. He had to have known that if his son would "sit every day for half an hour alone in the best room," his son would have had something of value to think about... and that some of the roots of those valuable thoughts would have come from the peasant father himself. The father seemed to be trusting the son to take from their tradition what was useful and then, in his own way, nourish others in his community.

You may feel quite different things from that story. There's no one who has the same inner story as you have, and you need times of solitude, times of being alone, to understand it.

Very young children can't tell us yet, "I need to be alone for a while," but it seems to be true for infants as well as adults. Tiny babies seem to need time just lying in the crib, staring at the ceiling, watching their own hands move, kicking, or cooing. In these quiet times, they seem to be getting used to who and what they are.

Toddlers, so busy on their explorations of where things are and how they come apart and go together, often find a quiet corner where they can sit and practice all the new things they are learning to do. As soon as they become comfortable with their new abilities, off they go again on new explorations.

For young children, comfortable solitude often means being near someone they love. It's only when they are a good deal older that they may seek out *aloneness* in their rooms or in another part of the house. For a long time before this, they may need to see or hear someone they love nearby. But it's still a form of solitude. Some children may simply lie down on the carpet, eyes open, seeming to be doing nothing at all. But you can be sure that inside they're doing things they need to do in order to go on growing.

Have you noticed how somewhat older children will suddenly stop an activity and sit on the grass, pluck at blades, contemplate insects, or just poke in the dirt? Then, almost as if an alarm clock had gone off, their reverie ends and it's time for a renewed burst of energy.

In medieval times, houses often had a room set aside for meditation, contemplation, and reflection. Nowadays, that room would probably be the "television room"—a place where you could go for rapid, disconnected, loud sights and sounds. The medieval room was one in which you could hear yourself think. Today's television room seems to be valued by many people of all ages precisely because it's a place where it's very difficult to hear yourself think.

One of the things I often wonder about is how those of us who make television programs could encourage the use of solitude. It seems almost a contradiction. Yet I think of the way books can help us by starting all sorts of trains of thought and then letting us follow them where we will. I wonder if television can ever do that? It certainly could do something to help human beings respect the need for quiet times.

When I'm on my travels, many people come up and talk to me— people I have never seen before but who feel that they know me because television has brought me into their homes. They have all sorts of things to tell me, but two recent comments made me feel very good about our work and its influence on people's need for solitude. One woman said, "Your program is our most peaceful half-hour during the day." A man put it this way: "At first I couldn't see what my children liked about your program, but I took the time to find out and now I know. You encourage people to feel...and take time to think about important things." Those people really gave me a good feeling.

Television, Children, and Violence

Many questions from parents have to do with the violence that is shown on television: How harmful is it? And what can we do about it? Researchers come to different conclusions; however, more and more they are finding direct corollaries between television violence and real-life violent acts. I personally am convinced that regular exposure to television violence *can* seriously hurt a child's emotional growth.

Most of us try to be careful not to let our children watch programs that are unsuitable for them. What is "unsuitable" is a judgment for you and for each parent to make. I do think all parents have a responsibility to make that judgment and to act upon it by placing off limits those programs they do not want their children to see. But even though we may monitor what our children are watching, there's no way to insulate them completely from, for instance, repeated news broadcasts about the killing of John Lennon, the children of Atlanta, the assassination attempts on President Reagan and Pope John Paul, the hunger strikes and battles in Northern Ireland, the riots in England, the assassination of Anwar Sadat, fighting in the Falkland Islands, bloodshed in Beirut—the list grows longer and longer even as I write. Not to mention insulating them from daily reports of local violence as well as violence in "entertainment" programming of all kinds.

Children can learn to cope with many scary things in life—violence on television included—*so long as they have caring adults at hand who want to help them.* Watching television with our children, and talking about it, is the best way to keep violence on television from becoming overwhelming and damaging. We may even be able to turn whatever violence our children do see into a positive experience, *so long as we see it with them.* We can, for instance, use it to help our children identify feelings, strengthen their own sense of self-control, sort out what's real and what's pretend, understand family values, understand more about cause and effect, and learn more about how the *real* world works.

Asking a child how he or she *feels* about a scary, violent TV episode can be the beginning of really important talk. Televised violence can arouse deep and strong feelings in all of us, but it takes young children a long time to identify such feelings as grief, anger, or fright in themselves, and even longer to learn to *manage* these feelings. Children need adult help. If you let your child know how you have similar feelings, and can talk about them, you can help your child learn to identify them too. You might want to talk about the violent adult behavior that you see on television, about how scary it can be when you feel so angry that you want to hurt someone, about a recent time when you helped your child stop before doing something hurtful, or about a time when you were proud of your child for finding a constructive way of expressing angry feelings. This kind of talk supports his or her own growing capacities for self-control.

My friend Steven, who's ten, told me that one day he'd felt so angry with his little sister that he'd felt like killing her. But, he added, he knew he wouldn't. When I asked him why he knew he wouldn't, he said, "Because I look at all the people who did that and other people really hate them. I don't want people to hate me." For Steven, as for most of us, the need for love and approval acts as a powerful control over destructive feelings.

When we adults supply loving and firm limits for our children's behavior, we give them a feeling of reassurance and safety. At nursery school one day, four-year-old Johnny started to hurl a block at a playmate who was getting in his way. Johnny's teacher quietly put her arm around him—a gesture of both affection and restraint. She said to him, "I can't let you throw that block, but I could help you build a block building with it." That teacher provided the limits Johnny needed and the comfort of knowing that if another child ever started to throw a block at Johnny, the teacher would stop that child too. Little by little, as our children borrow from adults' sense of self-control, they will learn to supply it from within (see page 150).

How do you suppose a child is likely to feel about the seemingly endless examples of *adults* on television who have no self-control themselves? The examples of adult rage that end routinely in injury and murder?

Through televised violence, we can certainly help children begin to understand what violence is real and what violence is "pretend." As you know, learning the difference between reality and fantasy is a big task for young children, and in this respect the world of television can be a very confusing place. Michael, a four-year-old friend of mine, thinks Bill Bixby really turns into the Hulk when he gets mad and that he really goes around smashing things and people. That's why we made five programs about superheroes for *Mister Rogers' Neighborhood*—to help Michael and millions like him sort out the reality and fantasy of programs like *The Incredible Hulk* (see page 115). Perhaps most important of all, we were able to let children know that neither anger nor any other feeling can turn us into someone else—that having a wide range of feelings, even conflicting feelings, is part of being the one person who we are. What we tried to do in our own way through television is something you, watching with your children, can do in your own way.

Whether we think the values shown on television are good or bad, they offer us an opportunity to help our children understand more about our own family values. We parents provide food and shelter and clothing for our children, and these things, in their own ways, express our values. So does the family car. And the family furniture, and the stereo (*and* the music that comes out of it) and the television set (*and* the programs on it). Whatever a child sees at home may carry with it the sense that it is condoned by the parents who provided it and therefore reflects the parents' values. We parents provide the television set in our home and that television often shows adults solving problems of all kinds. How do we feel about those problem-solving models? Do we want our children to believe that these models reflect our family values? When you see a destructively angry family confrontation on television, you might want to talk with your child about how angry feelings are handled in *your* family. When we talk with our children about things like this, we are passing on the values *we* think are important.

All television programming moves too fast for lengthy discussion while you are watching, but it's surprising how much you can say during commercials or between programs. Even just asking your child, "What do you think about that?" or "Why do you think that happened?" helps

turn your child from passive watcher into an active thinker, perhaps storing up questions to ask you at another time. Children need to know that actions and events do have both causes and consequences. When you and your child look for them together, television watching can take on another important dimension.

It's often hard to know what young children are thinking, so that makes it hard to know what they need to hear. I've found that asking questions before giving answers is often the best way to help children reveal just what their fears or misperceptions may be. When our children tell us about the violence they see on television, we may be in for some surprises. Sometimes we assume that they understand what we understand—and understand it the same way. For example, we as adults may see a violent police drama as a playing out of the old familiar concept, "Crime does not pay." We know what to expect, we accept the conventions, and our attention is mainly held by new variations on the old theme. Our children, on the other hand, who have none of this prior understanding and experience, may get from the same crime show the message that people are aggressive and violent, and that policemen shoot the ones who are "bad." You might find it revealing to ask your child, once the criminal has been caught, what he or she thinks will happen next. I've heard children say that the criminal is probably going to be spanked or sent to his room. If, on the program, the criminal is in fact about to be sent to jail, you could ask, "What do you think jail is?" That may bring some really unexpected answers, which you can then use to help your child know once again that anything can be talked about in your family.

What parents give their children will *always* be more important than what television gives them. Children who are loved and who feel they are lovable are the ones who are most likely to grow into loving, rather than violent, adults. Taking the time to help our children understand themselves, what they see on television, their world, and their place in it, is one way of showing love for them. It's a way of letting them know they are unique, valuable human beings who can learn to handle their own aggressive feelings in healthy, nonviolent ways.

Television, Children, and the Real World

In our own culture television is practically universal. It affects our relationships with our neighbors, our friends, and family. It's so widespread that there are some families in this country who buy a television set long before they install indoor plumbing, and what they see on their sets is what everybody else in the country sees on theirs. Television is in the real world; however, its portrayal of the real world is very *unreal*.

It's curious to consider, but that unreal, distorted view of the world is now influencing our opinions, shaping our attitudes, modifying our values, providing models of behavior, altering our buying habits... and participating in the raising of our children; so, in a very real way, television's unreal presentations become a real part of the real world.

The common culture of television doesn't have to be a bad thing just because it's so widely shared. People who have moved from one part of the nation to another have written to us reporting how delighted they and their young children were, not only to find that our television "visits" were being telecast in their new city, but that their new neighbors were discussing them and the children were playing about them. They wanted us to know that our being in their new home helped with the transition from the old.

Much of what is seen through the mass media, however, is dramatized mayhem, murder, debased sexuality, and an endless succession of real-life disaster, tragedy, and violence that comes to us through news and documentaries. When I was a child and my mother and I would read about such events in the newspapers or see them in newsreels, she used to tell me, "Always look for the helpers. There's always someone who is trying to help." I did, and doing so changed the way I saw them. I began to see that the world was full of doctors and nurses, volunteers, neighbors, and friends who jumped in to help when things went wrong. That was reassuring, and even amidst the violence that we may witness on television we might be able to help our children look for the many concerned and caring people in the world.

Potentially, for families, television can speak to the inner nature of the child and the parent. It can speak of issues in parent-child relationships and what it means to be a family.

Even people who live amidst great violence know that television's representation of the world is often a sick one. I once read about the vice president of a South Bronx street "gang." Two of her older brothers were sentenced to Attica for their involvement in a gang murder of a prostitute. Her "man" was fatally shot in a street fight. In an interview with *The New York Times* about violence on television, she said that right after a child has seen something violent on TV a parent should sit down and talk to that child about it. "Tell the kid that that's not the way life should be—that that's not the right thing to do." That's streetwise counsel, and it strikes me as very wise advice.

We all know, though, that there are millions of children who don't have parents who sit down and talk with them about what they've seen on TV, children who don't have families to help them deal with the feelings that are generated by television programming. Those feelings— if they are ones of stress and unresolved violence—can too easily be carried over into family life. I know this to be the reality, and that's why I have always felt it a duty to help resolve the stressful feelings we may evoke on *Mister Rogers' Neighborhood.* Sadness and fear and anger do exist in our Neighborhood, but so also do understanding adults who can help children distinguish between fantasy and reality, who can help children identify and manage their feelings, and who can encourage children to talk about those feelings with the real-life adults they love and trust.

Let's Talk About It is the name of a series of videotapes and books and booklets and other materials that we at Family Communications are producing for families to use at particular times of stress. We chose the title because it's a phrase that lies right at the heart of all the work we've been doing since *Mister Rogers' Neighborhood* started taking shape all those years ago. But the reason we're in business is not just that *we* want to talk to families. Not at all. Our main goal is to try to help parents and the children in their care to talk *together.* That's where the best talk takes place.

And there's a lot to talk about as children grow in their individual ways. There's sadness and disappointment, anger and frustration, danger and even death. Television gives us plenty of opportunities to talk about these things. What it doesn't give us as much is the chance to talk about love, compassion, commitment, integrity, the preciousness of life—all the many things that help make us feel good about being individual, unique human beings.

Television *could* meet real human needs. It *could* help children learn to recognize feelings and develop healthy ways of dealing with those feelings. Television *could* offer a wide variety of healthy problem-solving models. It *could* encourage children to look for their own inner worth, their family traditions and values. Television *could* help broadcast the value of childhood and communicate the fact that childhood lies at the very basis of what human beings are and what they can become. It *could* help children reflect on who they are and what they want to be.

Television *could* do all these things and sometimes *does* do these things. But so often it doesn't. Parents can and often do. That's another reason parents are so special!

CHAPTER 8:

SOME EARLY CHALLENGES

People are very different in their attitudes toward doing new things, particularly things that may be difficult and even frightening. When we're young, life is full of challenges, many of which we can't avoid in the normal process of growing up—challenges like going to the doctor, going to the dentist, getting a haircut, sleeping away from home, and going to school.

As we get older we usually have more choice about what happens to us. Some people tend to avoid the new because they feel more comfortable staying close to their neighborhoods and keeping to a familiar routine where there are few surprises. But we all know others who seem to seek out the new and challenging—trying new foods, visiting other countries, signing up for night school, climbing mountains.

How we dealt with our own earliest experiences has a lot to do with how we cope with the ones that come later—and with how we help our children encounter their first challenges. For instance, if we had a very fearful and difficult time getting injections at the doctor's office when we were little, and we really hated it, that is going to affect our ability to help our children through their own experiences with injections and doctors. Children pick up very quickly on how we are feeling at times that are difficult for them—to the point that our feelings become part of their feelings.

While some challenges our children face may make us anxious, they also present us with one of the great opportunities of parenting—the chance to resolve these lingering anxieties of our own. That's why I often say that "children offer us another chance to grow." Going through an experience with your child that was once frightening to you when you were a child allows you to find ways to comfort not only your own little son or daughter, but also the child that has remained within yourself. You're an adult now and you can use your adult perspective to make a difference in your children's present and your own past.

There are two ways that we can be really helpful to our children when they face something new and difficult. The first is to try to let them know what to expect. Children need to be told what to expect because they may not feel comfortable asking, or not even know how or what to ask. That's why I wrote a song that I sometimes sing on *Mister Rogers' Neighborhood* called "I Like to Be Told":

I like to be told
When you're going away,
When you're going to come back,
And how long you will stay,
How long you will stay,
I like to be told.

I like to be told
If it's going to hurt,
If it's going to be hard,
If it's not going to hurt.
I like to be told.
I like to be told.

It helps me to get ready for all those things,
All those things that are new.
I trust you more and more each time
That I'm finding those things to be true...

I like to be told
'Cause I'm trying to grow,
'Cause I'm trying to learn
And I'm trying to know.
I like to be told.
I like to be told.

There's the separation theme again—leaving and coming back—and as you think about times that are difficult for children, so many of them do include separation as part of the difficulty, even if it's as brief a separation as the one that occurs when a child gets an X ray taken. If that moment of parting comes as a complete surprise, it can trigger real alarm. If, on the other hand, you have talked it over ahead of time and your child understands that the separation will last only a few minutes and that you will be just around the corner, there may be no alarm at all.

When children know ahead of time what's going to happen—and *not* happen—they can prepare themselves for what's coming. They can think about it and get used to their feelings about it.

Encouraging children to do this kind of rehearsal through play is the other way we can help (see Chapter 5). Naturally, not everything in life can be anticipated. But whenever we have the chance, we parents can show our children that feelings are mentionable and can be manageable. By doing so, we encourage them to express their feelings after a difficult experience, too. They may feel sad or afraid or angry because of something that happened, and being able to tell us so is a really healthy kind of communication.

SOME EARLY CHALLENGES

Going to the Doctor

Your child may have been going to a doctor for checkups ever since birth, but this familiar routine can change when children have to change doctors or go to a specialist for the first time. Feelings change, too, as children grow, and it can be a real indication of how feelings and age levels are tied together when your child shows sudden anxieties when there doesn't seem to be any reason for them, or gets upset over routine procedures that have never caused upsets before. When that happens, we can be fairly sure that though the procedures haven't changed, our children's feelings about the insides and outsides of their bodies have.

It sometimes helps for a child to know that many doctors are themselves fathers and mothers with children of their own. Your child may like to hear that all doctors were children once and that they grew up wanting to take care of people in special ways. To do this they had to study and learn about people's bodies and people's feelings. Doctors are there to help people stay well and help people get better when they're sick.

If a child is suddenly unwilling to be undressed in the doctor's office, that might be evidence of a brand-new sense of privacy. Or it might be because a child feels a new need for the protection and security of clothing. It's generally wiser not to suggest there's a choice about things like this when there isn't (see page 206), but children sometimes feel better if they can feel they're helping a little. One way might be to say, "The doctor needs you to undress so he (or she) can make sure your body is healthy all over." They also might like to hear that they'll be able to put their clothes back on just as soon as the doctor is done.

You wouldn't think that the weighing and measuring part of an examination could cause much trouble, and it seldom does. Just recently, though, I heard of a seven-year-old boy who, with a group of children, was watching a program we made to show children what emergency rooms are like and what happens there. At the end of the program the children were asked which part they liked the least, and this boy answered: "The measuring part." Our staff consultant who was there thought he meant the temperature measuring or the blood-pressure measuring. The boy shook his head but refused to explain until the two of them were alone. It was the simple height measurement that he had hated most, because he was the shortest child in his nursery-school class. That story reminded me once again of something I think of often: There is *always* a reason for children's feelings!

Objects that intrude into the body are often especially frightening for a child. Both the mouth and the anus are basic, early, and important sources of body feelings; consequently, tongue depressors and rectal thermometers may be particularly threatening. Anything unusual inserted into the mouth may arouse a conflict between the natural urge to bite and a child's efforts to control that urge. A child's trying to control lower-body muscles at the time of toilet training may make a rectal temperature taking a really difficult experience.

Some parents have wondered why their children get upset when the doctor looks into their ears with an otoscope or listens to the insides of their bodies with a stethoscope. The otoscope may produce an unpleasant sensation as it probes into the ear, but it very seldom hurts,

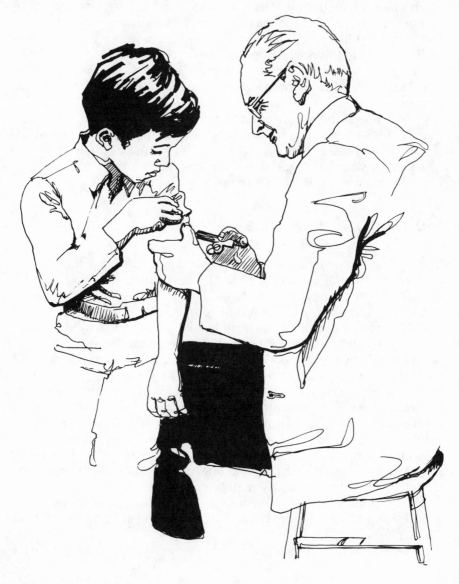

and certainly most adults find nothing unpleasant about stethoscopes (unless they're very cold to the touch!). The fact is that children may worry when doctors look into their heads and listen to their insides because they wonder if those doctors can tell exactly what they're thinking and feeling. Some doctors will let children try out these instruments for themselves, so that they can find out just what they do. It's important for children to know that no machine can read thoughts and feelings, that people's thoughts and feelings are their own to share or not to share with whomever they wish.

It's no surprise that children dread finger pricks and injections. They do hurt. There's nothing we can do about that except be honest and say that they "feel like a big pinch" or "a sting" (or however you think they feel). It can help to say, though, that the hurt usually goes away quickly.

There's something else troublesome about anything that punctures the skin, and that is children's common fantasy that what is under the skin may all leak out (see page 52). They need to know that this can't happen and that the doctor or nurse takes only a *little* bit of blood, that there's still as much as a person needs left on the inside, and that the skin heals and closes and won't let any more come out. Children who like playing with bandages often find it reassuring that bandages help keep everything inside that's supposed to stay inside.

Going to the Dentist

By the time all their baby teeth have come in, children should start to have regular dental checkups. Going to the dentist, for a young child, has a lot in common with going to the doctor, so knowing what's going to happen, and *playing* about it, are good ways to get ready.

Most often, the dentist will need to take only a good look at a child's teeth during this earliest visit, but it's an important visit because potential problems can be spotted and corrected before they get serious. As nothing much is likely to happen, this first appointment is also a good time for children to get used to sitting still in a dentist's chair and having someone peer and probe into their mouths. Because children's mouths are likely to be intense sources of feeling at this age, and because children are likely to be wrestling with their urge to bite, a dental exam may present a real test for a child's self-control. (Even children who have learned that control may feel angry when someone makes them open their mouths when they might not want to.)

If you think your child may be upset by a visit to the dentist, it's a good idea to talk to the dentist or hygienist about it in advance. They "like to be told," too.

There are many things children have to get used to in a dentist's office. Just the look of the place might be scary if a child didn't know what to expect: the bright light, the chair that goes up and down, the tray of sharp-looking instruments, the little hoses that squirt air and water or act like a vacuum sweeper. So often it's the small things that we adults have taken for granted that startle a child. A bib that suddenly gets clipped around the neck, for instance, could make a child wonder if he or she is going to be turned into a baby again. It's easy for us to overlook these details when we are right then dealing with our own *adult* memories and concerns about needles or drilling or pain.

It was exactly these small things that we decided to show on two programs about going to the dentist on *Mister Rogers' Neighborhood*, and the response from many people proved to us again what such simple preparation can do. One dentist wrote us to say that he could tell when these programs were broadcast each year because *new* children were less anxious. The children would even say, "That's just like what Mister Rogers showed me." Dentists say that the children are pleased by the recognition and seem to have a readiness to cooperate with what the dentist has to do. If our television visits can make that kind of difference, reassurance from *you* is likely to be even more helpful. Of course, your being right there with your child at the time is the best emotional support of all.

In the course of their dental care, children are likely to encounter tooth polishing, mouth impressions, X rays, painkilling shots, and the drilling and filling of cavities. If you talk to your child's dentist before each visit, these procedures don't have to come as a shock and you and your child can prepare for them.

Dentists tell us that the most important part of tooth care happens at home—and that's certainly true. Proper brushing and flossing and diet, for example, are keys to having healthy teeth. It's hard for young children to hold a toothbrush and work it around the mouth so that it does a good job, but we can encourage them from the start to begin the brushing by themselves, even though we may have to finish up for them. Using dental floss takes even more dexterity, but the habits our children learn very early are the ones that tend to persist as they grow. That certainly seems to be true about eating habits. It's likely that the way you and I eat reflects preferences we developed among the foods our parents offered us. Eating habits are hard to change once we get older and our tastes are formed. They *can* be changed, though, and caring for a child may be a good motivation for us to think carefully about what *we're* eating—whether we have become dependent on too much salt or too much sugar. Healthy eating, of course, is not only important for our teeth but for our total well-being; and, just as raising children confronts us with old feelings, it confronts us, too, with old habits—and a new chance to change them.

SOME EARLY CHALLENGES

Before your children's baby teeth begin to get loose and fall out, it's a good idea to make sure they know that this is going to happen. The chances are that they will have some friends whose baby teeth are already missing. For many children, losing baby teeth brings pleasure and pride; it's a visible sign that they are growing.

The notion of a "tooth fairy" who leaves a present in return for a tooth is fun for some children. It gives the lost tooth a kind of importance and value even when it's gone. After all, it was a part of the body. Other children prefer to save their baby teeth. If the tooth fairy is part of your family tradition, you'll be the best person to decide how much to make of it and when to let your children know that it's only pretend. You may find, though, as did one friend of mine, that your child has different ideas from yours about things like the tooth fairy. Although that little girl's parents had grown up with the tooth fairy tradition and looked

MISTER ROGERS TALKS WITH PARENTS

forward to recreating the game for their daughter, they found that she flatly refused to put her tooth under her pillow, because she "didn't want anybody sneaking into her bedroom like that when she was asleep."

Most children in our culture will meet many health-care professionals as they grow. As we and others give our children care, they can learn that they are worth taking care of. When children actually feel *that they are people that are worth taking care of*, they are much more likely to grow into adults who do take good care of themselves.

Going to the Barber or Hairdresser

What children seem to worry about most when they go to get their hair cut is that the scissors and clippers might cut something more than hair—something like ears or noses or any other parts of the body. Hair scissors are long and pointed, and it's not hard to imagine the fantasies a child could have when the blades are snapping and clicking all around the head but just out of sight.

Many parents cut their children's hair themselves. At the beginning, that may be easier for a child than going to a professional who is a stranger, and a loved adult should certainly accompany a child at least on that first professional visit. You will probably have trimmed your child's toenails and fingernails long before it's time for a haircut, and you might want to explain that hair and nails are alike in that they need trimming from time to time but that doing it *doesn't hurt*, and they all grow back after they're trimmed.

Once again, dolls and teddy bears can give you and your child a chance to do some pretend haircutting. And if you can arrange to take your child with you when you get *your* hair cut, that can also give him or her a chance to see what happens, to think it over, to ask you some questions. I've found it helpful to let children know that people who cut hair have been to schools to learn how, and that they had to practice and practice so they could learn to do it very carefully. A child may need to hear many times that *all* that barbers and hairdressers cut is hair. *They don't cut anything but hair.*

In one of our programs on *Mister Rogers' Neighborhood* I go to my barber for a haircut, and in addition to introducing children to the experience, I mention that changing our appearance doesn't change who we are—something children may wonder about, just as they may when they have an operation (see page 208). One father wrote me to say that for days after seeing that program his preschool son took an imaginary friend for imaginary haircuts. His father heard him reassuring his "friend" again and again that he would still be the same person after it was over. No doubt some parents find that a strange fantasy, but it's one that young children *do* have.

As with visits to doctors and dentists, small things at the haircutter's can be upsetting—like having to hold really still, the little bits of falling hair that are itchy on the neck, the chair that goes up and down, or even getting onto the little seat that the hairdresser may put between the arms of the big one. For one two-year-old, having a shampoo at the barbershop was the most difficult part of the visit. He was scared to be tilted backward in the chair; that was not the way it happened at home and it must have felt a little like falling. After his second or third visit, though, he said he thought the barbershop shampoo was better than home: The water and soap couldn't get in your eyes!

Even very young children, as they gain a firmer sense of how their bodies look, may be sensitive to the shape and length of their hair. They may have distinct preferences, preferences that don't always match those of their parents. There is a real issue here, and it can be a long-lasting one. A middle-aged friend of mine, for instance, tells me that when he visits his eighty-year-old mother, she is still almost sure to comment within the first five minutes on how she thinks his hair looks. Even when she doesn't say anything aloud, he still knows whether he's been given "thumbs up" or "thumbs down."

I asked him how it was when he was little. He told me he couldn't ever remember being asked about how he wanted his hair to look. "I was taken to the barber and my hair was cut according to my parents' instructions," he said. "That was that." Once, when he was in his twenties, he daringly had a brushcut, and he remembers how embarrassed his father was to go anywhere with him until it grew back to its usual length. (Sometimes it works the other way around, and young children are upset when their parents change *their* hairstyles. One boy I know was terrified when his mother came home one afternoon with a new puffed and frosted hairdo.)

How our children look does affect how we feel about ourselves as parents, and it's almost sure to reflect how our parents felt about us and how we felt about them. Identity and appearance are closely linked, particularly in early childhood and in adolescence, and how we handle the issue the first time around can have a good deal of bearing on what will happen when it comes up again later on.

When our children are small, we can certainly talk with them about how they think they want to look, just as we can ask them about the clothes they want to wear. While remaining true to our values and our sense of our own identities, we can generally find a way to allow our children to express at least some of their inner feelings about who they are.

Sleeping Away From Home

Some children resist going to bed anywhere, anytime because, of course, it means a separation. At least at home, this nightly separation has become routine and children have learned to cope with it in familiar and comforting surroundings and maybe with comforting rituals such as a bedtime song, story, or prayer. The dark corners and closets of their own rooms are known, as are the shapes of clothes draped over a chair and the nighttime sounds that are unique to each neighborhood, street, and house. At home, children can often hear the sound of their parents' voices nearby and have learned to trust that a call or a cry will bring someone loved or trusted to the bedside. When you think about it, by the time children are three, they have learned about a thousand times that nighttime will come, separation will take place, they will fall asleep... and that daytime will come again, they will wake up safely in their own beds, and the people they love will still be there to look after them.

But it's not surprising that fresh doubts may appear about this otherwise predictable sequence when the time comes to spend a night in a different place with different grown-ups. Many children make the transition through visits to a grandparent or relative, spending their first nights away from home in another place that is familiar. Even this kind of overnight visit can be difficult for some children.

When a child starts having a best friend, they may become almost inseparable, and it's a common occurrence for a mother to get a phone call from her son or daughter who is playing at a best friend's house asking, on the spur of the moment, to spend the night there. One mother told me what mixed feelings she had when she got a call like that from her five-year-old. Laura had never spent a night at a friend's house before, and though this mother's first feeling was one of not wanting to disappoint her daughter, she also realized she was very anxious at the prospect. She asked to speak to the friend's mother, and together they decided to choose another night for that first overnight, a week or so later. Her daughter's disappointment was short-lived and was quickly replaced by excited anticipation of the overnight to come.

"I don't know how it would have been for Laura if I'd said yes instead," that mother told me. "She might have been fine. But I knew from my feelings that I wasn't ready." As it worked out, both mother and daughter had time to think and talk about what it would be like to sleep over in a strange place. Together, they packed an overnight bag with a couple of favorite toys, and Laura's mother explained that different parents did different things for their children when they went to bed, but one thing Laura's parents would be certain to do was make sure someone would be there to look after her all night long. She said she'd like to hear all about it when Laura came home. Laura, as it turned out, had a good time and brought home many stories about what had been the same and what had been different at her friend's house. Laura's mother felt good about that visit, too.

Children do tend to know when they feel ready to try sleeping over, but everyone can get surprises. Carrie was four when she thought she'd like to spend a night at a friend's house and didn't seem anxious about it at all—even when her mother said good-bye to her. But the family in the house she was visiting had just had a new baby...and when Carrie's friend, in the darkness of their bedroom, told her that there were "little monsters outside the window," the visit came to an abrupt end. Carrie said she wanted to go home. Her mother came and got her. That experience didn't make spending nights away any harder for Carrie, though. It might even have made it easier, because she had learned that wherever she was, her mother would come and get her if she felt afraid.

I've recently learned how a new baby *at home* made the difference for a six-year-old's decision about spending the night away. Her friend's parents picked her up to spend the night at their house, which was only about a mile away. They had just gone a few blocks when Elaine said, "I didn't know you lived so far away." The parents explained that it wasn't really very far at all, but after a few more blocks Elaine said, "Boy, you really *do* live far away!" When they pulled up at the house, she had decided she'd changed her mind about wanting to spend the night. When asked why, she explained, "I just think I want to go home and spend the night in my mom's bed with the new baby." So it may not be anxiety only about new places that might upset overnight plans, but also anxiety about what might happen by leaving home—like losing a place in the family.

And sometimes there seems to be no reason at all that a child may be dead set against spending a night away from home. In that case, all we can do is respect that child's feelings until either they change or we come to understand what the problem is. Two friends of mine had a very gregarious little boy who loved to play with other children and who gave every sign of coping very well with times when he was away from the family. Nor did he seem to have any particular fears about bedtime or the dark. All the same, even though he would regularly have friends over to spend the night, he steadfastly refused to sleep away from home himself. It was only years later that he was able to tell his parents that the reason he wouldn't spend the night at anyone else's house was that he was afraid of what they might give him to eat and that he might get yelled at for not wanting to eat it. That boy was a very finicky eater and his finicky tastes were always a big mealtime issue in his own family.

Going to School

My very first school was a small-town school that had eight classrooms: one for each grade. It was the same school my mother and dad had gone to. Those desks and chairs and blackboards would certainly seem old-fashioned now! I must have had a good time there, because I have pleasant memories about it. I know I liked my teachers—Mrs. Curto, Miss Albert, Mr. Gallagher. And I was excited about learning to read and write. I made good friends there, too, and some of them are my friends even now. Of course, there's lots I can't remember about that first school of mine, but I feel sure that the good feelings I had about it really helped me want to go on learning.

Most children are naturally eager to learn and to join the world of the "bigger kids" who already go to school. But like other important times in our lives, beginning school can bring mixed feelings. Some young children may even imagine that being sent to school is a punishment. They may feel that somehow they are less important to the family because they're away from home, where all that's fun is going on. They may feel jealous of their younger brothers or sisters who get to stay home with their parents. When children feel uncertain about a new experience like this, it's quite common for them to behave in ways they did when they were younger. You may find your child clinging more closely to you than usual, thumb sucking again, or even forgetting his or her toilet training now and then. Such steps backward often precede big strides forward, and they generally pass quickly. If you can remember uncertain feelings when you first went to school, talking honestly with your child about them can be a real help.

Because starting school can represent such a large change for a child, it is best to put off any other significant changes you may have been contemplating—even rearranging furniture or redecorating a room. Familiar home life can mean a lot to a child at this time.

Here are several ways parents have found to make the first days of school more comfortable for their children.

- If your child already has friends in the neighborhood who will be going to the same school, you might arrange with other parents for the children to get together and play before the school year starts. You could even encourage them to play about what they think school will be like.

- Some parents call the school to see if they can arrange for their child (together with a few friends) to tour the school building and meet the teacher.

- Children usually like to know their address and family's phone number. It's reassuring to hear that this information could help them get home if they ever got lost.

- You could walk or ride with your child to the school and back, just to show the route he or she will take.

- Your child might like to meet the school crossing guard. The guard can become an important new friend.

- An unhurried morning routine at home can help your child to get ready—and feel ready—for school without haste or anxiety. Sending him or her off with a cheerful "Have a good day in school!" or "See you after school!" is much more encouraging than an admonition like, "Be good!"

- Some children like to take a special container for their pencils and erasers with them to school. It could be one you have made together. That, or some other personal belonging, can be a comfort if your child feels homesick.

- One mother I know put a photograph of the whole family in her son's lunchbox. It could just as easily go in a notebook or jacket pocket. The photo was a reminder that they would be together again at the end of the day—that home would be there when it was needed.

A five-year-old who didn't want to go to school explained to me that it was because he "didn't know how to read and work with numbers and that's what you do at school." I've found out since then that his belief that you already had to know those things *before* going to school is a common source of anxiety for preschool children. Others worry that there won't be any time for play, and they need to be assured that teachers not only understand that children *need* to play but that teachers also know that many forms of play are good ways to learn. Children need to be assured, too, that teachers are there to help children find their way around—to the bathroom, for instance—and they may find it comforting to hear that teachers, like other nonfamily caregivers, were children once themselves and may have children and grandchildren of their own. The reason they wanted to be teachers is that they are grownups who like children and like helping them learn.

Going to school, of course, will mean learning not only numbers and letters but also some new rules. I think it's helpful to explain that some rules, like not running in the halls, are to keep children safe; others, like raising your hand when you want to talk, make learning easier by ensuring that everyone gets a turn to talk. You may have similar rules in your house and for similar reasons.

There are many things that children wonder about when it's time for them to go to school. Here are some frequent questions I've been asked:

- Will I have to eat things I don't like at lunchtime?

- Will I have to fall asleep when it's nap time?

- What happens if I'm bad?

- Will I get to play on the playground?

- How will I know what time it is?

- How can I make friends?

- Are there birthday parties at school?

- Why do classrooms have so many kids?

- How will I be able to sit still all day?

- How will I be able to follow so many rules?

The end of the school day is usually an exciting time for your child and a time when he or she needs you to listen to what went on—what was fun, what wasn't, what was easy, what the other children did, what the teacher said. Taking a short time-out *really* to listen can both give you insights into how things are going at school and give your child the sense that you care about his or her life at school and that you are proud of the ways he or she is learning and growing. There were some days I remember that our sons didn't want to tell us anything about school, but they knew that when they were ready we'd most likely be ready to listen.

Once your child goes to school, the teacher is in many ways the most important caregiver other than you that your child will have. The relationship between the three of you can be best if it's a close one. You certainly need to know your child's teacher so that you can better understand what your child tells you about school, and so that you can feel comfortable and confident talking with the teacher about your child's progress. But it's just as important for your child's teacher to know you. That's because young children and their first teachers are likely to have an emotional relationship unlike relationships with other teachers later on: It is often especially intense because it is highly colored by your children's feelings about *you*.

When I think of my years working as a kind of teacher at the Family and Children's Center of the University of Pittsburgh, I can remember many times in my early days when a child did something that evoked a reaction in me that really surprised me. At these times I felt as though

I was acting like someone else. As I thought more about it, I realized that the child I was working with was doing his or her best to get me to act that particular way. The more I found out about the child's family—especially the father—the more I understood that young children often transfer their feelings about their closest caregivers onto their *teachers*. I was talking to a male teacher friend about this phenomenon the other day. He recalled some instances from his preschool teaching experiences that confirmed my own:

- The girls in his class tended to go to a female teacher for permission to go to the bathroom or to talk about things they felt were personal.

- One boy, when he wanted to do something special, would always come to my friend rather than to a female teacher. This boy's parents were divorced, and he lived with his mother, who was responsible for everyday limit setting. When he visited his father, though, he was allowed to do more or less what he wanted to do.

- A little girl in my friend's class was particularly shy with him and even seemed frightened when he approached. In this case the girl's father was a trucker who was seldom at home, but when he was, he assumed the role of a very strict disciplinarian.

Children do tend to transfer their ideas about who grown-up people are from their own families. They *will* expect a woman teacher to be in many ways like their mothers and a man teacher to be like their fathers. What's more, they will be very skilled in evoking the behaviors they expect. It can be a real help to your child's teacher (and consequently to your child in school) to know something about you, your relationship with your child, and your family life. It can help a teacher respond appropriately to a child's behavior or know when a sudden change in behavior indicates a call to you to talk it over.

Teachers particularly need to know about sudden or unusual stresses in your child's family life. Hard times at home are likely to influence the way your child is adapting to life at school.

The older your child gets, the more other people will become involved in helping your child grow. As these relationships take shape, your child needs to feel you are on his or her side—not that your child is always *right*, but that, no matter what, he or she is always *loved*. It is through children's trust in their parents that they can come to trust other grown-ups who will be helping them with the early challenges in their lives.

SOME EARLY CHALLENGES

CHAPTER 9:

HOSPITALIZATION

When our younger son was two, he had to have hernia surgery. We learned of a hospital that would do the surgery on an outpatient basis: go in in the morning, go home in the afternoon. The whole thing, which was meant to be a "routine procedure," turned into a very difficult experience for my wife and me, and a traumatic one for our son. In fact, it was several years before we all felt that we understood and had even begun to resolve our feelings about it.

In our case, we were not prepared for what was going to happen. Not knowing what to expect, we were not able to prepare our son. When we arrived at the hospital, he was abruptly taken from us with no preoperative sedation, and he was wheeled screaming to the operating room. We later learned that it took forty-five minutes to put him to sleep. Those forty-five minutes have been a recurring nightmare for him and for us ever since. It must have seemed to him that he had been snatched away by strangers who then did things to him that were painful and terrifying. I'm sure, too, that he was deeply sad and angry that we seemed to have abandoned him just when he needed us most.

It didn't have to be that way, and now, twenty years later, many hospital staff people and parents alike are more sensitive to the emotional needs of children and their families. There is even a Washington-based national organization, the Association for the Care of Children's Health, which has made the emotional well-being of hospitalized children its central concern.

Materials to help families through the hospitalization of a young child were the first that we produced under the *Let's Talk About It* title (see page 184). For me, the project offered the opportunity I'd wanted ever since our son's terrifying experience. We have now produced videotapes on going to the hospital, having an operation, wearing a cast, and on what an emergency room is like. We created little picture books for children to remind them of what they had seen in the tapes, and we also wrote booklets for both parents and hospital staff. We even printed large color posters of "Mister Rogers" that could be put on the walls of corridors or waiting areas or any place where a child might feel scared or lonely and need to see a familiar face. These materials are being used in some five hundred hospitals across the country. That reinforces my belief that adversity can generate creative energy that, in turn, can result in help for others.

I would like someday to broaden the scope of what we have done to include families whose children face prolonged hospitalization, life-threatening illnesses, or alarming procedures like cardiac catheterization. So far, though, we have been able to deal only with the more routine types of hospital experience. But at least we have made a beginning, and I would like to share with you some very practical ways in which, we learned, children can be helped to cope.

HOSPITALIZATION

Going to the Hospital

The circumstances of hospitalization can intensify many scary things that young children are already normally worried about. I've mentioned them all in other places in this book—fear of separation, concerns about body wholeness, feelings of being small and vulnerable, the struggle for self-control, the fright that comes with scary fantasies. All these anxieties can be aroused when somebody has to go to the hospital.

Few parents can be with a child as much as they would wish when that child is in the hospital. There are commitments to jobs and to other children at home, and there are the necessary everyday chores that must be done. When we can't be with our children, though, we can let them know why *and when we'll be back.* Such a large part of the fear of separation is that it may be forever, and one of the main ways children learn to cope with times of separation is by learning (through experience) that "going away" can be followed by "coming back." Telling your child when you're going to come back may not prevent tears and anger when you leave—at least, not to start with. But as you come back again and again when you say you will, your child is likely to develop the trust and anticipation that can make your times away more manageable.

We found that one of children's commonest (but often unexpressed) fears is that their separation not only from you but from *home* will be permanent. They're afraid that they won't ever leave the hospital. They may need to hear over and over again that they will be going home just as soon as the doctor decides they are well enough. Even then they may harbor some deep doubts about whether that is so. In one of our video cassettes, we made that fear the one most on Daniel Striped Tiger's mind as he faced a trip to the hospital. Daniel even feared that his clock house wasn't going to be there when he came home—somehow it would have gone away. I have heard one suggestion that I think could be very helpful for coping with fears like Daniel's. In this family, the parents encouraged their child to make pictures for a scrapbook about home with an instant camera. All the time the child was away in the hospital, she had pictures with her of the people and things that meant the most to her. Her parents were able to keep assuring her that when she came home she would find everything just as she had left it.

These parents did something else that turned out to be really helpful, too. With the same camera, they encouraged their daughter to take pictures of the people and places she saw in the hospital. On her return home she showed these pictures to all her friends and talked about her experience and her feelings, gradually becoming more comfortable with her memories as she did so.

Hospitals impose their own times of separation no matter how available parents may be. Nighttime is often one. Sometimes all we can do is let a child know that there will always be someone nearby and that there are nurses who stay up all night to make sure children are safe while they sleep. That can be very comforting. And then there are the times when parents have to stay behind while a child is taken away for treatment. It may be possible for your child to take something along—something very small from home, or a reminder of you. The most important thing for your child to take, though, is the knowledge that you'll be waiting when he or she returns.

Many fears about the hospital come from not knowing what to expect. Hospitals are confusing not only because of their size, but because of their unfamiliar sights, sounds, smells, and the seemingly endless number of people who come and go through their halls. There are now many books that introduce children to hospital life, books you can find in most libraries and bookstores. Reading them with your child is a good way to begin talking about hospitals. Of course, you may have personal recollections of your own that you can add to those conversations. Knowing what it was like for you when you went to a hospital *and came back* will have special meaning for your child. Your recollections may not all be pleasant ones, and if you can talk about the times that you felt scared and sad and angry, you'll be letting your child know that these feelings aren't strange or "wrong," and that talking about them with you is something that's all right to do.

The best descriptions of the hospital you can give are those that describe concrete details and the things that will be different from the way they are at home. Children are likely to wonder how they will eat, where they will sleep, whether there will be a bathroom, and who will be with them. These questions, and the many, many more your child is likely to have, can be answered most helpfully by a preadmission visit to the hospital, if you are fortunate enough to be using a hospital that offers such visits. A preadmission visit is a tour for children and their parents of some of the hospital facilities. It's usually conducted by a hospital child-care specialist or a nurse. At the end of the tour there's usually a time for questions. But whether you are preparing your child in cooperation with the hospital or all on your own, it's most important to start talking about the hospital a couple of days before it's time to go. We all need time to get used to our feelings about something new and time to think up the questions we feel we really need answered.

Then there are all the "What's going to happen to me?" kinds of questions. Here we need to begin by learning what *we* need to know; adults can have scary fantasies, too. All parents should feel free to ask their child's doctors whatever they feel like asking—about their child's illness, about the details of necessary medical procedures, about the hospital or staff, or about anything whatsoever that is a source of worry.

The more we know the real answers to our concerns, the more we're likely to feel comfortable and confident in answering our children's questions. Of course, there will always be times when we may have to tell our child, "I don't know." (There may be times, too, when our children may ask us difficult questions about life, health, or death.) If we really don't know the answer to a question, we can promise to find out. If we're not sure how to answer, we can say something like, "Let me think about that and then we'll talk about it later." That way, we can use the extra time to get advice from friends or professionals we trust. But when we say, "We'll talk about it later," we must be sure to do that. Promises need to be kept as well as we possibly can.

Above all, we need to be honest with our children. There are, for instance, honest choices we can give our children that may help them feel at least a little in charge of what's happening to them. They may be small choices such as, "Do you want the back of the bed up or down?" or "Would you like the table here or there?" They can be more important choices, too, such as "Do you want the shot in the right or left side?" But when there is no choice we must not let them think that there is. "The nurse is going to give you a shot now, okay?" sounds like a choice, but in reality it isn't; the shot is going to be given, "okay" or not. Nevertheless, we can make a child feel less of a passive victim when we enlist his or her active cooperation, such as by saying: "We need you to hold really still for a minute."

And we need to be honest about pain, too. "Is it going to hurt, Mommy?" is a question no one likes to answer when it *is* going to hurt. At a time like that a helpful answer might be, "Yes, it will hurt, but the doctors and nurses will try to make the hurt go away as quickly as they can."

Having an Operation

The apprehension that most of us feel at the thought of having an operation tends to be a pervasive sense of vague alarm, and because it is not readily describable, it can be very difficult to deal with. But if we can (at least to some extent) identify our own feelings, it will be all the easier for us to help our children cope with theirs. As we try to come to grips with our fears as adults, we are likely to find that some of them are long shadows cast from our own childhoods. Once we understand that, we are much closer to understanding our children.

Is that old, old fear of separation part of what we feel? It almost certainly is. As *I* think about it, I focus on the specific separation that would take place as I was being wheeled out of my hospital room on a gurney and, in a strange place surrounded by strangers, *separated from consciousness*. I can imagine that trip to the elevator and into the operating room vividly because it's a trip I've taken before. I can see the rectangles of fluorescent light pass by above me. I feel helpless, strapped onto the cart, pushed along by someone I don't know and can only glimpse upside down, not in charge of anything that is about to happen to me. The pre-op shot has made me quiet and disoriented, but I can still feel an undercurrent of panic and a desperate, urgent need: *I want someone I love and trust right now!* The child who is still within me is crying. I can hear him ever so clearly screaming, *"I want my mom and dad!"* But neither mom nor dad, nor my wife, nor a son, nor even a trusted friend will be there right then. What comfort can I find?

That's worth thinking about when we wonder what comfort we can offer a child who is about to go through this experience. Memories will be somewhat different for each of us. But there's something I hear within myself that I believe is commonly shared: I find at least some comfort in having left someone I love at my hospital-room door, someone who has promised to wait for me and be there when I return. I can only guess why this should be comforting. Perhaps it's because it lets me look beyond the experience of unconsciousness to a time when it will be all over. Perhaps I somehow feel that though *I* will not be conscious, I will still be part of someone who *is*. Perhaps it is simply that I know there is someone nearby who cares. And perhaps it's all of these things as well as others I can't identify. But I know the thought is comforting.

The chances are that your child's surgeon will come to meet your child well before the time of the operation—possibly the day before. This is an important visit and one you should try to make sure takes place. In the videotape we made about having an operation, we showed such a visit. On our tape the surgeon explained to a little girl what she would see in the operating room. He talked about the bright lights, about the table she would lie on, and how everyone would be wearing green smocks and masks. (When I talk with children, I like to add that although the doctors and nurses will be wearing masks, "you'll still be able to see their kind eyes.") He explained that the little girl, too, would have a special mask to breathe through, and that the air in it would smell a little different because of the medicine that would put her to sleep, and keep her asleep, until the operation was over.

Some children have a real concern that they might wake up before they're supposed to, right in the middle of the operation. For most adults that fear may not be very strong, but that's only because adults can bring reason and logic and knowledge (and possibly experience) to bear on it. I can say to myself, "Millions and millions of operations take place and I've never heard of anyone waking up in the middle of one. Why should it happen to me? What's more, anesthesiologists are highly trained people who know what they're doing; of course they wouldn't let that happen!" But if you couldn't think these thoughts for yourself, as young children can't, you'd need someone you trusted to tell you these things in ways you could understand.

Our work with children has taught us to be very careful when we liken the effects of anesthesia to sleep. For one thing, the phrase "being put to sleep" may have associations with the death of a pet. For another, sleep is something children know people can wake up from anytime—especially if someone touches them. We've found it helpful to say something like, "The doctor will give you a special kind of medicine that will make you go to sleep. It's a medicine that keeps you asleep and you can't wake up until the doctor decides the operation is all over. Then you *will* wake up."

We shouldn't ever forget the waking-up part. Perhaps you can still feel a lingering doubt about that, too. I know I can.

Something many of us prefer not to confront straight on is the most obvious part of having an operation: the fact that someone is going to take a sharp knife and cut our body open. It's a rare person who does not feel squirmy at the thought—let alone at the sight on film. As I've mentioned before, uncertainties about our bodies—whether they can come apart, whether the insides can fall out, whether *all* our blood can leak away when the skin is broken—are universal anxieties of early childhood and ones we have to go on working through again and again. It's natural that having an operation should bring them right up to the surface once more. As adults, we have probably had many chances to work on these feelings, but an operation can come at a time in a young child's life when these fears are still new and urgent.

Hard as it may be, we need to be direct and honest about what an operation is. One explanation that we have found children can often understand and accept is: "An operation is a way for doctors to help people get well. It's a way for them to fix something that needs fixing on the inside." A child might ask you: "Are they going to cut me all open?" A helpful kind of response might be: "The doctors will make a little cut right where they need to. As soon as they've fixed what they need to fix, they'll close the cut back up. The cut will heal just the way other cuts and scrapes do." It's part of being honest to let a child know that there will be a hurt for a while after the operation is over. They are likely to feel better about that if they know beforehand that the hurt from an operation, like other hurts they have had, will get better every day.

There's one concern that I learned about only through my work, a feeling that our consultants confirmed is common to many children. It may seem strange to adults, but many children do fear that an operation will change who they are—that they will come back from the operating room a completely different person. Not all children have this worry, but it's a common enough fantasy for you to keep it in mind as you talk with and listen to your child.

Going to the Emergency Room

When an accident or high fever forces a sudden visit to a hospital emergency room, no one is likely to feel prepared for the event. It was this that led us to make a segment for *Mister Rogers' Neighborhood* on going to the emergency room—a segment we then packaged separately on videotape and now offer as part of the *Let's Talk About It* materials. We hope that, in time, this tape will find its way into many hospitals and schools and centers that serve children. We have already heard from several parents who told us it was very helpful when their children had accidents. The following letter tells about a child having an emergency experience *before* seeing our program:

> *Two days ago my four year old son fell off the sliding board in the playground at nursery school and broke his arm. We had a very harrowing day, going through both the Medical Center emergency room and the hospital emergency room, three sets of x-rays, shots, and eventually anesthesia and setting of the arm in a cast. Although I tried to explain what was going to happen and whether it would hurt or not, and even though he was very brave and courageous through most of the ordeal, by the end of it our son was frightened and crying.*
> *Yesterday I put on your show and we saw Queen Sara fall down and hurt her arm, and you took the children through the emergency room. Robin was very excited and said over and over that "I was there" and "That happened to me." It meant a great deal to him and I know it explained a lot of what happened in a way that was clear to him.*

Thinking and talking about a difficult experience is *such* a help in coming to terms with our feelings before, during, and after!

In the program we made, I show a local hospital's emergency department and talk with my "television friend" about such things as waiting in the waiting room, getting weighed and measured, having blood pressure and temperature measured in the triage room. I notice the sound of children crying and mention how it's okay to cry when you feel hurt and scared—that it isn't "just babies who cry."

I ask a doctor about X rays and we go into the X-ray room together to have a look. The doctor explains how the camera works, the need to stay still and to be alone for a moment, and the buzzing sound of the X ray being taken, and we look at an X-ray picture. Knowing how alarming all the X-ray equipment can be, we watch a boy having an X ray, to show that it doesn't hurt and that the camera doesn't even touch you. We also make a point of saying that although an X ray can show what needs fixing inside of you, it can't see your thoughts and feelings.

We talk about stitches. Another doctor explains stitches as "special sewing to hold the edges of a cut together more firmly." We certainly don't pretend that the anesthetic shot isn't going to hurt; we say that it can sting a whole lot but only for a short time, and that then the actual stitching doesn't hurt.

"Some children need help in staying still." That's how we present the "papoose board"—as a helpful device. I lie down on one and the doctor shows how the straps fasten. I say that I think it would be hard to remember to hold very still if you were scared and hurting, and that I suppose many people who come to the emergency department are feeling hurt and scared. "That's true, Mister Rogers," the doctor replies, "but the nice part about working here is that we have so many ways to help children get better."

And of course we emphasize that children do go home from an emergency room visit—as soon as they are well enough, and often the same day.

In that particular program we didn't deal with broken bones and casts because we had already done that on another tape in the *Let's Talk About It* series. It might be helpful for you to know the most important things we covered there:

- We emphasized that while bones can break, they also heal; they're *not* like a broken toy that can't be fixed.

- We explained that casts are a kind of hard bandage that helps people heal faster.

- We showed that it doesn't hurt to have a cast put on, but it might feel warm and heavy for a while.

- We said that casts do limit a person's motion, but added that there are still a lot of things a person in a cast *can* do.

- We showed what it's like to have a cast taken off and how the cast cutter makes a loud noise but *doesn't cut anything but the cast.*

- We let children know that the part of the body that was in the cast might feel stiff for a while but that the stiffness goes away.

All loving parents find it hard to see their children in pain and many of them have reactions they cannot control at the sight of a child's wound or broken limb. Doctors, of course, know this and tend to keep parents away from their hurt child at times that are likely to be particularly painful or difficult. We do need to be realistic about our limits, but so often a moment of crisis in our children's lives enables us to do more than we think we can. To the extent we can stay with a hurt child through the ordeal of medical procedures we should do so because nothing can replace a parent's presence, voice, and touch as sources of comfort.

A father told me of his trip to the emergency room with his six-year-old son, who had badly cut his hand. When the doctor came for him, the boy began howling and crying. "It will be all right," the doctor reassured the father. "It won't take long. Just wait right here." The doors swung shut behind the boy and the doctor. The father sat in the waiting room listening to his son's sobbing and screams of "No! No! Don't touch me! Don't touch me!"

Well, that father barged right into the room where his son was and, over the understandable protests of the doctor, insisted on staying next to his boy's head. He did explain that he wasn't squeamish and would stay out of the doctor's way, but made it very plain that this was exactly where he was going to be while the suturing took place. His presence didn't stop his son's hysterical screaming; nothing did until the local anesthetic took effect. To this day, that father doesn't know for sure how much comfort his presence really provided, but he does know, even ten years later, that the incident is one important component of his continuing close relationship with his son.

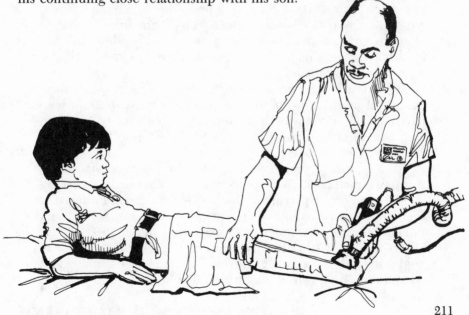

Hospitalization and Play

Encouraging children's play before and after important events in their lives is something that helps them understand and manage their feelings. Here, while we're talking about hospitalization, I want to underline the therapeutic value that playrooms in children's hospital units can have *during* a child's hospital stay.

I've found that not many adults know that these playrooms are often supervised by highly trained people. One such person, Mary Donnelly, was our chief consultant as we produced our *Let's Talk About It* materials about hospitalization. Mary, at the time, was director of the Children's Activities Department at Children's Hospital in Pittsburgh. She had earned a master's degree in child development and is now patient representative at Children's Hospital in Washington, D.C. Mary has worked with hospitalized children for more than ten years. Her experience has taught her that play in the hospital, like other forms of play, may look like a simple channeling of energy, but in fact "becomes a therapeutic situation when play helps the child to deal with the situation at hand."

Here's how Mary described her hospital's play program in Pittsburgh:

Its purpose is to provide a familiar and friendly environment in which children are made to feel welcome no matter what physical or emotional limitation the child has on a given day. Playrooms are designed to reflect this and provide enough space so that children can participate whether they are ambulatory or in a wheelchair, cart, stroller, or a bed. Moving from a hospital room to a playroom gives the child a feeling of mobility, a change of atmosphere, and an opportunity to join with other children in play activities which closely resemble those enjoyed at home or in nursery school.

To children who are feeling the effects of separation from home and family, a loss of routine or control over events, or who have fantasies about why they are sick or about what will happen to them, the playroom is one place where these feelings are recognized and understood.

In a typical playroom setting, one child may be vigorously painting a picture in vivid colors, while another may be dealing with separation by playing in the housekeeping corner or using the toy telephone. Another's energy level may only permit him to listen to a familiar story or to work on a simple puzzle. Still others may, at first, only wish to watch the other children or to hold a toy. All these reflect the choice the child has made and are appropriate levels of play which should be encouraged.

"Expressing feelings through play helps to make hospitalization an ego-building experience," says Mary, and as we worked together we came to agree that in addition to plenty of opportunity to talk and play, these are the things that hospitalized children need the most:

- They need to know what to expect.

- They need to know that there will always be someone they can trust nearby.

- They need to have their concerns and questions dealt with honestly.

- They need to have their feelings recognized and understood.

- They need to understand that they will return home as soon as the doctor decides they're well enough.

When it's time to go home, your child will undoubtedly be happy to go. For a while, though, life at home may not be quite the same as it was. Most children go on wanting extra attention, and it may even seem to you that your child has taken some steps backward in development—clinging to you, thumb sucking, or bed-wetting. Brothers and sisters may feel jealous of the recovering child and angry that he or she is still claiming more of your time than anyone else, particularly because they have already been putting up with your absences at the hospital. In most families, this period of readjustment is a necessary transition back to everyday normality and it can't be hurried. Everyone's feelings need time to even out. Plenty of talk and plenty of play will go on being good ways to help family life settle down. When it does, you may see in your recovered child signs of new mastery, strength, and independence. And you may find, as a family, new closeness and pride for having come through a difficult time together.

When a Parent Goes to the Hospital

As so often happens in our work at Family Communications, some of the best descriptions of the delights, sorrows, or uncertainties of being a parent come to us in letters. Here is one we received from a mother who, when she wrote, was facing a time of separation from her family because of an operation:

I will undergo elective surgery in two months. The hospital stay should be five to seven days. I am concerned about the separation from my children, Michael, almost 4, and Susan, one year old. Susan is a nursing baby. I can arrange to have a private room so that the kids can visit, and so Susan can nurse when she visits. However, I still feel that this is not enough. I don't think children really realize that mothers get sick or that mothers sometimes have to leave the home and family. I can only imagine what the baby will think when I am not at home for several days. I'm particularly worried about how she'll react at night when she can't snuggle in bed and nurse.

When I was pregnant with Susan, I felt so proud of my preparation for her arrival. Michael knew all the terminology and even visited the obstetrical ward and nursery with me. He stayed home with Daddy and other family so as not to feel displaced or confused while I was hospitalized. He visited me several times, and we spoke on the phone when he awakened and at bedtime. However, he did sob over the phone and once refused to come up to my room from the lobby. I thought, though, that we were communicating our feelings quite well. Several months later, however, Michael suddenly said that he never really believed that I was coming home again.

There's so much to think about in that letter, and one of the strongest feelings I get from it is that Michael and Susan have very caring parents who truly strive to understand children's needs.

The separation that will come during that time of hospitalization *is* going to be hard on everyone. What a difficult time it will be for the mother, as she adds her anxieties about her children to the loneliness of her separation from her husband and all the worries she is bound to have about herself. The children's father is going to have his hands full with his work, and his head will be full of the concerns about looking after a small child and a nursing baby and arranging help for the times when he's at work or at the hospital. I'd like to think there might be a grandparent nearby.

Michael, at four, already has a lot of feelings to work on just because he is four (see Chapter 3). He's only recently experienced a similar separation, *and*, what's more, has been sorting out how he feels about having a baby sister. He may be feeling very competitive with his father right now and extra-protective of his mother.

As for Susan—she may just be beginning to understand that she really *is* a separate person from her mother, but it's still going to be a new understanding. On top of that she will have to start a transition to bottle feeding, and make that change *without* the familiar encirclement of her mother's body, with its comforting sights and sounds and smells.

Are these children at risk? I trust that they're not, but they are facing one more of life's challenges. Growing through them began for these children at their birth, as it does for all of us, and that process will continue all their lives, even as it's continuing for you and me right now.

I feel confident that Michael and Susan *will* grow through their mother's hospitalization, because it's clear to me that they have parents who will let them know what to expect, who will be honest with them, who will offer loving support, and who know the value of talking about feelings. Michael was able to tell his mother that he had never really believed she was coming home from the hospital the first time she was there. That's something that almost every child must wonder about, particularly those children who may have known or heard of someone who did not come home from the hospital. But Michael's mother told him she'd be home and she did come home. She'll tell him again this time, and although he'll be sad and maybe even angry about her absence, I think he'll find his separation from her more manageable this time around.

Accidents and illnesses are part of almost everyone's life and so, too, are pain and fear and separation from the people we love. We may never be able to prepare our children fully for times like hospitalization, but we can certainly care enough to try. Feeling cared for and cared about is one of the very best ways to feel prepared for *anything*.

CHAPTER 10:

VERY HARD TIMES

There are times when going away is followed quite naturally by coming back, but there are other times when this is not so. It's three such times—moving to a new home, divorce, and death—that I'd like to think about now.

Moving, divorce, and death are, of course, very different kinds of experiences one from another; but whether it's a home, a family structure, or a loved person, the loss is for good, the grief can be profound, and it may include a good deal of anger at having had something taken away, as well as sadness that it's gone.

Life's circumstances are likely to confront us with losses of many different kinds even when we're very young. It may be "only" the loss of a treasured teddy bear or soft blanket, but we need to remember that the word "only" is one *adults* use: That kind of loss at an age when a child feels the bear or blanket to be an important part of himself or herself can seem a very serious loss indeed. How parents respond to their children's early losses is going to become really important to them as they grow. If we can bring our children understanding, comfort, and belief in a brighter time ahead when they need this kind of support, then they are more likely to grow into adults who can find these resources within themselves later on.

For a child, moving through life within a family may be a little like being in an airplane: There may be a lot of rough weather outside, and the plane may shake around quite a bit, but inside you're safe. Sad, scared, and angry, perhaps, but within the special atmosphere of a loving family, even these feelings are safe. When a child learns to trust that there is a loving caregiver right there to help in rough times, he or she can weather most any storm—and ultimately be stronger for the experience.

Moving

Compared to those of a great many families, the moves that my family has had to make have been few and without more than the usual amount of stress that any move is likely to bring. When our sons were three and one, we moved to Canada for a year and then moved back to Pittsburgh, where we had been living, into the house we had left. A year or so later we changed houses, but within the same general neighborhood, and there we stayed for the next seventeen years. So, for most of our working lives and for most of our children's growing up, we were settled and close to our roots and to many of our relatives. I'm grateful for that stability and full of admiration for the many, many families who have learned to cope with frequent uprootings from close friends, family, and places where they were happy.

It's hard to find the typical moving story, but all the families we have talked with found their experiences with a move to be difficult, hectic, and to some degree disorienting. A few had really unpleasant memories and recalled their times on the move as nightmares of physical and emotional strain. Most, though, found that they were able to cope with their moves and looked on them as more of life's inevitable challenges—not that they were necessarily easy or welcome events. Almost all parents we talked with worried about the effects of the move on their children. Would they be able to adjust to a new place, a new school, new friends? How would they be affected by having to leave the places and people they had come to know?

I've been fortunate to work with many friends and colleagues who really care about the way people grow. I have learned much from them! One such friend is Linda Philbrick. Some years ago Linda and I helped start a children's center together. She now teaches child development in New York State, where she lives with her husband and two sons. Linda has a great deal of firsthand knowledge about moving, and it's clear she has grown through the many moves she has experienced. She has also thought a great deal about what a move means to children, and we asked her to write some of her thoughts so that you could share them. I hope her firsthand account will be helpful to you and your family if and when it's your turn to make a move.

As the daughter of a civil engineer, I moved often as I was growing up. Until I was almost six, we never lived in one place for more than a year—and we moved four more times after that. "Home" was a series of interesting places, including a house on stilts at the edge of a jungle in Panama and a tin-roofed bungalow in the smoldering heat of the Indian Punjab.

My family approached each new move with a spirit of adventure, eagerly looking forward to the stimulating experiences that were a part of our mobile life. We read history, explored museums, met fascinating people, and had fun together. And yet each time I had to leave a place that had become familiar and comfortable, I experienced a deep, aching sense of loss, as if somehow part of me had to be left behind.

Integrating those losses into my personality was an essential task for me in early adulthood, and trying to understand what moving means to children has been a fundamental part of my own search for self-understanding.

It may help to understand how deeply a child can feel disrupted by a move to know that a child's earliest awareness of *self* is interwoven with the awareness of his or her surrounding world [see Chapter 2]. As children get a little older, they may

form a deep and intimate attachment to an object—a blanket, perhaps, or a teddy bear. We think we now know that these objects are another important part of children's growing understanding of "me" and "not me." These objects are in between. Or, more accurately, perhaps, they are *both*: a part of the outer world that, through touch and taste and feelings of comfort, are also part of the inner "me." Children may feel the same way about rooms and particular pieces of furniture (my very own bed, the chair where Daddy sits). And so we come back to the effects of moving, an event which separates children from familiar people and things. A move may be a potential disruption to a child's very sense of self. In *The Widening World of Childhood* Lois Murphy includes a description of the feelings of a three-year-old whose family was moving from Kansas to Iowa: "Molly's self-feeling seemed to be intense at this point and seemed to be connected with everything she had been a part of or felt close to—she seemed to think of losing her room almost as if it were part of her body; she did not want to give it up to anyone else."

When the object which the child feels particularly close to cannot be taken along, as Molly's room could not, the sense of disruption can be severe. However, when the object is portable and can be taken along, it may play a very important role in helping a child feel he or she belongs in a new location. I saw this happen with one of my own children, and by seeing it in him, I came to understand that a similar process had happened to me also.

When Whitney was eighteen months old, his father and I both completed graduate school and we moved from Pittsburgh to Poughkeepsie, New York. At the time of the move, Whitney clung tenaciously to either me or his father at all times, and insisted on keeping the other in sight. He wasn't taking any chances that either parent would go away without him. In the first days in the new house, Whitney at least had his "very own crib" because we had brought it with us, lashed to the top of our tiny car. Even so, he would only fall asleep in my arms in a borrowed rocking chair. Even with our constant attention he cried a great deal and was generally miserable—and so were we.

But his behavior changed dramatically when the moving van arrived and the furniture from our former home was carried into the new house. Whitney greeted a carved Victorian sofa, covered in yellow velvet, with a crow of delight. His few words were clearly inadequate to the occasion, but the inflections of his babbling made it obvious that this was a reunion with an old and important friend: "How are you? You don't know how I've missed you! I'm so glad you're here!" The sofa was indeed an old friend. It had been one of his favorite objects since early infancy. It had shared in all the developmental milestones of his first year. He used to get stuck under it in the process of learning to crawl (which, at first, he did backward). He learned to stand by pulling himself up against it. Soon he learned to climb up into it and then to walk back and forth along the seat, "talking" to it and poking his fingers in and out of the holes and scrolls of the elaborately carved back.

That sofa had deep symbolic meaning for Whitney. Besides having shared in so many of his important achievements, it also was the place where I had sat and held him and the place where, later, he had gone by himself to enjoy the feeling of being held. As we watched him clamber all over it in the new house, we realized that its presence was a real reaffirmation of his sense of self. Whitney had a lot more feelings about the move to work out, but from the time the sofa arrived he was much more comfortable and began taking his first emotional steps toward accepting his new home.

For my part, I knew that one of the first steps I had to take was to find an Oriental rug for the living room. Looking back now, I know why this was so important to me: My mother was always picking up rugs wherever we went—Chinese rugs, Indian rugs, Iranian rugs. She used to laugh and say, "I'm just like a bedouin tribeswoman. I just roll up rugs and when I get where I'm going I unroll them again." It was a good description; we children used to say that if we had to wait in a train station more than an hour, mother could make it feel like home. So when I came to making a home, I, too, needed a rug.

But although I've scarcely ever seen an Oriental rug I didn't like, I couldn't find one for our new house in Poughkeepsie. We went to Syracuse and Rochester and New York, and we had several rugs sent to the house to try out. None seemed quite right... until the day we were watching some men flipping over rugs at a sale at Sloane's. A flip—and there it was, unmistakably, the one I had to have. And so the rug came home. When a friend suggested that for the price of the rug I could have furnished the entire room (which was still empty except for the rug and the Victorian sofa), I just said to her: "It doesn't bother me. I really like it."

Not long after, my mother came to visit, and I proudly showed her my prize. I told her how long we'd looked and how I'd known, instantly, that this was the one. She gave me a knowing smile and said: "It's so much like the rug you grew up on. Take a good look next time you come home." I did, and sure enough, it was as close a copy as you could ever expect to find. My mother's rug, like the grandfather's clock in the song, was "bought on the morn of the day I was born" from refugees in Panama and was on the floor of all nine or ten homes where I grew up. As I learned to crawl over its brightly patterned surface, its color and design had become firmly imprinted on my memory—but on such an early layer of memory that, twenty-five years later, I couldn't have recalled them if I had tried. That early memory

MISTER ROGERS TALKS WITH PARENTS

surfaced, though, in feelings of comfort and warmth and security when I saw its near-duplicate. That pattern was backdrop to so many of my early achievements, but it was more than part of my childhood. It was part of *me*.

I know full well the dangers of generalizing from one's own experience, but I believe that these kinds of experiences are commonplace in this society where we shed houses and neighborhoods like snakes shed their skins. There may be no way for most of us to get at the roots of the strong feelings that accompany moving, but we should at least know that those feelings are real and that they are important. There are many ways we can deal with these feelings, too, but all I'd like to suggest here is the way that I have come to believe is the most important of all: We and our children can work on our feelings together. Parents tend, naturally, to worry about how they can best help their children through a difficult time. Too seldom they acknowledge the importance of their own feelings and often overlook the help they have available from the children they are concerned about.

Looking back on my experiences, I'm reminded of the help I got from a four-year-old Japanese boy who joined a nursery school class that I was teaching in the children's center that Fred Rogers and I helped to start. The boy's name was Isao, and he came from Japan speaking no English. Only a few weeks after arriving in this country, he found himself away from his family during a large part of the day. He had to cope not only with a strange culture, but also with the unfamiliar environment of an American nursery school. Isao spent a lot of time those first days in the block corner building things, but he was only able to play when I sat beside him in a chair. The content of his play seemed so emotionally charged for him that he was able to play only in the presence of an adult he was beginning to trust.

I'm sure that any teacher would have had certain childhood experiences that would have helped her understand Isao's feelings. For me, as I watched Isao struggle with the blocks to build an airplane, the symbol of his transition from one culture to another, I found myself once again overwhelmed by the feelings I had as a child when we moved from the United States to India. I remembered forcefully the barriers of the strange language and the strange culture, and I remembered, too, how hard it had been to come back home again to a country where I no longer really felt at home.

Being the teacher of all the children in that nursery school, I often had to leave Isao's side. When I was not with him, he stopped his play. Sometimes he would come to me, take me by the hand, and lead me to the chair in the block corner so that he could get on with the serious work he had to do. Since we had no language in common, I couldn't speak to him, but we communicated easily in the shared language of play. Those times with him were important for me; I knew his play was helping me understand better what the difficult times in my childhood had meant to me. Again and again memories surfaced that I thought had vanished forever. I reexperienced events and places, I was flooded with sights and sounds and feelings from so long ago. And by the time Isao had begun to settle in, had learned to say "juice" and "o.k.," my own early moves had become a more comfortable part of me, too.

Moving to a new home will always be a stressful event for a family, but talking about how you feel about it, as well as helping children express how *they* feel, can do a lot to keep a feeling of family togetherness just when everything seems to be flying apart. Encouraging children to play about the move, to draw pictures about it, or to collect old snapshots for a scrapbook of the place you're leaving—all these are activities that can be helpful to both of you. Finding time for these kinds of activities in the midst of those frantic days when there are 1,001 details to attend to is never easy. Some of these activities can be done once you have decided to tell your children about the move and before the hectic time begins. But even in the midst of chaos, it is necessary to create short spaces of time away from the packing, the boxes, and the lists, when each of you can work on keeping your sense of "self" intact and your shared feeling of "family" healthy and strong.

Stressful times often bring opportunities for growth. Through a move, our children can learn so much about separation and togetherness, regrets and expectations, about saying good-bye to someone familiar and saying hello to someone new. A move can be a chance for us to help them develop coping skills they will call on throughout their lives. And as for ourselves, we can benefit from one of the constant rewards of living and working with children: They give us a chance to relive certain times in our own early development. By helping a child grow through experiences that are hard, we move closer to the resolution of our own unfinished issues of growing up.

What Linda writes has so much meaning for all difficult times and for so many different kinds of growth. Her own ability to cope with all those moves and later help others was enhanced by the good feelings she felt from the people she loved best. Children pick up on and share

MISTER ROGERS TALKS WITH PARENTS

their parents' emotions. If parents feel optimistic and enthusiastic about a move, then the chances are that their children will share that enthusiasm and optimism, even though they may have sad and angry feelings as well.

I'm not suggesting that we hide our true feelings from our children by pretending to feel something we don't. If we feel no enthusiasm for a move, if all we feel is sad and angry, then we need to let our children know that—and work on those feelings together. Above all, we need to let our children know that they are not the cause of our upset, that they are loved, and that together the whole family can try to make the best of a bad situation.

I talked with one family not long ago who were facing a move from Pittsburgh to the West Coast. The father was an intern at a hospital here, and now he was going out to a strange place to open his own practice. He was frankly apprehensive about taking that big step in his career. Pat and Karen had made good friends in Pittsburgh. As Karen put it, "We're leaving things behind reluctantly... but, we feel, for the better."

As 've talked, it seemed to me that they were trying to handle their move in very constructive ways. For one thing, they had decided to make the actual move itself as pleasurable as possible—to regard it as an opportunity for a kind of family vacation.

They'd decided not to spend whole days driving, but to drive in the mornings and then take the afternoons off to do something together. "We want to camp and see things," Pat explained. "We may never drive back to the East Coast again, and it's such an opportunity if you can take the time to go to the Grand Canyon or whatever, to make it a vacation as opposed to 'something you have to go through.'" Karen added, "We'd like to leave Ian and Domenic with the feeling that the trip out was a pleasure, that it was done slowly and gave them enough time to adapt, so that when we get there they're not exhausted mentally and physically and unready to do the things we'll have to do."

Even while looking for the good things a move west might bring, Pat and Karen were realistic and accepting of their own feelings and those of their children. Pat had this piece of advice for parents in the same situation:

"When you talk about leaving and the sadness that you feel, I think it's important to communicate to the child that the sadness is natural and it's okay to feel that way. Don't deny the sad feelings. Sometimes it's easy to go too far the other way and make it all sound like a great thing and that feeling sad is wrong. It's very natural to feel sad and all of us are going to feel sad. We've told our kids that if they feel like crying when we drive out of the driveway for the last time, it's okay to cry, and those are perfectly natural feelings."

Karen remembered a dinner-time conversation about friendships. "Ian was asking about leaving his friends," she told me. "He was saying that he didn't want to leave his friends. He liked them and he wanted them to be his friends forever. I think one of the things you can say to a child is that just because you leave a friend, it doesn't mean he's not your friend anymore. You can communicate with letters or maybe a phone call. Even if you don't keep contact, you still can feel the friendship you felt with that friend. That seemed to help at the time, because I think for children, making friends is probably the major thing in their minds."

Something else Karen said struck me as really important. "I think that even after we've gotten out there and begun to settle down, there will still be feelings of loss and feelings of insecurity. I guess the job isn't over once you've arrived. There's lots left to do." That's so true. There's always lots left to do with the feelings we have about any loss, and we go on working through them again and again as we go on growing and facing new experiences.

Pat was reflecting on the uncertainties of his own future at the time. "There's a need now to make a change of my own," he said. "I've got to get out and set up practice. There are lots of things about that you'd just as soon not face, just as soon not have to deal with. But you can't not deal with them. And I guess that just like Ian and Domenic will get support from Karen and me and each other, I'll be looking for support, solace, and familiarity from them. There will be an awful lot of things we have to do when we move out there. What we hope to do is communicate to the kids that it's possible to make a change like that."

When the members of a family are supporting one another the way Pat and Karen and Ian and Domenic are, it *is* possible to make big changes in life.

Divorce

For a couple with young children, divorce seldom comes as a "solution" to stress, only as a way to end one form of pain and accept another. I have heard from many divorced people how they experienced a feeling of near-total rejection—from their own parents, from relatives, friends, society, and even the church. Most, though, were fortunate enough to have *someone* to lean on, and many were brave enough to seek out a professional caregiver (i.e., minister, rabbi, psychologist, pastoral counselor, psychiatrist) when they feared their own emotional resources were not up to the job of coping. For almost all these people, the feeling of failure was a major part of their anguish—not just failure as a partner in a particular relationship, but failure as a person. On top of that came a nearly overwhelming load of guilt—not only for their responsibility for an unhappy relationship, but for making a decision that they feared would ruin their children's lives forever.

So many people wonder, "Why did I get married in the first place? Why in the world did I do this? Why did I put myself and my children through it?"

But deep and dark misery was only part of these people's stories. A woman told me how divorce brought her to the verge of a nervous breakdown, how there were times when she couldn't get up from the couch and couldn't see any point in doing so. "I was in such pain," she said, "and my children could see that I was, and I could tell them I was, but that's as far as I could go." Then she added: "It took a while before we could all communicate our pain to one another. But that brought us closer."

Another woman told me how much she had come to hate herself during her divorce. "I doubted everything about who I was," she said. "I thought I had been a phony to myself, a liar. I was angry at myself for the years I'd wasted, for how dishonest I thought I was, for how unaware I was. I went through all that self-hatred." Then she went on: "But I hung in there. You can't help but learn about yourself, and I really did...and I have a feeling I'm going to keep learning."

A man I talked with said that during his divorce he felt that the bottom of his own private universe was falling out. He could remember days when he wondered how he managed just to put one foot in front of the other. "You just do it," he said, "and then you look back over time and wonder how you did it." Later he remarried, choosing someone with whom he could talk about those bad times, someone who could "understand that over the years, as you continue to grow in your adulthood, you continually rework these things."

Earl Grollman is a nationally known family counselor, a rabbi and educator, and a special friend of mine. It was encouraging to hear someone with his long experience confirm that the despair of divorce does not last forever, that out of it can come growth and compassion. He is firmly convinced that even in the midst of great pain we need not lose hope. Divorcing husbands and wives, Earl says, "go from a we-relationship to an I-relationship, and they feel like half a person. And then, after perhaps two years, they begin to understand that 'I can still be a person even though I'm no longer married. I am still a parent, I am still a loving person, and I can give love in return to my family.'" They can also learn, as I know Earl agrees, that they are still lovable, too.

As I think about conversations I've had with people involved in divorce, four major things come to mind.

The first is that in order to be able to help our children, we have to be able to help ourselves. Part of this means being neither too judgmental about ourselves nor too demanding of our emotional strengths. Even though it may be natural to feel both failure and guilt, it is very important to be forgiving of ourselves, too. Some people attempt to go through a divorce with a constant "stiff upper lip." Divorce brings pain and anger and sadness. Pretending that those feelings are not there doesn't fool anyone and certainly not ourselves. I believe feeling the pain, venting the anger within healthy limits, and openly grieving is an important part of the healing process for adults as well as children.

Earl Grollman once told me, "I think the most we can give our children, if they are going through a divorce, is the right to *feel*." One of the best ways to give our children that right is, first, to give it to ourselves. For instance, the parent might say, "I am going through some difficult times. When you see me upset, just know that way down deep I love you and the upset isn't caused by you." When our children see us expressing our emotions, they can learn that their own feelings are natural and permissible, can be expressed, and can be talked about. That's an important thing for *all* children to learn.

Many people have also found that a good way to help themselves is to try to be open to help from others. Most found it hard at first, but the more they shared their thoughts with accepting, trusted "others," the better they seemed to feel. Children, relatives, and friends can all help remind us that we are still lovable... and capable of loving.

Professional counseling can be very helpful, even though the decision to seek it may be difficult. Some people think that seeking professional help is an admission of weakness, but I don't believe that's true. In my experience it's usually the strong and the emotionally healthy who can seek—and accept—help when they need it. And *everybody* needs help sometimes!

Something that I hear over and over again is that children think *they* are the cause of the divorce. Young children may think a divorce happens because they are bad. Or because they actually wished, one day when Daddy was angry, that Daddy would go away and never come back. (Children, naturally, seldom talk about these fantasies, and un-talked-about fantasies that actually "come true" can become a serious psychological burden for years.)

Divorce is a grown-up problem. Our children are not responsible for making it happen. There are many things children accept as "grown-up things" over which they have no control and for which they have no responsibility—for instance, weddings, having babies, buying houses, and driving cars. Parents who are separating really need to help their children put divorce on that grown-up list, so that children do not see themselves as the cause of their parents' decision to live apart.

Something else that most people involved in divorce tell me is important: Children need a lot of help understanding which relationships are changed by a divorce and, more important, which are *not*. A young girl told me that she was afraid that the divorce in her family would mean she wouldn't have her grandparents anymore. One little boy wondered whether, if he stayed with his mother, his dog would have to go live with his dad. One mother found it helpful to sit down with her daughter and go through all the roles her little girl had: daughter, sister, niece, granddaughter, friend, and so forth. As she did, they were able to talk about which relationships the divorce would change and how, and which would stay the same. She was able to start helping her daughter understand that while men and women may decide to stop being husbands and wives, they *never* stop being mothers and fathers. Or grandmothers and grandfathers. Or aunts or uncles or friends. And that although Mommy and Daddy don't love each other anymore, they both still love their daughter, just as they always had and always would, and that they would go on working *together* to look after her.

Supporting the ongoing relationships in a child's life, the relationships that bring love, care, and nurturance, is probably one of the best ways to help a child weather a divorce.

Several parents have told me about the damage that can be done by speaking badly of the ex-spouse, whom the child still loves and needs. One woman in her late twenties recalled how, when her parents divorced and she was only eight, her mother kept her from seeing her father—and how much that hurt. He was evidently a very fine man. "If I had had the chance at the time to see my father every weekend," she said, "it would have just been a blessing, an absolute blessing." And she added: "To deprive a child of that, an adult must have a great amount of hatred—not just for the father, but for the child."

Thoughtful, sensitive people don't seem to find it easy to talk about their experiences with a divorce, and almost everyone I've met has recalled how very hard it was to talk about it at the time—especially to their children. Nevertheless, one final thing seems sure: Children, even though they need only limited explanations of why the divorce occurred, do need to know what to expect in the future. Parents need to reassure their children on these points *repeatedly*.

It's often hard to know what a child under stress needs to hear, and when we are under stress it can be hard even to find any words at all. Many people who work with children have found it useful to answer a child's question about something difficult with a question of their own—one that lets them know what the child is really concerned about. A child undergoing surgery might ask: "How are they going to take my tonsils out?" and it might be useful to ask in reply, "How do *you* think they're going to take them out?" One little boy I know answered that question by saying, "They're going to take a knife and cut my neck all open." As soon as his parents understood his scary fantasy, they were able to calm his anxiety with the much more reassuring reality of what was going to happen.

The same can hold true when children ask questions about a divorce. "Why did Daddy go away?" might be the occasion to ask, "Why do *you* think Daddy went away?" If the answer is, "Because I was bad," or "Because he doesn't love us anymore," the adult is in a better position to provide the responses that the child really needs to hear. That's why on *Mister Rogers' Neighborhood* I often sing "I Like to Be Told" (see page 186). It speaks to the needs of everyone. Knowing what's ahead helps us prepare for things by thinking about them, and for children, by *playing* about them (see Chapter 5). "What you don't know can't hurt you" is *not* always true. One eleven-year-old boy was sent across the country to "visit his grandmother"—a visit that became extended to an entire year. When he finally came home, he found that his parents had been divorced and that he was expected to live with his mother, who was now involved with another man. His well-meaning parents had wanted to spare him the unhappiness of the divorce. Instead, they gave him an emotional shock that left scars for years.

At the time of a divorce almost all children wonder, "Who is going to look after me?" and "Where am I going to live?" Children who are left to wonder about these very basic things are likely to make up their own fantasy answers, which may be a lot scarier than the truth. Even when these kinds of details may be uncertain, a child can find comfort by simply knowing that the family is going to work out these things together, that "there will always be someone to take care of you, and we'll let you know as soon as we've decided what we're going to do."

But even with simple answers to simple questions, children may need to hear them again and again. Particularly at stressful times, a child may not be able to "hear" what we're saying the first time we say it. And just as children find pleasure in hearing, over and over, the same scary story that ends well, they may find increasing comfort in having you talk often about what may seem to them to be a scary future.

I am grateful to all the people who have talked with us and written to us about their divorces. For many, it was truly painful to relive what they had been through, but they were willing to reexperience their hurts and their tears in the hope that someone else might find the agony of divorce a little more manageable. A true expression of caring!

I think that most people want to have a perfect life for themselves and their children. They certainly don't want their families ever to have to go through the tragedy of divorce. Yet when it is inevitable, there *are* people who care and who can help, and there are loving ways to help children as one human being brings strength and support to another.

The work our company does with families, not only through *Mister Rogers' Neighborhood* but now through the many different materials we produce for both adults and children, often makes me very proud to be human. Again and again I have seen people in great emotional or physical pain, and I am repeatedly amazed by the courage they can find in adversity. Not by being stalwart and seemingly untouched by circumstance, but by having the courage to *be*, fully, and the courage to *feel*, and the courage to reach out for help and keep on going, putting one foot in front of the other until times get better again.

Death

My first recollection of anyone close to me dying is when I was six years old. My Grandfather Rogers worked as a plant engineer in a steel company and was a very strong man. He died very suddenly. It had never occurred to me that such a strong person would ever die.

I was his only grandson, and he always told me he wanted to take me fishing, but he never got to.

I remember how still he looked as he lay in his casket, but what I remember most clearly about Grandfather Rogers' dying was my own father's crying. It was the same day I saw the open casket in the living room, and I had gone upstairs to the bathroom when I saw Dad in the hall with tears streaming down his face. I don't think I had ever seen him cry before. I'm glad I did see him, though, because many years later, when he died, I cried; and way down deep I knew he would have said it was all right.

As I write this, I feel my connection with all of the many relationships of my life. All four of my grandparents and both my parents have died, but I know now that as long as I live some qualities of each of them— those qualities I have chosen—will always be a part of the person I am. That feeling of connection can come upon us unexpectedly. I remember that one day, when I was an adolescent making my own teenage efforts to be someone in my own right (someone separate from my parents), all of a sudden I started to cry about Grandfather Rogers dying. I don't know what sparked it, what sudden juncture of feeling and circumstance and recollection, but I cried. And just now I looked up from my writing to a favorite painting that hangs on my office wall. Up until this very minute I thought the reason I liked it so much was simply that it's an appealing picture of a child and it was painted by a friend. Those *are* reasons I like it, but it has just now come to me what "inner drama" that picture has evoked all these years: The painting shows a six-year-old boy back from a fishing trip, with a rod in his left hand and a fish in his right. At least in my fantasy, Grandfather Rogers can take me fishing.

My mother's father, Fred Brooks McFeely, was in his eighties when he died. I was working in New York, and I flew home to see him when the doctors told my mother he was dying. I was sad that he didn't even know who I was by the time I got to his bedside, but he told me about "a grandson" of his who was working in television in New York, and he sounded very proud. He was always "Ding-Dong" to me—a nickname that stuck after the day he taught me the nursery rhyme, "Ding, Dong, Bell."

As a youngster, I loved Sunday afternoons at Ding-Dong's farm. I was a city boy and used to a fairly formal life, which meant keeping things neat and in place. The farm had old stone walls running around it, and I wanted more than anything to be allowed to climb them and walk along their winding tops. When I was eight, Ding-Dong let me do it—over the protests of my parents. "If the boy wants to climb the stone walls," he said to my mother and father, "then let him climb the stone walls. He has to learn to do things for himself." I had the time of my life. My delight was obvious, and Ding-Dong shared it.

"Fred," he said, "you made this day a special day by being yourself. Always remember there's just one person in this world like you...and I like you just the way you are!"

I did remember that, and I pass that message on to my television friends each time I make a new program for *Mister Rogers' Neighborhood*. When we produced our series, *Old Friends...New Friends*, we even recreated that afternoon at the farm when I climbed the stone walls. A lot of what I've tried to work through in my own life has become material for programs. Some of my richest experiences have come out of the most painful times—times that were the hardest to believe could ever turn into anything positive. Everybody goes through times like that. And when we're going through them, we wonder if they will ever end. It's harder than ever to be available to our children at such times— to talk with them, to listen to them, and to provide the kinds of comfort *they* need.

If we have been able to prepare our children for death before a serious loss occurs in their lives, it's likely to be easier to cope when such a time comes. Plants die and can give us a chance to explain that when they do, they won't grow or bloom anymore. A pet bird may die and you can help your child understand that it won't breathe or move anymore. It might be an opportunity to say that when bodies are dead they are often buried in the ground, and that's what you might even choose to do with the body of your pet bird.

Your child may hear of someone's death in another family and suddenly realize that people die, also, and that you might even die, too. "Will you die, Mommy?" is a question that most children ask sooner or later. "Yes, I will," we might say, "but not for a long, long time, and I

hope to be here just as long as you need me." The questions may continue: "But if you did, who would look after me?" And of course that's the major question for a child—a child who naturally does need to be taken care of.

A colleague of ours, Hedda Sharapan, has made talking with children about death one of her special interests and skills. Her own father died not long ago, and she has two young children. Because of her experiences, we asked Hedda to write down what she thinks is most important in talking with young children about death, and I'd like to include her voice in our "conversation":

When my father died my two daughters were four and seven. I had already begun working professionally on the subject of talking with young children about death, but that time was still painful and difficult for me because it was *my* father's death and *my* children. I remember many moments when I was uncertain about how to answer their questions, or when I wondered what was the wise way to include them in the funeral rites. How often I wished for magic words that would make everything all right for them, that would make them smile again! I learned more from that experience than I could ever have learned from conferences or from books. In retrospect I see that it was often my children who were my best teachers. When I was open to them, by sharing some of my feelings and encouraging them to communicate their thoughts, they helped me know what they needed.

Sometimes, in trying to anticipate our children's pain and sadness, we tend to want to protect them, even to the point of not wanting to tell them about a death in the family. "Jeffrey's only two and a half," one mother explained. "He really wouldn't understand what it's all about." Another mother felt that her daughter would be overwhelmed by the news of a grandparent's death. "Cheryl loved her grandmother so much," she told me. "It would crush her to know that she died." Though the decision not to tell a child is understandable, we do have to ask whether it is really in the child's best interests.

Children's sensitivity to "vibes" is extremely keen. At a time of sadness in a family there are so many facial cues, so many disrupted schedules, new people coming and going, lots of conversations to overhear, and a general aura that clearly states something important is going on. Even if a young child is sent off to stay with a friend or neighbor, the chances are that he or she will know that this sudden visit is because something important has happened at home. Feelings of exclusion can be much harder for children than feelings of sadness. Not only does exclusion bring a sense of rejection, but it can also result in children misinterpreting what is going on. Uncertainty can arouse anxiety.

We need to remember that when there are unanswered questions (or even unspoken ones), children will find their own fantasy explanations. Often these fantasies are scarier than reality. One child who did not understand about burial decided that her grandfather's body had been placed in the attic, and that was why the attic was a forbidden place to play. It may well be, then, that one of the best kinds of "protection" we can give children is to provide them with simple and straightforward answers to their questions and ample opportunities to let us know what questions they have. It is precisely because young children don't understand what death is all about that they especially need us to talk about it with them.

It's not unusual for children to ask the same kinds of questions again and again before the answers become real to them. This can be especially true in a child's attempt to understand the finality of death. The young son of our neighbor helped bury a pet fish not long ago. A few days later, he peered closely at the several remaining fish in the tank and asked: "Which is the one that died?" Asking the same question again and again allows the child to test the answer and gradually understand.

Some years ago on *Mister Rogers' Neighborhood* we produced a program that dealt with the death of a goldfish, and Hedda was on our staff when we made it. As I go to feed the fish in the aquarium on that program, I notice that one fish is lying on the bottom of the fish tank. I try to revive it, but I can't. I explain that it's dead—that it can't breathe or swim or move anymore. Wrapping it up in a piece of paper, I take it outside to the garden and bury it. As I'm doing so, I tell about a time when I was little and a dog I loved—Mitzi—died. I talk about how sad I felt, and how I cried, and how my dad told me we'd have to bury her body. I didn't want to; I wanted to go on pretending she was alive. But we did bury Mitzi. I tell my "television friend" how I used to play with a stuffed toy dog after that, pretending it would die and come alive again, die and come alive again, over and over, and that little by little my sadness grew less. Mitzi became part of my memories, and I show my friend a snapshot of her.

In the make-believe part of that program, the trolley won't work anymore. It's just off its tracks, but some of the puppets worry that it's dead—until their friends help them understand that things that aren't alive can't die.

What we are saying there, gently, is that whatever *is* alive *does* die.

The response we received to that program was really encouraging:

• One mother wrote, "My son was very attached to a cat who died. He never realized that his cat would not come back. . . . Since that program he has been much happier with our present cat. The show explained a difficult experience and the feelings involved as well."

• A three-year-old asked his mother to tell us: "When your fish died I told Mommy I missed my grandpa and I knew my grandma was very lonely. God gave him a new body in a special place people can be when their bodies die, but fishes and bodies that don't live anymore can help make new flowers grow."

• The widow of an astronaut told me that she had watched the program with her daughters in Houston, and after the program was over, the girls were able to talk with her for the first time about the tragic accident in which their father died.

I waited a long time before I felt I was ready to produce that program, and once I did, it turned out to be a very personal expression. Much of my creative drive at the time came, I'm sure, from the grief I was feeling over the death of a dear friend, Emilie Jacobson. Emilie often worked with us in the days of *The Children's Corner* and then again in the early years of *Mister Rogers' Neighborhood.* She was our "poetry lady," who read and wrote poems for us. In those hectic days we didn't have the luxury of taping the programs ahead of time and editing when we wanted. Emilie was short and stocky, with gray hair and a very British accent and a magnificent sense of humor. What a trouper she was!

Emilie helped us all to feel good about who we were, and of course that kind of friend is the toughest kind to lose. She often quoted a poem by the late American writer, Douglas Malloch, and it became her trademark. Here are the first and last verses:

> If you can't be a pine on the top of a hill,
> Be a scrub in the valley, but be
> The best little scrub by the side of the rill,
> Be a bush if you can't be a tree.
>
> If you can't be a highway, then just be a trail.
> If you can't be a sun, be a star.
> It isn't by size that you win or you fail.
> Be the best of whatever you are.

Emilie, at seventy-five, was important in the lives of my sons. She lived only two blocks from us. When she had some free time, she would come over and read to them. They were eleven and nine when she died, and we all went to her funeral together. Our younger son said that he hoped the casket would be open when we went to the funeral home, but it was closed. At one point he told us that he heard a knocking and that "Miss Emilie" wanted to get out. It's very difficult for all of us, and certainly for children, to imagine life really stopping.

Most young children, for instance, can't imagine that the body functions that are most important to them (at their age) will really stop at death. "Who will give Grandma her dinner in the grave?" and "How will Grandma go to the potty under there?" are questions young children have asked. They didn't mean to be rude or hurt anybody's feelings. They really wondered, and at the time of a death, they'll be wondering about a lot of things—as Hedda has found out:

> Most children want to know what death is like. They may equate death with stillness, but may ask if you can see or feel cold when you are dead. These questions may catch us off guard, but they are all part of a natural curiosity about the physical aspects of death. Letting our children view an open casket may be a particular source of worry for us, but even here, it can turn out that the reality of a dead body is less frightening than a child's fantasies about it. Children may startle us by wanting to see "what dead looks like." They may even want to touch the body to see "what dead feels like." They might even ask, "If we sat Grandma up, what would happen?" or "What's under the blanket where Grandpap's feet are? What makes it so puffy there?" They might want to know what is inside the hearse. (Many funeral directors have become accustomed to children's needs to know things like that and can help us provide answers to such questions.)
>
> While trying to be simple and direct in response to our children's wonderings, we do need to think carefully about the words we use: Children tend to take what we say literally. If, in an attempt to explain death, a parent has likened it to sleep, then it is not surprising that a child may assume that death is something from which you can wake. Or if, instead of using the word "died," we say that someone has "gone to sleep forever," a child may begin worrying that he or she may never wake up some morning. Our euphemisms can be troublesome for young children! What, for instance, are they supposed to understand when they hear someone has "lost" a father or a daughter? And there's one example of children's literalism I came across recently that really taught me the importance of trying to find out whether a child has correctly understood what we've said. In this instance, a family was trying to prepare their young son for a visit to a funeral home where the boy's grandfather was awaiting burial. They explained that Grandpa's body would be lying in an open coffin. The boy was very anxious—until he saw his grandfather in one piece. He had expected his head to be missing and only his body to be there.

Children's fantasies about the reality of death can be frightening for them, that's for sure, and so can their *feelings* about a death—particularly the feeling that they may in some way have been responsible for the death of someone they loved. (It's like the responsibility children feel when their parents get a divorce.) No matter how much we love someone, there are times when we get angry with that person. When children are four and five, aggressive urges tend to be strong, and if a child of that age happened to be angry with a parent, and that parent happened to be killed in an accident, that child could have a terrible struggle wondering how much his or her anger had been responsible for the parent's death.

"Scary, mad wishes *don't* make things come true." (See page 64.) I've sung that song many times with my "television friend" and I'll go on singing it occasionally in the knowledge that somewhere a child will be watching who really needs to hear that right then and there.

And children may be angry *because* someone died. They can't understand why someone they love would leave them. I've certainly known children who felt that way. I've sometimes said to them, "It can make a person mad to have someone go away and not come back, can't it?" I've had children nod in reply, as if to say, "Yes, *that's* what I'm feeling." Then I might say something like: "Well, a *lot* of people feel mad when someone they love dies." Just identifying a feeling and hearing that there's nothing wrong with it seems to be a big help to a child and to make it possible for him or her to talk more about it—then or later. When that time comes, we may find it possible to explain that the person who died didn't go away on purpose and that "your mom really loved you and I'm sure she'd want you to remember that."

I trust that you'll find your own ways to say these things, ways that are comfortable for *you*. Who you are will always mean more than the words you say to your children; nevertheless, your own unique words can help at a confusing time like a death in the family.

As at other stressful times, our children's feelings may become part of their play. I know that some parents are uncomfortable when their children "play" about death right after a family member has died. They feel it shows an insensitivity on the child's part. But just the opposite is true; children who play about death are feeling so sensitive about it that they are using the best means they have for coming to terms with what death means and how they feel about it. Play is one way children *grieve*, a way that is necessary and appropriate for them. And sometimes children's laughter seems most inappropriate to grieving grown-ups. Usually that laughter just says that the children are feeling very, very anxious around all these very, very sad adults. They wonder what's going to happen next, so they try to break the tension with a laugh.

Grief takes an individual form for each of us, and every family has its own ways of grieving together. I believe children find it helpful to

VERY HARD TIMES

be included in at least parts of their family's traditional rituals. They need to feel that they *belong*. I know that was true for me when Grandfather Rogers died. My family always let me play the piano for family gatherings, and when the minister came to Grandfather Rogers' home for family prayers before the funeral, they asked me to play a hymn. I remember feeling that I had a part in what was happening, and I remember hoping that Grandfather Rogers was proud of me. I still hope so.

Here's how it was in Hedda's family, in Hedda's words:

Many of us have worried about whether our children should attend funeral services of someone they loved. Are they too young? Will it be traumatic for them? There really are no set answers, but I have come to believe that even very young children can benefit significantly by sharing in at least some of the rituals that attend death—if we have prepared them for what to expect and have been open to their questions.

Funerals provide a structure for the early days of grieving. They provide a time for the sharing of grief, and they bring a sense of closure and finality that, sooner or later, we all have to accept. Funerals are a time for venting emotions and bringing relief, and I believe children need that relief, too.

Though parents are the best judges of how their children should participate in a funeral, we all need to consider whether at least some participation in the rituals may not be healthy for them. A first-grade teacher I knew once asked her class: "If you had two wishes, what would you want?" One of her pupils responded: "To go to a funeral and to a wedding." The boy, who had been excluded from a family funeral a short time before, clearly felt a real need to see what went on at these two important milestones in life. Another boy, a five-year-old, was not allowed to participate in his grandfather's funeral. For a long time after, whenever he heard an announcement of a funeral at church, he begged his mother to take him—to *anyone's* funeral.

The decisions aren't easy, and in addition to considering what may be best for our children, we need to stay responsive to what is best for us. When we are under the stress of bereavement, we may feel overtaxed by the constant need to cope with our young children's questions and fears and upsets, not to mention the demands of their daily routines. Although our seven-year-old, Amy, was with us through my father's funeral, we decided that four-year-old Laurie should go and stay with her four-year-old cousin at his house. Although she didn't attend the actual funeral and burial, we did take her with us to the funeral home beforehand, we did explain what would happen at the funeral, and I promised to take her to the cemetery at a later date.

I found it easy to postpone that visit, but when we did go together one autumn afternoon, the experience turned out not to be the devastating one I had anticipated. As we walked over to my father's grave site, I explained to Laurie that this was where we had come after the funeral service to bury the casket. She looked up at me and poignantly asked: "Why wasn't I here then?" I explained, as I had before, that funeral services and burial services are long and that there are long speeches and that I thought it might have been boring for her to have to sit through them all. But perhaps we would have gained a lot by being together then. It reminded me of the experience a friend of mine had when she had to tell her nursery-school class that one of their classmates had died. She said that she gathered the children around her and felt a compelling need to have one of them sitting on her lap while she explained what had happened. During those difficult moments, she told me, she could feel herself drawing on the vitality and freshness of the young child she was holding. Our whole family felt the same thing whenever the children were close by at the time of my father's death.

As the members of a family grieve and bring one another comfort, there is one thought that I feel can be helpful to grown-ups and children alike: Sadness isn't forever. I'm not suggesting that we remind ourselves of this in order to lessen our grief. On the contrary. The knowledge that time *does* bring relief from sadness and that sooner or later there *will* be days when we are happy again may allow us to grieve more fully and deeply when we need to.

That knowledge may even make it more possible to accept the comfort of feeling close to people who have died by talking about good times we remember having had with them, or by looking through scrapbooks of snapshots, or by having some of their favorite possessions around us. Memories and mementos can make us very sad because, of course, they remind us that *things* are as physically close as we can now get to the person we loved. Having that measure of closeness is a comfort, though, and allowing ourselves the feelings that go with it is a way to help the deep sadness of separation pass.

Young children don't know that sadness isn't forever. Just as it can be frightening to them to feel that their anger might get out of control, so it's frightening, too, for them to feel that their sadness may overwhelm them and never go away. That "the very same people who are sad sometimes are the very same people who are glad sometimes" is something all parents need to help their children come to understand.

And what about heaven? People have sometimes asked why I didn't mention heaven in the program we made about death. Like so many things in families, I think the question of what happens after death is best talked about within a family's own traditions and beliefs. Naturally, I have my own beliefs about it. I'm convinced that our souls are accepted and received *exactly as we are* in the most incredible loving way. We just don't have any earthly words to describe it. Another thing I feel sure about is that there is nothing to fear once we have died. I talk very naturally with my family about such questions. Our sons will probably form their own beliefs and use them when they talk to their children. But they'll certainly know how I have felt. That's the way I think is best—expressing beliefs in the context of the family.

　　　　　　MISTER ROGERS TALKS WITH PARENTS

It's only natural that there are many things we find hard to talk about. But I've often said that anything human is mentionable, and anything mentionable can be manageable. The mentioning can be difficult, and the managing, too, but both *can* be done if we are surrounded by love and trust. It obviously was true for Hedda:

> For me, the closeness and love and trust I felt with my husband, my mother, my sister, and my friends are what helped most, and I think that atmosphere is what helped our children most. This is not to say that the time of my father's death was a time without resentment, irritability, and even anger. But even so, no one tried to talk anyone out of his or her feelings, no one denied them. We supported each other as best we could, doing whatever seemed most comfortable at the moment, and together we came through a time that was hard for us all.

It is our relationships with others that can sustain us when, during very hard times, we feel we are near the end of our own resources. Many people find it difficult to receive such sustenance, though, even when they need it; we'd all like to feel self-reliant and capable of coping with whatever adversity comes our way. But that's not how most human beings are made, and it's my belief that the capacity to accept help is inseparable from the capacity to give help when our turn comes to be strong.

CHAPTER 11:

FAMILY OCCASIONS

Family gatherings are often a focal point for the traditions that each family hands on from generation to generation. For a young child, they bring a gradual awareness of his or her place in a larger group, and that awareness is likely to produce some surprises.

In the first year or two of life a child is working hard on understanding that he or she is a separate and individual self. That is a large step to take, but that large step is immediately followed by another large step: having to work on where that new self belongs in relation to a mother *and* a father, *and*, possibly, to brothers and sisters who force the realization that Mommy and Daddy are someone else's mommy and daddy, too. Family gatherings present an added set of relationship puzzles: that Mommy and Daddy have brothers and sisters and even a mommy and daddy of their own; that they are Cousin Harry's uncle and aunt; and that Grandma is Grandma to Cousin Harry as well. Learning to accept the fact that affection is *shared* within a family isn't always easy for a child, because it may seem to diminish the love that's available for "me." But it's through that struggle that we can all come to understand that love is different from, say, cookies. Cookies can be shared only so far until they're all gone. It's wonderful to grow to the point where we know that love is just the opposite: The more love is shared, the more there is to give.

I wonder how many grandparents realize how deeply confirming their presence can be to a young child—just as my mother's father was deeply confirming to me (see page 232). In a relationship with a grandparent, a child can be freed of a lot of the daily expectations that are part of home life, that are *necessary* for growth at home. A grandparent is a very special kind of ally in a child's search for an identity that includes being lovable and loving. When "Ding-Dong" McFeely overrode my parents' objections and gave me permission to walk on his stone walls, he didn't undermine their authority. Life at home went on as it always had. My parents were still my parents. What he did was let me know that it was possible to have different kinds of loving relationships with different people, and that I had a special place in this world as a grandson in addition to a special place as a son.

And the presence of a grandparent confirms that parents were, indeed, little once, too, and that people who are little can grow to be big, can become parents, and one day even have grandchildren of their own. So often we think of grandparents as belonging to the past; but in this important way, grandparents, for a young child, belong to the future.

There are many kinds of events that become occasions for family reunions: the Fourth of July, Thanksgiving, religious holidays, family milestones. But when a child is very young, I think it is the simple coming together of the family that means the most. Family reunions help children learn again and again that there are many people in this world who can love them just the way they are.

FAMILY OCCASIONS

Family Get-togethers

Some parents worry about taking their young children to big family gatherings where they may not be comfortable. As we all know, the most delightful children can, under stress, become quite unpredictable and even difficult. We can't, after all, expect children to be quiet and cooperative all the time. Part of the problem for children is, I think, not knowing what to expect. Even adults feel more comfortable when they are prepared for a new situation—whether it's going to a party or starting a new job. If you're planning to go to a family party in a house that's strange to your children, you might want to tell them what you know about the house and what memories you have from other times there. You could talk about the other guests, particularly the ones you grew up with, and about the things that you did together as children. If you can recapture the feelings you had as a little one at large family get-togethers, it may be comforting to your child to hear that you, too, sometimes had mixed feelings. It can be helpful, too, to let your child know that he or she will have choices and will be allowed to stay at least a little in control of what happens. For example: "Grandma always likes children to sit on her lap. If you want to, that's fine. But if you don't, you could just tell her that you may feel like it later but not right this minute." You can emphasize, too, that you're going to be there with them all the time, and if they feel funny about something they can come to you and let you know.

Family dinners can be very long for a child! Some families have made a tradition of calling a short time-out for the children after the main course when they can leave the table, stretch, play, and then return for dessert. Other families put children at a table of their own nearby, which can give them a sense of importance, closeness, and yet freedom from undue adult constraints. And if they don't like Aunt Sally's candied yams or Grandma's mince pie, do they have to eat it? The issue of "eating everything that's on your plate" can become a big one in some families (see page 197), and it's one of those issues that each family, quite properly, deals with in its own way. My wife and I encouraged our boys to try a wide variety of foods, but we never felt comfortable about forcing them to eat things they clearly didn't like. Generally, we could find alternatives that would give them a healthy diet while not turning the dinner table into a battlefield. Our tastes change as we grow, and I wonder if we're not likely to become healthier, happier eaters when we're older if we were allowed, within the boundaries of what's good for us, to find our own way when we were young.

As for Grandma's mince pie... if our children are old enough, they might be able to thank Grandma for making it and tell her they might like it better when they're a little older. If our children are too young for that, it can be our job to say it.

There's one suggestion I've heard that I think can be really helpful for children during long family gatherings, and that's to give them a place of their own, a place that's safely out of the way of the adults—a place where they can go to do their kinds of things. It could be a place outside, a quiet room with some books and toys, a blanket spread out on a bedroom floor, or just a space behind the couch in the living room. What matters is that the children know it's a place for *them*.

Nothing, though, can replace your child's need for you. When our children become overstimulated, exhausted, fretful, or just plain out of control, the chances are that they need to borrow from our self-discipline. Often we can see the signs of trouble before the situation gets out of hand, and that may be a good moment for some quiet time together— to go for a walk, to look at the moon, find some blocks or crayons, anything that will give your child time to let his or her strong feelings subside within the security of your presence. Once in control again, your child may fall asleep, want to go on playing alone for a while, or choose to rejoin the group. But the crisis of feeling overwhelmed will have passed. The worst feeling anyone can have is the sense of being out of control, and when parents step in to help at times like these, they are reaffirming for their child that his or her feelings are *safe*.

Birthdays

When a baby is born, its parents often feel that they would like to give that baby a perfect life. It's a very natural feeling, but of course not a realistic one, especially if "perfection" means a life that is always happy. Our children will sometimes hurt and suffer no matter what we do. They will have stomach pains and growing pains, feel jealousy, disappointment, and all the rest. Very early in our children's lives we will be forced to realize that the "perfect" untroubled life we'd like for them is just a fantasy. In daily living, tears and fights and doing things we don't want to do are all part of our human ways of developing into adults.

Nevertheless, the fantasy within the hearts of many loving parents persists, the fantasy that says, "Certainly there's something perfect I can give to my children. Even if it can't be the whole of life, maybe it can at least be one day each year." And many parents choose their child's birthday for that day. Consequently, the day is filled with fancy presents and events. Unfortunately, days like that often bring tears and fights, disappointments on many fronts, with parents feeling at the end of the day that their children never appreciated any of it. There's a letdown that turns that "perfect" day into a most imperfect disappointment. And yet, in practically every home, the very next year, the very same thing happens: The longing always remains in parents' hearts to create something perfect for their child.

One thing we may not realize is that it can be hard for a child to receive too much of anything—gifts, food, attention—at one time. I can remember birthdays and Christmases when I received so much of everything that I felt overwhelmed. I couldn't express it in words when I was little, but my feeling was, "How can I make up for all this? How can I ever say thank you enough? How can I ever be good enough in return?" It was an oppressive feeling, even amidst the joy of the day. Parents, without knowing it, may have parallel feelings. Their investment of time, money, and comfort can lead them to expect their children to give them back an overabundance of happy feelings. If their children don't respond with absolute joy, and if the day is marred by fracases and upsets, they may feel, "We did all this for you, and why aren't you happy? Why can't you be *good* for once!"

Birthdays are more likely to be happy days if we are responsive to how our children need to feel rather than to what our children think they want. Children need, for instance, to feel important, and a birthday is a grand opportunity to let a child feel "in charge." One way we can do this is to let the birthday child choose something for the whole family to do. It can be very helpful for you to offer some reasonable suggestions, like going out to a farm, making a picnic, going to a puppet show or a circus, or visiting any of the places in a town or city that have been set up for children's enjoyment. What matters most is that it be something of the child's choosing, to which you can agree, and which the family can do together. Often, such events have to be postponed to the nearest weekend. If that's the case, the child's actual birthday could include a family birthday breakfast, a chance for the child to decide on the supper menu, and a family reading of a favorite story before bed. These are the sorts of simple things that come to my mind, but each family can devise alternatives of its own.

When the weekend celebration comes, and if it includes a children's party, many parents have found it wise to be wary of creating an overabundance of *people*. We all know that large groups of five-year-olds can generate a lot of stimulation that often ends in tears and exhaustion. If you feel uneasy about such large groups, you might want to ask your child about just a few particular friends. "Would you like to ask Mandy, Eric, and Kate to come over for cake and ice cream? Is there anyone else you'd specially like to invite?" That way, you can probably keep the size of the party down to a number that is comfortable for both you and your child. I know parents who allow their daughter to invite just as many friends as the number of years she is old. When their daughter was three, she invited three friends. At four she invited four. That seemed to work well.

Birthdays are meant to be "You Are Special!" days that both celebrate the arrival of a particular person into this world and express our continuing joy in having that person among us. Don't we all have a longing to hear this from the people we love? Isn't this a very different longing from the one we have for material possessions? Parties and presents, of course, have their place as a traditional part of birthdays, but when we let them become what birthdays are all about, we have missed a once-in-a-year chance to give our child a strong and special confirmation of the importance of his or her place in our family.

That Winter Holiday Season

The winter holiday season is meant to bring us warmth of many kinds at the coldest and darkest time of the year. It's meant to lift our spirits, bring us good cheer, draw us together in our traditions and rituals, ease our burdens, and renew our hopes. And so it can. But I know from experience that the "comfort and joy" of the season can be very elusive indeed.

Last December, a friend of mine wondered aloud whether it was worth celebrating anything anymore at that time of the year—Christmas, Hanukkah, New Year's, *anything*. The way she put it was that along about Halloween she feels she's stuck behind the wheel of a car she can't control. By Thanksgiving she's going forty miles an hour, by mid-December she's racing along at eighty, and on Christmas Day she always runs into the same brick wall. "No matter what I do," she says, "I wake up at the end of the holiday season feeling like I've been in a collision. Our family is an emotional, physical, and financial wreck!"

Not all parents feel so pressured during the holidays, but so many have told me of their overworrying, overworking, and overspending! As I've listened to them, I've found once again the widely shared, deep, and natural desire to make the holiday a single perfect day for their children—that same desire that can so easily lead to birthday overload. In the case of the winter holidays, though, that desire is fanned to a great blaze by media of every sort in every town and virtually every household in the country, affecting our reason and emotions, exploiting all five of our senses, evoking joy and sadness, hope and despair, and, along with them, loads of guilt. The cruelest and loudest message of the season, shouted from millions of television sets, newspapers, and magazines, seems to be: "To spend more is to love more . . . and to be more dearly loved."

There's a universal longing, one that everyone shares, parents and children alike, and that is the longing to have something to give that is acceptable to others. Reviewing my own feelings about Christmas helps me recognize the depth of this longing. Everyone wants to feel that he or she has something to offer. The most depressing feeling in the world is that of having nothing to offer... nothing that's acceptable.

The way a mother receives the simple touch of her infant's hand at her breast means so much to that infant's beginning feelings of having something acceptable to give. The way parents receive a child's early "productions" in the toilet gives that child beginning notions of how welcome his or her actions are. And so it is with all our development. We collect clues all along the way as to how acceptable—how lovable— we really are to others. An important question, it seems to me, is how we can begin to turn holiday celebrations into the giving and receiving of positive clues as to how "acceptable" we and our children really are to one another.

Over the years, families tend to develop their own ways of observing these seasonal celebrations. There's certainly no *right* way for a family to celebrate Hanukkah or Christmas, other than the way that happens to suit us, our beliefs, and our traditions. I have heard of families deciding to celebrate Christmas in July in order to avoid winter's commercialism and bustle. I remember one family when I was growing up who didn't celebrate Hanukkah or Christmas or anything. It just wasn't part of their tradition, but they had other things they did together, other times of giving and receiving, at other times of the year.

Among the people who came to America from Poland, for generations there has been a family tradition that consists of passing out wafers to each family member, from the eldest to the youngest. After everyone is holding a wafer, the eldest, perhaps the grandfather, begins the ceremony by breaking his wafer against all the others, expressing loving wishes for the holiday, leaving a fragment of his wafer with each family member, and taking a fragment of each of the others as he goes. By the end of the ceremony, each member of the family has broken and shared his or her wafer with every other member. Only then are the wafers eaten, so that the family truly shares a common bread and confirms that what each person has offered is acceptable to all the rest.

I have been asking friends to tell me what made holidays special in *their* families. What they cited were:

- things that were familiar and traditional;

- things that were done before the holiday itself;

- things that were done together;

- things that had personal associations;

- things that reflected the real inner needs of young children; and

- things that didn't cost much money.

I like to compare the holiday season with the way a child listens to a favorite story. The pleasure is in the familiar way the story begins, the anticipation of familiar turns it takes, the familiar moments of suspense, and in the familiar climax and ending. So, too, with holidays. When we think back to our early holidays, we usually find many strong memories of rituals—secular or religious or both—memories that we associate with the season's unfolding. Often these memories are far stronger than what we can recall of the actual day itself. There is, after all, so much more to a story than its end.

One family told me how, starting on the first day of November, they all get together in the evenings and start making greeting cards. They

use potato halves in which they've cut designs that will "print" when dabbed first in paint; felt-tip pens; crayons; and anything else their children can work with, like paste and pictures cut out of magazines. Our adult sense of perfection may tell us that these cards don't always look neat and professional, but have you ever noticed how a homemade card stands out on a mantelpiece crowded with the store-bought kind? When this family goes visiting, and, in someone else's home, the children see a card they've made, they not only feel proud, but, in that moment, are reliving the pleasure they had as they made it.

Many families mentioned preholiday baking as one of their family traditions. The children, from their earliest years, helped knead the dough and decorate the holiday treats. Children's cookies aren't always as "fragile" as the ones an experienced cook might make, but they are edible and their acceptance demonstrates to the child that he or she has something to offer that others are willing to take into themselves and make a part of their own celebration. There is a deep, deep correlation between the making of food for others and the giving of love!

And those handmade presents that children often bring home from school: They have so much value! The value is that the child put whatever he or she could into making them. The way we parents respond to the giving of such gifts is very important. To the child the gift is really *self*, and they want so much for their *selves* to be acceptable, to be loved.

My own two boys always looked forward to going out to get the tree and decorating it. From the time they were big enough to stand up, they helped with the ornaments. In those early years, when we finished, the bottom branches were always laden with decorations while the top branches, which the adults decorated, were relatively bare. Our favorite ornaments are still those the boys made in nursery school out of rope, clay, yarn, pipe cleaners, and paper. Naturally, the result is never a sleek, sophisticated tree like those you might see in magazines. "Chef" Brockett, who appears regularly on *Mister Rogers' Neighborhood*, and his wife always stop by our house at Christmastime. They are very artistic people who invariably decorate their tree with great care. They often make good-natured fun of our tree. "Well," they'll say, "this year we'll give it a C-plus." Ours *is* usually a homely tree, but it suits us just fine.

From earliest childhood, my younger son, John, insisted on helping drag the tree out of the car and put it on its stand. Every year as we came in the door, he heard his grandmother Byrd call out, "Did you get any loose branches for me?" (She used those extra branches to decorate the mantelpiece.) The first Christmas John was big enough to bring in the tree all by himself, he came in hollering, "Hey, Nana Byrd, I got you some loose branches!" and Nana Byrd gave him a warm hug. At moments like these you realize how much family traditions mean to children and how very important the little things are.

FAMILY OCCASIONS

For one of my friends, December 15 was the day when he and his father and brother set up the electric-train set, which then stayed up until New Year's. He vividly recalls the excitement of seeing it again each year, of putting it together and getting it to work. He remembers the hours spent in his dark bedroom making the engine and the cars go fast and slow, through the tunnels, past the lighted buildings and the station where the signalman's arm went up and down. He can still hear the sound of that little whistle, still smell the lubricating oil, still see the lights reflected on the artificial snow in that magical landscape. In a world where adults were always in control, this was *his* world—a place where he could make things happen, even to making the whole train crash if he wanted to. Being in control of that toy world was a powerful experience for him right then...and it was a Christmastime experience.

By the time that friend had children of his own, his train set had gone the way of many other childhood toys, but he started buying and making components for another one. Each year for Christmas he would give his children something new for *their* toy landscape, and that little present turned out, year after year, to be the one they most looked forward to opening. As he told about this experience, I realized once more that it's not how much we give our children that counts, but how much whatever we do give *means* to them and to us.

It's been my experience that children's favorite presents are often ones that in some way reflect what they are feeling or need to feel. Very young children who are still trying to understand what is inside and what is outside themselves are frequently fascinated by things that have well-defined insides and outsides—boxes with lids, anything that has doors, drawers, and compartments. I remember giving a three-year-old a pair of play pliers and a puppet whose mouth opened and shut on hinges. As it happened, this boy was working hard right then on mastering the urge to bite. I could see how much he liked the presents.

When children are still preoccupied with containing their own body fluids, they may play delightedly for hours with things that pour or simple toys, like an hourglass, that have sand that runs. Doll figures and cars have always been popular because these toys answer young children's need to be in control, to feel in charge. They allow children to practice being grown-ups, too, and that's something all children *need* to do.

Miniature cooking utensils and hand tools (even real, safe second-hand ones) give children that same opportunity to practice. They may also carry a strong association with the things that loved parents have and use—an attraction that can hold true for gifts of clothing as well. I remember a three-year-old girl who was enamored of her grandmother's fur hat. I'm sure she loved that hat for many reasons. Its warmth and

MISTER ROGERS TALKS WITH PARENTS

the softness of the fur may have suggested love, gentleness, and all sorts of happy feelings. But she probably admired it most because of its strong associations with her grandmother. At Christmas, her perceptive parents managed to find an inexpensive rabbit-fur hat to give to their daughter. And how she loved it! For that little girl, having a fur hat like her grandmother's was the very best present of all.

One small boy I know asked his parents for Scotch tape for Christmas. His parents were sensitive enough to know that he really meant it, and they got some for him. He used that tape to make many things. When children make requests like this, we need to listen extra-carefully before deciding whether our notions of value are more appropriate than theirs. What fits a child's needs is not always the most attractive thing in the toy shop.

Why, then, do we overspend on expensive toys with batteries that run down and plastic pieces that break? Probably because we have heard our children say they want them, and no one wants to disappoint a child. No one *wants* to, that's true, but an important part of being parents is helping our children cope with disappointment—a skill they will need all their lives. When I was five, I wanted a parrot very badly! But that year there was a big parrot fever scare and my mother flatly refused to buy me one. Even though she helped me to understand her fears, I was terribly disappointed. But that early disappointment didn't hurt me; it helped me to deal with later ones.

No one can go through life without disappointments, and children have a healthy way of using play to help work through them. A little girl who wants a puppy may play out her unfulfilled wishes by making believe with a stuffed toy dog. The boy whose father can't afford to buy him that fancy remote control automobile race game will probably get more lasting satisfaction out of a couple of dime-store cars he can push around all over the house, carry in his pocket, and park under his bed. So often children do want things their parents can't afford, but I think it's a useful lesson for them to learn, and learn early, that there are limits to what people can have. It's helpful for children to know that there isn't an endless source of money in the family. There's nothing inappropriate about telling a child, "We don't have enough money to buy that this year. We need the money we have to pay for the house, for food, for clothes, and for the other things we need to take good care of you and us. There just isn't that much left over." If parents are willingly supportive, they can help a child face disappointment and grow from it.

Some adults have told me of holidays when, because of sickness or other troubles, they simply couldn't rise to the occasion—and they felt inadequate and guilty for not being able to do so. The simplest rituals became chores and the supposed joy of the season was a major depressant in itself. Well, depression isn't only an adult affliction. When children's feelings are in turmoil, they, too, can find holiday card making or cookie baking beyond their inner strength.

We each develop our own ways of coping with these times. Some people grit their teeth and push on. Others settle for doing less, or plain give up on that holiday that year. When we can be honest about how we are feeling, and if we are able to let go a little, we may often be surprised at how other family members can shoulder the tasks we may have come to think of as particularly our own. Many parents have found, to their astonishment, what strength their young children can supply and how, when we let them make a holiday happen for us in their own ways, they ease one common cause of depression that is uniquely an adult's: that sad feeling of lost childhood.

Holidays do have a way of evoking the sadness of life's passing, even as we celebrate and rejoice at the best of times. There is a powerful nostalgia in memories and in the bittersweet recollections of the children we once were. With the family gathered around the festive holiday table, we can't help but reflect on the changing cast of characters. Great-grandparents and grandparents have died, new children have been born. Where we may first have attended these gatherings in a high chair, it may now be our turn to sit at the head of the table.

I am glad that the religious services leading up to Christmas were a central part of our family celebrations, because I know now that they helped me learn to feel comfortable with this passing sequence of the generations. Oh, I can remember squirming in services when I couldn't understand their significance, and our boys, when they were little, didn't find sitting still and keeping quiet any easier than I had. But I wanted them to have what I knew I had had, so they always went along with my wife and me. Joining in adult things and doing as adults do was something I knew that they, like all children, longed for. Much more than that, though, I wanted them to have the comfort I had found in the rituals of our faith and culture—the slow growing knowledge that even as all living things will die, some things will also endure.

*   *   *

In thinking about family times together, I realize that I have come back to the very best reason parents are so special—the place we started out so many pages ago. It is because we parents are the holders of a priceless gift, a gift we received from countless generations we never knew, a gift that only we now possess and only we can give to our children. That unique gift, of course, is the gift of ourselves. Whatever we can do to give that gift, and to help others receive it, is worth the challenge of all our human endeavor.

Songs
and
Music
from
MISTER
ROGERS'
NEIGHBORHOOD

**Lyrics and Music
by Fred Rogers,**
A.S.C.A.P.
Music Arranged by
John Costa, A.S.C.A.P.

Won't You Be My Neighbor?

It's Such a Good Feeling

Fox-trot, lively

It's such a good feel-ing to know you're a-live. ___
good feel-ing to know you're in tune. ___

It's such a hap-py feel-ing: You're grow-ing in-side. ___
It's such a hap-py feel-ing to find you're in bloom. ___

And when you wake up read-y to say, ___
And when you wake up read-y to say, ___

You Are You

Voice: I eat and you do too. You sleep and I do too. I wake up and you do too. So we two do so much the same, But I'm Mis-ter Rog-ers, And you have your name.

Chorus:
You are you and I am I And we will al - ways
You are you and I am I And we will nev - er

262

Everything Grows Together

Everything grows together
Because you're all one piece.
Your nose grows
As your ears grow
As your arms grow
As your hands grow
As your fingers grow
As your legs grow
As your feet grow
As your toes grow
As the rest of you grows
Because you're all one piece.

This is a cumulative song. Each time, the singer adds a new part of the body and then repeats all those that have gone before. (#3-8)

3. nose grows as your
ears grow as your
arms grow as

4. nose grows as your
ears grow as your
arms grow as your
hands grow as your

5.
6. etc., adding fingers,
7. legs, feet, toes
8.

*Tag after last verse.

You Can Never Go Down the Drain

©Fred M. Rogers 1969

Children Can

Who can crawl under a ta - ble? Who can
wake up ev - 'ry morn - ing And be

sit un - der a chair? Who can fit____ their feet in
read - y right a - way? Who can no - tice all the

lit - tle shoes____ And sleep most an - y - where? Who can
ti - ny things____ That oth - er peo - ple say? Who can

268

play
make

ver - y much long - er,
the things they play with

Play much hard - er than grown-ups ev - er
Some-thing dif - f'rent for ev - 'ry sin - gle

dare? You're a child____ so you can do it. You can do it an - y-
day? You're a child____ and you can do it. Chil-dren do it an - y

where. Who can way.____ Roll in the grass,____ Squoosh in the

mud. Lick an ice cream cone,____ Sing to a

269

I Did Too!

Allegretto

Verse

Did you ev - er fall and hurt your hand or knee? Did you ev - er bite your tongue?_____ Did you ev - er find the sting - er of a bee Stuck in your thumb?

Moderato

Chorus

I did too. It seems the things that you do,____ I did too when

I was ver-y new. I had lots of hurts and scares and wor-ries When I was grow-ing up like you. Did you ev - er trip and fall down on the stairs? Did you ev - er stub your toe?_____ Did you ev - er dream of great big griz - zly

bears Who would-n't go? I did too. It
seems the things that you do,___ I did too when I was ver-y new.
I had lots of hurts and scares and wor-ries When I was grow-ing up, When
I was grow-ing up, When I was grow-ing up like you.

You're Growing

1. You used to creep and crawl real well But then you learned to walk real well. There
2. hands are get-ting big-ger now. Your arms and legs are long-er now. You

was a time you'd coo and cry But then you learned to talk and, my! You
e-ven sense your in-sides grow When Mom and Dad re-fuse you. So you're

al-most al-ways try.___ You al-most al-ways do your best. I
learn-ing how to wait now. It's great to hope and wait some-how. I

like the way you're grow-ing up. It's fun that's all. You're

274

3. Your friends are getting better now.
   They're better every day somehow.
   You used to stay at home to play
   But now you even play away.
   You do important things now.
   Your friends and you do big things now.
   I like the way you're growing up.
   It's fun, that's all.

   Chorus

4. Someday you'll be a grown-up, too
   And have some children grow up, too.
   Then you can love them in and out
   And tell them stories all about
   The times when you were their size,
   The times when you found great surprise
   In growing up. And they will sing
   It's fun, that's all.

   Chorus

Sometimes People Are Good

1. Some - times peo - ple are good, And they do just what they
2. Some - times peo - ple get wet, And their par - ents get up -

should, But the ver - y same peo - ple who are good some - times Are the
set But the ver - y same peo - ple who get wet some - times Are the

ver - y same peo - ple who are bad some - times. It's fun - ny but it's
ver - y same peo - ple who are dry some - times. It's fun - ny but it's

true. It's the same, is - n't it for Me and...?

3. Sometimes people make noise,
   And they break each other's toys.
   But the very same people
      who are noisy sometimes
   Are the very same people
      who are quiet sometimes
   It's funny but it's true.
   It's the same, isn't it, for
   Me and. . .?

4. Sometimes people get mad,
   And they feel like being bad.
   But the very same people
      who are mad sometimes
   Are the very same people
      who are glad sometimes.
   It's funny but it's true.
   It's the same, isn't it, for
   Me and. . .?

5. Sometimes people are good,
   And they do just what they should.
   But the very same people
      who are good sometimes
   Are the very same people
      who are bad sometimes.
   It's funny but it's true.
   It's the same, isn't it, for me. . .?
   Isn't it the same for you?

Good People Sometimes Do Bad Things

Good peo - ple some - times think bad things,
Good peo - ple some - times wish bad things,

Good peo - ple dream bad things, don't you?
Good peo - ple try bad things, don't you?

Good peo - ple e - ven say bad things, Once in a while we
Good peo - ple e - ven do bad things,

do. Once in a while we do.

Has an - y - bod - y said you're good late - ly?

Has an - y - bod - y said you're nice?

And have you won - dered how they could, late - ly,

Won - dered once or twice? Did you for - get that

It's the People You Like the Most

What Do You Do?

What do you do___ with the mad that you feel___ When you feel so mad___ you could bite? When the whole wide world seems oh, so wrong___ And noth-ing you do seems ver - y right?___

What do you do?_ Do you punch a bag?_ Do you pound some clay or some dough? Do you round up friends for a game of tag?_ Or see how fast you go? It's great to be a-ble to stop When you've planned a thing that's wrong,_ And be

283

Sometimes

3. Sometimes I don't feel like going to bed.
   I don't feel like getting right up sometimes.
   Sometimes I don't feel like wearing my shoes.
   But sometimes isn't always.

4. Sometimes I don't feel like sometimes I do.
   I feel like I don't like to feel sometimes.
   Sometimes I don't and sometimes I do.
   But sometimes isn't always.

The Truth Will Make Me Free

What if I were ver - y, ver - y sad And
What if I were ver - y, ver - y an - gry And

all I did was smile? I won - der af - ter a
all I did was sit And ne - ver think a - bout

while What might be - come of my sad - ness?
it? What might be - come of my an - ger?

Where would they go, and what would they do, If

Wishes Don't Make Things Come True

3. Everyone wishes for scary, mad things.
   I'd guess that you sometimes do, too.
   I've wished for so many
   And I can say
   That all kinds of wishes
   Are things just like play.
   They're things
   That our thinking has made—
   So wish then
   And don't be afraid.
   I'm glad it's certainly that way, aren't you?
   That scary, mad wishes don't make things come true.
   No kinds of wishes can make things come true.

You've Got to Do It

never see it through 'Cause the make - be - lieve pre - tend - ing just won't
you who have to fall (sometimes) If you want to ride a bi - cy - cle and

(spoken)

do it for you. You've got to do it.
ride it straight and tall. You've got to do it.

Ev - 'ry lit - tle bit, you've got to do it, do it, do it, do

it. And when you're through, you can know who did it, for you did it, you

295

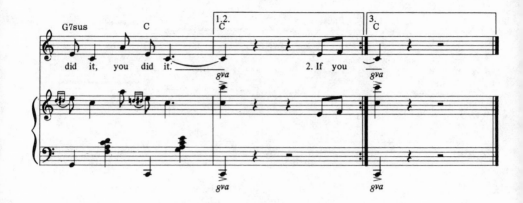

3. If you want to read a reading book
      and read the real words too,
   You can't simply sit and ask
      the words to read themselves to you.
   But you have to ask a person
      who can show you one or two
   If you want to read a reading book
      and read the real words, too.

   Chorus

4. It's not easy to keep trying,
      but it's one good way to grow.
   It's not easy to keep learning,
      but I know that this is so:
   When you've tried and learned
      you're bigger than you were a day ago.
   It's not easy to keep trying,
      but it's one way to grow.

   Chorus

Everybody's Fancy

Tempo di Fox-trot

Some are fan - cy on the out - side.
Boys are boys from the be - gin - ning.

Some are fan - cy on the in - side.
Girls are girls right from the start.

Ev - 'ry - bod - y's fan - cy. Ev - 'ry - bod - y's fine.

3. Only girls can be the mommies.
   Only boys can be the daddies.
   Everybody's fancy.
   Everybody's fine.
   Your body's fancy and so is mine.

4. I think you're a special person
   And I like your ins and outsides.
   Everybody's fancy.
   Everybody's fine.
   Your body's fancy and so—is—mine.

Going to Marry Mom

Medium Fox-trot tempo

1. One day I said, "I'm real - ly going to mar - ry,
2. told my mom, "I'm real - ly going to mar - ry,

Real - ly going to mar - ry, real - ly going to mar - ry," One
Real - ly going to mar - ry, real - ly going to mar - ry," I

day I said, "I'm real - ly going to mar - ry,
told my mom, "I'm real - ly going to mar - ry,

Real - ly going to mar - ry my mom. 2. I
Real - ly going to mar - ry you. 3. She

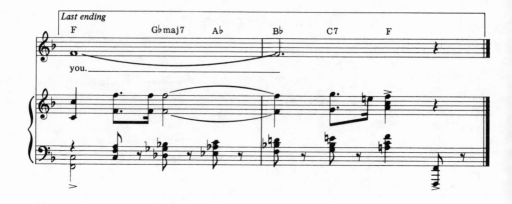

3. She smiled, didn't laugh, said, "I hope you will marry,
   Maybe someone like me."

4. "But you see," she said, "I'm already married,
   I'm married to your dad.

5. "And as you grow more, more like your daddy
   You'll find a lady like me.

6. "And she'll love you as I love your daddy
   And she will marry you.

7. "Then she will be the wife and the mother,
   Of your own family.

8. "And I hope you will have little children,
   And they will be like you.

9. "'Cause mothers and dads have special love for children
   Especially children like you."

10. That's what mom said when I told her I would marry
    Told her I would marry her.

11. I'm glad I told her 'cause I really often wondered
    Who my wife would be.

12. Now I'll just wait and look for my lady,
    And I'll just wait and see.

13. And I will grow up just like my daddy
    And my wife'll be looking for me.

14. And when I get married my mom'll be the granny
    The prettiest granny in town.

15. It all works out if you talk and you listen
    And your mother cares about you.

16. It all works out if you talk and you listen
    'Cause someone cares for you.

When a Baby Comes

301

It's You I Like

It's you I like, It's not the things you wear, It's not the way you do your hair— But it's you I like, The way you are right now, The way down deep in-side you—

Not the things that hide you, Not your toys ___

___ They're just be - side you. ___ But it's

you I like, Ev - 'ry part of

you, Your skin, your eyes, your feel - ings Wheth - er

Pretending

I Like To Be Told

2. I like to be told
   If it's going to hurt,
   If it's going to be hard,
   If it's not going to hurt.
   I like to be told.
   I like to be told.

INDEX

About the Authors

Fred McFeely Rogers, known to millions of American families as "Mister Rogers" of *Mister Rogers' Neighborhood*, was born in 1928. He graduated from Rollins College with a B.A. in music composition and became a creator and producer of television programming for children. In addition, he found time to complete his theological studies at the Pittsburgh Theological Seminary and was ordained as a minister in the United Presbyterian Church. He also took the Masters program in Child Development at the University of Pittsburgh. The Rogers family—his wife, who is a concert pianist, and their two sons—live in Pittsburgh.

Barry Head, a freelance writer, has been associated with Fred Rogers for ten years. British by birth, he graduated from New College, Oxford, and spent several years as a journalist and magazine editor. His articles and short fiction have appeared in such national publications as *Harper's Magazine, Mademoiselle,* and *Redbook*. He is the co-author, with Neil Paylor, of *Scenes From a Divorce* (Winston Press). In addition to developing a wide range of media materials for children and families, he has worked in public affairs television and documentary film. He is the father of two sons, and makes his home in Pittsburgh.